From Ocean to Desert

From Ocean to Desert

A Spiritual Memoir

Janet Sunderland

SHANTI ARTS PUBLISHING
BRUNSWICK, MAINE 04011

From Ocean to Desert
A Spiritual Memoir

Published by Shanti Arts Publishing
Cover and interior design by Shanti Arts Designs

Cover image is comprised of three photographs: *[schoolhouse, lower left]* David Goodrich, Lower Fox Creek School in the Tallgrass Prairie National Preserve, 2013. National Oceanic and Atmospheric Administration Photo Library. Public Domain; *[desert scene, right]* Andrew K. Pepper, Saguaro National Park, 2012. Wikimedia Commons. Creative Commons License; *[ocean, upper left]* Lee Sharon, 2015. Wikimedia Commons. Creative Commons License

Shanti Arts LLC
193 Hillside Road
Brunswick, Maine

www.shantiarts.com

Printed in the United States of America

ISBN: 978-1-947067-93-0 (softcover)
ISBN: 978-1-947067-94-7 (digital)

Library of Congress Control Number: 2021942052

For my husband, Cliff,
whose promptings made this journey
possible long before I knew him

CONTENTS

ONE

WASHINGTON, D.C.

The hot wind plastered a crumpled newspaper against my leg as I crossed DuPont Circle toward P Street. Peeling it off, the headline, Hurricane Moving Up Coast! unsettled me. Would a hurricane come this far inland? The knot in my chest tightened, but sixteen men sitting around a table at the Better Business Bureau to judge my restaurant dream were more threatening than a storm. I understood storms. They could skip over land or make a new path or bring needed rain.

"Nice business plan," one said. "Other investors?"

"A business contact is looking into possibilities," I said, my actor smile in place. I didn't say he sat at my bar during happy hour or that I'd refused his goodnight kiss after a dinner to go over said business plan.

Stopping on my way down P Street to stuff the newspaper into a trash bin, I saw one of the regular homeless guys wave from across the street. "Hey, Pretty!" I waved. He was far enough away I didn't have to stop and chat. Besides, how can you whine and feel sorry for yourself to a one-legged homeless man? That made me smile, more rueful than charming, so I waved again, and the knot in my chest softened.

Good reminder. Shake it off. You'll figure it out. My mantra most days.

At the door of my building, cool air swept me across the lobby as an elevator door opened. The doors closed, and I shrugged out of my suit jacket. No one joined me on my ride to the seventh floor. Keys in one hand, jacket in the other, I walked down the hall and opened to quiet. Pushing the door shut with my heel and stripping to skin, I wrapped in a sarong and stood at the windows in a cool shaft of air. This south wall of windows, sliding open to sky, had sold me on the place. So had the quiet. I watched as an airplane silently lifted over the Potomac into a clear sky.

Three years in D.C. Was I was settling down? An interesting possibility given the history trailing behind me like some old stripper's purple boa, shedding feathers at every step. My lopsided grin traced laugh lines from mouth to eye in the window's reflection. At least I could amuse myself, momentarily anyway. I'd sent my stepdad the business plan, extolled my successes, asked for seed money. When? Two years ago? Had I been working on this restaurant idea, minus success, that long? But Dad had died. Not as young as my father when he'd died, but Dad's death left another empty space above my head.

I leaned my forehead against the cool glass. Another crossroad. I could feel it building like a wooden crossbar in my chest. But to where? I never knew, only knew the feel, the where written on the reverse in ink destined to remain invisible for an unspecified span of time. How long would I keep wandering, three years here, three years there and there, searching, always searching, never knowing exactly what it was I looked for?

Love? Love created more problems than it solved.

Shoving open the window, I lifted my face to the sky, "What do you want with me?"

"What am I supposed to do?" I yelled louder at something I hoped would listen.

The phone rang.

"Hi, it's Catherine," a familiar voice said. "There's a spiritual teacher in Bethesda this evening. I'll drive. I can pick you up in an hour."

"Sure," I said. We talked a moment more. How had the interview gone? Was I making headway? Maybe. But it will take time. What else could I say?

After hanging up, I picked up a corner of my sarong and cleaned the forehead sweat streak from the window. The sarong needed washing anyway. I'd bought it in Mexico City, two doors down from my apartment.

Remembering Mexico revived memories of Gloria as she blessed me. I didn't know she was a *curendara* (healer) before the blessing, although others on the Mexican film crew had come to her, indicated an injury, and she'd touch and murmur as I watched in the makeup mirror. After the movie wrapped and I'd returned to New York, I longed for Mexico. So I went back. Gloria invited me to her home, washed me with handfuls of rose petals drenched in blessed water, scrubbed my head, my arms, water streaming down my face. She said a new path was open for me. I stayed in Mexico for three years. Now new paths seemed in serious short supply, and somewhere between Mexico and here, I'd lost track of myself.

I turned from the window. A book inched itself into falling from my over-full bookcase, an old copy of *Alice in Wonderland*, read so many times the pages were smudged. After repositioning it, I ran my hand along the spines. One entire shelf held books on the Divine Feminine. *When God Was a Woman*, a comforting title. I didn't need a judgmental God; I did enough of that to myself, although I had managed to keep a copy of the Bible through all my moves. My whole life in a bookcase. Was there ever a time when books weren't in my life? When we moved to Grandpa's big house in Barnes, Kansas, shelves bowed with books. His stacks of *National Geographic* magazines gave me glimpses of a wide and wonderful world: tribal villages and snow-crested volcanoes, leopards, gazelles . . . no wonder I became a wanderer. Most of my childhood books tracked someone's search: Alice, Zane Gray, the Bible, The Book of Knowledge, heavy in my hands. Quests were quests, regardless of the destination, but they'd never shown me how to make a living. Except for Jason, Jason and his Golden Fleece, which, when you got right down to it, now seemed in serious short supply.

Pulling myself back to the present, I headed for the shower.

CATHERINE BUZZED MY APARTMENT, AND I WENT DOWN TO MEET her. She looked fresh and happy, her chestnut hair curling over her shoulders. We drove to the Bethesda suburbs.

"Thanks for the ride," I said. "I haven't had a car since New York, an old brown and cream Chevy." I grinned at the memory of driving the old highway from Kansas to Austin and stopping at Alcoa Springs where cold, fresh water bubbled over a rocky creek. I'd perfected rolling a joint as I drove, wrists on the steering wheel, and on one trip, picked up a young and lanky hitchhiker. We flirted and told stories all the way to Waco where he disembarked.

"What happened to it?" Catherine said, drawing me back from trailing through my mind's story.

"The hitchhiker? Oh. The Chevy. Got impounded in New York. I'd moved back and forth, Kansas to Texas, to Los Angeles, to Austin, New Orleans, New York. My two sons learned to drive in it. By New York, it was pretty beat up. I tied the trunk shut with a rope. Still had Texas plates, a Texas drug-runner look to it, I guess you could say."

I'd spent most of my life explaining where I'd been when, but thankfully, Catherine simply laughed. "You ever think about getting another?" she said.

"Nah, the Metro's okay. Cars get me into trouble." I laughed with her.

Catherine parked outside a two-story house, white with glossy black shutters. Inside, she knew several people and stopped to say hello. I felt out of place and secured myself against a wall. I'd never been good at parties, even if I knew people, and I had never learned how to do small talk.

Lagging behind and following her up a short stairway, we entered into what looked like a sunroom except the windows were covered in heavy, cream-colored drapes, muffling outside noise. Twenty-some women settled on floor pillows; the room hummed with air-conditioned summer. One woman, her hair ribbon-tied at the nape of her neck, sat in a kitchen chair in the middle of the room, hands folded in her lap. Although I'd agreed to come, I didn't really understand what was going to happen.

"Hello," she said. "I'm Alissa." She smiled. "If you don't mind, please remain quiet for a few moments as I go into meditation."

She seemed to fall asleep, her chin, resting on her chest, rose and fell with each breath. Without preamble, she lifted her head, eyes open, but unfocused.

"Well. Good evening," she said.

Her voice, not wispy but soft, began teaching: love is the primary energy; we reincarnate into family groups in order to complete patterns. My years of journal writing, years of reading spiritual books and counseling had taught me buckets about family and relationships. Except why.

After teaching, she opened the session to questions.

I shifted on the floor and blurted without thinking. "My father died when I was eight. I keep messing up. Do I have to go into past lives and dig out all that stuff? How am I supposed to heal? What am I supposed to do?"

My questions tumbled too fast to edit.

Her eyes locked on mine.

"Forgive yourself."

Forgive myself? Myself? But ... but ... words ping-ponged inside my head.

She turned, continued teaching: "It does no good to look backward. Humankind does not have the capacity to remember all that has passed. Our task is to forgive one another and forgive ourselves."

Others asked questions. She continued teaching. I waited, shifting on the floor. My desperation forced me to speak, but I formed the question carefully, word by word.

"I've been working on a plan to open a restaurant, but I can't find investors. Is that what I'm supposed to do?"

"Tell me the date of your birth."

I told her.

"The placement of planets at your birth makes it difficult for you to succeed in a public venture such as a restaurant. Your work lies with the internal, more subjective skills. Like healing. You would make a very fine healer."

"My sister's the healer, not me. She lives in Hawaii."

"You would do well to go to Hawaii."

The thump in my chest felt like a giant pink hibiscus had burst into bloom. I glanced down, expecting petals to drift across my bosom. The newspaper warning flashed through my mind. This wasn't precisely a hurricane, but enough to knock me off balance.

Others asked questions. I didn't hear them. With all my therapy, all the meditation and dream work, my body had never reacted like that.

What's a person to do once a heart opens like a flower?

I dithered. Like Alice, but without a Cheshire Cat.

THE WEEKS INCHED ALONG, BARTENDING, TEACHING PRONUNCIATION at the ESL school. Along with dithering, I filled page after page in my journal, trying to make sense of how and why I'd lived my life as I had, and what, exactly, forgiving myself meant. Jeanne, the sister a step younger, had asked me to come to Hawaii many times. I said no many times. She and Robert had lived on Hawaii Island for years; my stepdad and my mother visited each winter before Dad died, and even now, each winter Mom went back.

What would I do if I went to Hawaii? How would that make me a healer? I couldn't even heal the knots of pain I carried, the shame, the anger. The mistakes. At seventeen, I'd married against Mom and Dad's wishes. I knew it was a mistake, unfair to the young soldier, but I had to change my life, and I didn't know how except to marry and leave the farm. He was big, sandy-haired like my father; I was pretty and had learned how to hide behind my face.

But I'd never learned how to stop being angry.

The weeks inched along, bartending, teaching pronunciation at the ESL school. I often rode my bicycle down to the mall to feel wind whip through my hair. One day, I parked and chained the bike before climbing the steps to the Lincoln Memorial to sit, look out over the mall, and see into the far edges. If my dreams were pointing to death and transformation, which death and what kind of transformation? I had meditated, traveled into my body to vision quest in the way I'd learned early in therapy, and occasionally, walking to the Metro, I'd hear my name called and I'd turn. But no one there. Which piece was missing?

I knew I'd always heard a voice, or as always as I could remember. It started after my father died, as if death gave me the freedom to be chaotic. Could I have decided that at eight years old? Or was it what grew in me? Memories are like quicksilver; they can slide away at the slightest touch. Yet even now, these many years later, I could still see the moment my mother received the phone call. "He died?" she said, her voice raspy. And while I stood at her side, grasping her skirt below a very pregnant belly, what my memory sees is the entire dining room into the kitchen, from the wide north window across the polished dining room table, carved-back wooden chairs set neatly, to the kitchen bar where she stood, receiver pressed to her ear, me beside her.

A laughing family of parents plus four children began straggling up the steps of the memorial. The tallest, and probably oldest, a boy, bounded up two steps at a time. The father held a younger boy's hand while the mother held a young girl's hand and crooked a baby in the other arm. "Tom. Slow down!" I heard the father call. But Tom didn't. The father released the younger brother to run after him and took the young girl's hand to relieve the mother.

I watched Tom dash past me as the younger brother struggled to catch up and wondered if, as they grew, they would remember this trip and tell stories of Washington, D.C. and how Tom wanted to climb up and sit in Lincoln's lap as he was now endeavoring to do. The father's sharp "Tom! Stop!" did, actually, stop him as if the different tone in the father's voice was more a signal than his words.

As I climbed back down the stairs and unchained my bike, I wondered about fathers and signals and what that might lead to if your father dies young and most of your signals are others' stories. Before he died, when we moved from Arkansas to Barnes, Kansas, there's a story of my mother marching into Mike's Pool Hall late at night, demanding my father come home. Mother was tiny, four-foot-eleven, and the image of her marching into a pool hall is at odds with her Quaker upbringing. My aunt tells the story of my father singing, "I didn't know God made honky-tonk angels," on some drive to go fishing, a song embedded in me. Perhaps my years of tending bar were a holdover.

The Barnes house belonged to Grandpa Joe. He was the depot conductor in town. His wife, my grandmother, died shortly before we moved up from Arkansas. I barely remember her, even when I look at her photo. Maybe her death is why we moved. I never asked. The entryway had a small foyer between two doors, a place we stamped off snow or mud or bugs on the carpet square before pushing through heavy swinging glass-paned doors into the hallway. To the left of the hallway was the dining room and kitchen and to the right a long living room with an alcove where the upright piano sat with my music open, waiting to be practiced. Straight ahead of the foyer, a stairway led to a landing with a paned, oval window, fracturing light beams, and a turn up the last flight to the upstairs bedrooms.

How is it, I wonder, I can remember that house in such detail when I have lived so many places? How is it I can see that eight-year-old girl standing beside her mother? Perhaps because that moment, that exact moment, fractured my life into what I have become.

My first big dream came shortly after my father died when monsters chased me down the street. Stumbling and clawing my way to our porch, I woke before they reached me, but I wasn't safe... *not safe not safe not safe*.... I studied my dreams and wrote them into each current journal, which meant lugging boxed journals with me every time I moved. There lay my memory's recall, a companion, perhaps, to the same chaotic brain that funneled the voice.

The one thing I could remember, without any prompts, was when journaling began: an autumn afternoon in Texas before moving to join my soldier husband in Germany, the sun-washed yard flooded in the whisper of migrating monarch butterflies and Doris Lessing's *The Golden Notebook* open on my lap. I couldn't keep four notebooks, but I could keep one. And had. For decades.

Wrestling the bike onto my building's elevator, I ascended to my apartment in the sky. At least that's what I called it. My seventh-floor apartment was above all the surrounding buildings, and the wide windows looked out over rooftops, but mostly the windows were filled with sky.

The Mexico initiation meant something, but I couldn't see where it led. I kept meditating and I kept dreaming.

Scattered dreams of *this man*, as I named him, began to show up. I entered a cathedral to find refuge and saw him, dressed in white, looking into a mirror. In the reflection, he nodded yes. I shook my head no. He nodded yes.

I'd not exactly had good luck dreaming up men.

Four years after divorcing my kids' father, I dreamed Bill Joyce. The dream took me wandering through a circus where I bought a gondola ticket from a dark bearded man, his face shadowed by a screen. We rode the bumpy gondola together, but he jumped off, and I had to scrabble up my books and parcels to leap after him. That dream was the reason I stayed even as life became one long circus as we moved from Austin to Los Angeles to New Orleans to New York, where I was cast in the movie that took me to Mexico and where I stayed after it was over, and lastly to Washington, D.C. Finally, I ran away—or more precisely, walked away—from love in all the wrong places, as the song goes.

To say the least, I was cautious of dreams. Was this man a problem or a puzzle? Life was a puzzle, with spaces left between all the pieces.

SOME WEEKS INTO DITHERING, THE CROSSROAD APPEARED.

"You have to stay," Frank said, squinting at the wall clock on the back bar. My happy hour shift had come to its quitting time. "Beth's sick. She can't come. If it's not busy, I'll let you go in a couple of hours."

It got busy.

Working nights meant music cranked up beyond happy hour levels by a DJ who only knew loud; colored strobe lights flashed along the walls; the standing-room-only packed with inexperienced drinkers who spent a lot of money on liquor, got sloppy, rarely tipped. This night no different. Since the bar was off K Street, just a couple of blocks from the White House, congressional interns came through in clumps, and a young man, whom I'd already served, bought several more drinks. As he scooped up the change, two dimes slid on the bar. He carefully picked them up, one by one, and dropped them in a vest pocket.

"Didn't your momma teach you how to tip?" My anger often ran to sarcasm.

He looked up, startled, his eyes trying to focus on mine to see if there was a joke he'd missed. There wasn't. He complained to Frank. It wasn't the first time I'd snapped at a man too drunk to realize he was being stupid. Frank fired me but not until the bar closed.

Anger had been my talisman for so long.

It was decidedly time to visit Ouide Bolen, a counselor I'd seen off and on after leaving Bill Joyce. Jungian trained, she encouraged my dream journaling, self-guided meditations, and my questioning. I made an appointment. She was happy to see me.

After I'd whined about my life, I said, "I'm tired of asking for someone to love me!"

Ouide leaned into the corner of her big leather armchair and tipped her head. Her hair, blended into the leather's brown, framed smiling eyes. "You can ask for anything you want as long as you're willing to take no for an answer."

Her response was like swat up the side of the head.

"Be willing to ask for what you want. If someone can't give it to you, ask someone else. Allow yourself to open up. You don't have to fight. Allow life to happen," Ouide said.

And how was I supposed to do that?

Home, I clapped on earphones for the steady drumbeats that led me on a visioning quest. Traveling forward through a long, dark tunnel, I arrived at a house under construction. I walked up to this man, brownish hair, about my height, who gave me a one-arm-around-the-shoulder hug. He was involved in the construction. I looked up at the roof and sunlight caught me full in the face. Pulled back into the tunnel, my arms reached out.

Not knowing what anything meant was familiar territory, forced to remain still when all of me strained to move forward.

Jeanne phoned. "Come to Hawaii," she said when I complained about being fired. "There's hotels. You'll find a job."

I shrugged. "Okay."

Nothing held me in D.C. My older son had moved to Denver; my younger son in Georgia.

I talked to the director of the ESL school where I taught part-time. "Jane, I want to go to Hawaii. I don't really know why, but I want to go. I'm sorry if I complicate your schedule."

"It's okay," she said. "I'll miss you. Put up a notice on the bulletin board. New students have started to arrive for the next term. Maybe one will sublet your apartment."

I put up a notice.

Two days later, a Korean student phoned, wanting to sublet the apartment. My daughter-in-law was Korean. Koreans kept things clean. I told my pronunciation clients I was leaving. International people understood moving on.

I needed to tell Cynthia so called her in Austin. She and I had been friends for years after we met working on the McGovern campaign for president. The night of the election, as state after state turned red with only one small square of blue, we left campaign headquarters and walked the streets of Temple, Texas, talking the stories of our lives. She was slender, willowy, with luxurious long and wavy dark hair. I didn't realize she was African American until one day, visiting in her apartment, she said something about her father being the first African American Attorney General in Texas. I can still see that day: Cynthia sitting in an overstuffed chair with an open window behind her, white silky curtains billowing around her. "Your father is Black?" I blurted. She looked at me and smiled. Her skin was more like coffee with a lot of cream. Driving home that day, I worried about that, wondered if we could still be friends. A couple days later, I asked her that same question: "Can we still be friends?" She burst out laughing. "Of course we can." And we were. Not only friends, but best friends. Together we went to the first women's convention since Seneca Falls in Houston, Texas, sat together in workshops, voted together.

When I lived in Manhattan, Kansas, after divorcing my husband and moving home to enter K-State, I'd drive the old Highway 75 south to Texas. Cynthia in Austin was always my destination. I even moved to Austin for a couple of years after K-State, but then I met Bill Joyce and more wandering ensued until I went to New York and from there was seduced into Mexico to make a movie and met Gloria and stayed in Mexico for over three years before moving to D.C.

Well, put that way, it's no wonder her voice sounded harsh.

"Hawaii?" she said. "Why are you going to Hawaii?" I told her the message from the spiritual teacher, Alissa. After long years of friendship and watching me wander off to one place or another, I expected her to understand I'd always come back, but each time was like the first time. "I'll write," I said. I always wrote, but each of my leave-takings was like forever.

Three weeks passed in a blur: boxes of books and incidentals shipped to Hawaii; lists made for the subletting student. My friend Willy drove me to the airport with two packed suitcases.

As the plane lifted over the Potomac, I looked out the window and glimpsed my apartment building. The rooftop swimming pool, blue-eye gleaming, studied me as I headed into unknown territory sans plan.

TWO

North Kohala, Hawaii Island

The plane reached altitude and leveled off. I heard the seat belt sign ding and the snap of a briefcase opening. The woman sitting in the aisle seat removed papers, flipped down the tray table, and began writing.

The past three weeks had exhausted me, so when the steward passed, I asked for a pillow and wrapped in my shawl. I slept, missing the meal, the movie, and the clouds, until the pilot's voice announced our descent into Los Angeles. Keeping my eyes closed and gingerly rolling my head back and forth, I released the tightness in my neck.

"Are you all right?" a voice said.

I opened my eyes and turned to the woman in the aisle seat. She smiled, but her eyes held a pinch of concern around the edges.

"Yeah, I think so," I said. "I guess I slept a long time."

"Yes, you did, but you kept breathing regularly, so I guessed you were just really tired."

The laugh that welled out of me surprised us both. "I was. What time is it?"

She glanced at her watch. "Not quite eleven . . . L.A. time."

I nodded. "Okay. Thanks."

I'd left one city in the morning, taken a four-hour nap across America, across farmland, mountains, desert, crossing nearly three thousand miles to arrive in another city before lunch. Homesickness stabbed. The student in D.C. had probably picked up keys to my apartment, shopped for groceries, brought in his books or papers. Already my home wasn't mine. A place, only, where someone else lived.

I watched as we made our approach over Los Angeles and remembered seeing the city at night, years before, during an aspiring for stardom period. I had moved to L.A., following hope, and now I followed some heart-opening-like-a-flower fantasy that might not be any more founded in reality than the star-struck dreams.

The woman from the aisle seat nodded as we deplaned. I hadn't talked to her more than our brief conversation as I woke, retreating into the solitude of the past weeks as I'd prepared to leave, shy of saying what I was doing, since I didn't know, shy of saying I'd deserted the restaurant plan since I'd told everyone who would listen I was opening a restaurant.

The beehive quality of the airport stunned me. I stood near one wall, reading the flight information monitors to get my bearings. I was hungry and I had to find my next gate. More than two hours yet before boarding for Kona, but I felt rattled by the noise of flight announcements, the undercurrent of music, the cries of unseen children, snatches of conversation as other, surer passengers strode by, and the sudden beeping insistence of a passenger cart. My body twitched as if it were being pushed, but it didn't know a direction.

"May I help you?" a voice said at my side.

I looked into the face of a tall, brown-skinned man. I had the fleeting impression he might be East Indian or Pakistani. "I need to find my flight to Hawaii," I said and heard the frantic tone in my voice.

"Which airline are you flying, madam?"

"United."

"That board is not here. If you will allow me, I will show you," he said, dipping his head in a very careful, and slightly sideways, bow.

I walked with him to another bank of monitors where he showed me the flight number and explained the gate location.

"I will walk with you to the turning of the corridor," he said, "and you will see."

We walked together silently, the noise in the corridor subsiding as if some safe cocoon were shielding us. At a conjunction of hallways, he indicated the direction to take, described the signs to look for, smiled briefly, and said, "You will find a small, quiet restaurant just near your gate. You might like to eat there. Goodbye." He bowed again with the same slight turn of his head.

As he walked against the tide of moving people, I noticed he wore a long, brown jacket, like a Nehru jacket. I hadn't remembered to thank him, and, I realized suddenly, I hadn't told him I was hungry.

I found the quiet restaurant. Two strangers had offered concern: the woman on the plane and the man in the brown jacket. I didn't often allow anyone to help me and had responded to the woman on the plane in that manner, shutting off conversation. But the man reached out in a vulnerable moment, and I'd not only allowed his help, I'd changed my usual brusque manner of response. The man's offered peace lay around me, and I didn't understand what had happened other than a simple act of kindness.

After a very long flight, Jeanne met me at the Kona airport. We drove to North Kohala on a tarmac highway across black lava, black on black, as if a heavy wheel had rolled through and flattened a road—no easily discernible boundary between tarmac and lava. Out my car window, beyond the stretch of black, a forested mountain reared up. On Jeanne's side, the ocean.

Scattered white rocks shaped curves over the lava. "What are those white rocks?"

Jeanne glanced over. "They spell out names or messages. If someone takes a new lover, they move the rocks." She laughed. "That's the road to the Ritz Carlton." I whipped around to see the sign disappear behind Jeanne's window. Turning to watch for white rocks, I recognized a heart, a plus sign, a name. White rocks spelling out "Lalani loves" swept by. We reached a stop sign. A wooden directional sign pointed right to Waimea, left to Hawi. Jeanne turned left.

"There's a heiau over there," Jeanne said and lifted one hand from the wheel to point through her window.

"What's that?" I said, looking at the rectangular shape of land and rock.

"A temple. We'll go down sometime and walk around. Can't climb on it though. It was Kamehameha's and sacred." She turned right at a gas station, passed scrubby trees clinging to rocky road banks, and topped a rise. Through the open windows, I smelled grassland and sea. The land leveled and ocean spread to the horizon. A double rainbow arched over placid waves.

"Look at that," Jeanne said. She grinned and ran fingers through her short-cropped red curls.

Wind rustled the wild grasses and sent my hair flying as we traveled the coast road. If Jeanne took this every day to the Ritz Carlton with the windows open, I understood why she'd cut her hair short. I might do the same. No curves in this highway, rather another straight blacktop road. Sometimes the ocean lay twenty feet away and sometimes a quarter-mile down the slope. Rocky outcroppings studded the grass, or a house set back on a hillside, but mostly miles and miles of grass and ocean. The rainbow traveled with us, sometimes brighter, then fading. We turned onto Puakea Ranch Road and drove downhill toward the ocean. She stopped at a wide, low, sand-colored house and parked in the circular drive.

Jeanne pulled out the suitcases and led me across a stone walkway between shallow pools. Water tinkled and water lilies breathed fragrance. But no time for dawdling as I trudged behind her, pulling one suitcase as she pulled another. We passed the kitchen, gleaming in sunlight, a wall of windows, a glimpse of sea beyond the slope of a hill, and down the hallway to a room where my tall and lanky brother-in-law Robert, wrench in hand, balanced two corners of a metal bed frame between his knees. I recognized the frame from the hoard of antique furniture they'd bought in Kansas and stored in the farm's old chicken house before shipping it to Hawaii.

"This is your room," Jeanne said.

Boxes I'd sent from D.C. were stacked in a corner. Did he want help? Robert shook his head. Lia arrived from school and wanted to drive me to Hawi, past the house where she'd grown up before the Puakea house, to Nakahara's General Store where I bought my first muumuu, a green leafed print, full length, while Lia shopped for supplies. After checking out, Lia pointed to the post office window and Robert's medical office behind the general store. I nodded and looked. We whirled back to Puakea, picked up Jeanne, and the three of us went to a movie in the old theater, a dark, wooden, barn-like building.

"We'll sit here," Jeanne said about halfway down the aisle. "The front rows are for the kids. They aren't padded."

Lia's curly hair bounced out of its knot and down her back as she pointed to the ceiling's studded nails. "This used to be a canoe house. Can you see the shape?" I nodded, and about halfway through the movie, nodded off. As we left, I confessed to falling asleep and missing most of the movie.

"Oh . . . yeah! Poor thing," Jeanne said. "It's after midnight where you're from. I forget you only arrived today. It feels you've been here always."

That evening, in the kitchen, Jeanne cooking, kids at the bar, me helping with homework, she said, "You're what I've always wanted: two of me!"

As night descended and I fell into bed, I briefly pondered how long and full one day could be.

I woke early. Outside my bedroom window, the patio stretched along the side of the house. Three steps down from the patio, a pool, and beyond the pool, a hillside of grass-waving pasture met the blue Pacific as it crawled toward the horizon. Maui's tip poked up, distant and green. The trade winds ruffled the trees, slanting from wind the same way trees on the farm slanted; the sky childhood familiar with clouds floating by. A Kansas in the summertime sky.

On Sunday, Robert wanted to go snorkeling. I'd learned to snorkel during the New York years when Bill and I lived on St. Lucia one winter, but the wide Pacific is a different beast. Below the Puakea house, waves crashed against rocks and cliffs, but Robert drove to a small bay where the waves broke at far edges and gentled as they brushed the rocky shoreline. Jeanne and Robert swam out to deeper water. I paddled fins languorously, grateful to feel salt water buoy me, to drift and watch. Sudden movement focused my eyes on an octopus, maybe a foot long, as it darted from rock to rock and slid to invisibility. A school of bright yellow fish with pointed dorsal fins waved past my mask's window, behind them a school of slender, striped green and yellow somethings. I could name the Caribbean fish, the seahorse, trumpet fish, angel fish, but this world was so much bigger. If a small octopus lived here, might a big one?

An octopus was an imagined challenge; the reality of paradise another.

Puakea lay on the island's dry side, so each morning, I checked my shoes to make sure no centipedes had taken up residence. Jeanne taught me how to pick 'em up with tongs, cut them in half with the pair of scissors kept at the back of the toilet, and flush the halves.

One night, a cloud of mosquitoes attacked. Robert and I found the standing water and drained it. And then the ants! Tiny ants traveled in long trails across the porch and into the house. I swept them up and plugged holes and they kept coming. I swore they'd lift the house and carry it away if given half a chance. They finally gave up. Out of fear at my frenzy or a change in routes.

Putzing became my life: laundry for five people, sheets and towels for Robert's office; a daily check of the pool vac to make sure it was working; sweep the patio; cut Jeanne's roses and put them to chill; write a letter; jump in the pool and swim laps; watch the cat stalk invisible prey.

During an afternoon home from the hotel, Jeanne said, "There's a workshop on Brain Gym in Kona. I know the teacher. Why don't you go? You wanted to learn muscle testing."

A week later, detailed directions in hand, I dropped Jeanne at the Ritz Carlton and drove to Kona. I'd glimpsed wild and loose goats on the lava field during the drive from the airport, now I stopped for three loose donkeys crossing the road. My body grinned all over. Hawaii and Mexico. Home. At the workshop, I realized my left brain made pictures, and the cross-crawl exercise made memory more accessible. Anything that allowed me to access memory was a plus, and the cross-crawl exercise anchored memory in my body.

Soon, Halloween arrived. Robert, master-stitcher of wounds, sewed up an alligator costume, complete with snout and long tail. The cooking duties fell to Jeanne, Lia, and me, while Robert and Daemion sprayed tangled cobwebs from doorposts, lintels, and corners. For the party, I wore a white silk jalabiya a Saudi friend, Fatimah, had given me. Parties at the house meant hordes of people, but the veil allowed me to lurk at the edges in wallflower mode.

November blew in. Rain sloughed, battered the patio doors, seeped into pools under the sill. The trees whipped their faces toward the house. We spread towels on the floor to sop up water. When the rains stopped, snow lay on Mona Loa.

The next morning, Jeanne and I put on jackets for our walk up to the gate, dodging cows lying on the sun-warmed tarmac, calves huddled against their sides. "You know, when I left Mexico, I sensed a change coming, and I wanted to see it. How am I supposed to see? I don't even know what to look for!" I could hear desperation in my voice.

We parted on each side of a paired cow/calf and rejoined five paces past, Jeanne watching ahead, me with my head down, pondering. "Maybe I need to be more specific when I make requests," I said. Jeanne laughed. Her nose and cheeks were glowing pink. "I mean, in D.C. stuff happens, but I'm in Hawaii with no plan. I'm expecting some great spiritual something. A calling? And I don't even want to be a spiritual leader."

"Maybe you need to write a book called the reluctant master," she said.

"Maybe. If I can ever figure out what to master in."

Many of the books I'd boxed and left in my D.C. closet were from the early searching years when I lived in Texas, met Cynthia Alexander, organized women's study groups, and argued for women's equality in work and in the God-head: Joseph Campbell and Robert Graves, Monica Sjöös. They wrote of the holy as partnered masculine and feminine energy. If I had a spiritual path, I wanted one like that.

We returned to the house, me pondering, Jeanne accepting my silence. Every spiritual path I'd practiced had some rule or another, mostly several, I couldn't follow. And none had spoken of equal male/female energy.

That afternoon, a letter arrived from my friend Sandy. She wrote, "Are you pushed by your past or pulled by your future?" I didn't know. I stared at the letter in my hand. Whenever someone asked me, "What do you see yourself doing in five years?" I couldn't answer. As a kid in Sunday school, I heard "Have faith." Faith in what, I wanted to know. "In God," they said. "What does that mean?" I said. No one told me.

Was faith hoping someday something would make sense and I'd understand what I was doing?

Sitting at my Smith Corona, I began to answer Sandy's letter when Robert knocked. "Want to come visit Kindy? I did his gall bladder surgery a couple of weeks ago and want to check on him. He said he'd give me some red ti leaves." Adventures with Robert always beat pondering.

We drove to Pololu where the road ended and parked at a rock wall. Ocean yawned to the horizon. I almost missed my step down from the truck, staring, as I was, at the expanse of water. It seemed bigger than at Puakea, overwhelmingly bigger, and I tried to figure out which way I faced, toward which part of the North American continent. I knew Hawaii Island was more or less on the same parallel as Mexico, but we were at the top of the island and at an angle slanting northeasterly. Robert was already walking across the road toward a wall of shrubbery. I turned from the ocean to follow him through a half-hidden gate.

"Kindy!"

A white-haired man pushed open the screen door and started down the porch steps, one careful step at a time, bracing himself with a cane.

Once on solid ground, he opened his palm and showed Robert four small, narrow glass bottles, stained and streaked with dirt.

"Opium bottles," Kindy said. "From the twenties. Found them when we dug the new cesspool. Here, Doc. Dig that." He flipped his cane tip at the edge of a red ti leaf. Robert dug. "Back in the twenties, Hu Lee sold opium for gold pieces and made a half million dollars." When Kindy laughed, his bushy mustache wobbled. It seems Mr. Frank, the banker, had convinced Hu Lee to rent a safety deposit box. But Mr. Lee didn't trust the banker, so he welded forty-six pounds of gold together and left it in his box. Each week, he'd go to the bank, lift at the corner of the box, test the weight. When his son was ready for college, Lee pulled out the box, but all he found was forty-six pounds of lead. "Course, Hu Lee couldn't say anything or they'd find out how he got that much gold." Kindy pulled off several limes and handed them to Robert. "Here. Got choke limes on this tree. So anytime I wanted to get Lee going, I'd say, 'Hey, Lee, what about that Mister Frank?' 'Ooooooh, Mi'ter Frank!' he'd say. 'He bad man!'" Kindy laughed so hard he wobbled on his cane. Robert reached out to steady him.

"What are choke limes?" I said. Kindy laughed again. "Too many!" he said. "Choke means too many." He led us to a palm tree, reached up his cane, and knocked down two green coconuts.

"Doc, hand me that machete leaning against the porch." Robert brought the machete and with the swing of a much younger man, Kindy sliced off the tops so we could drink the coconut water. "Ever had a star fruit?" he said, pulling a yellow waxy lobe from another tree. He held it under my nose and I sniffed sweet sunshine. When I bit into it, juice ran down my chin.

The Kindy trip plied us with coconuts, star fruit, red ti plants, avocados a bag of limes, and stories, but not one word about his surgery. We loaded the truck.

"Want to see the beach?" Robert said. I hadn't noticed a beach, but I nodded. He led me on a steep climb down a trail of shifting rocks and lava chunks to a narrow curve of black sand where waves rustled. I found a disk-shaped piece of volcanic stone, small enough to rest in my hand.

"Pelé either welcomes or she drives you away," Jeanne said when I showed her. "You are welcomed. That's a gift from Pelé."

The next weekend, Robert wanted to visit the Goddess Pelé and show me Kilauea, the active flow at the bottom end of the island and recently busy. We arrived at dusk. It wasn't what I'd envisioned, fire and rocks shooting into the sky; instead, a Niagara of fire flowed down the volcano's sides from vents below the jagged top. Robert stopped near Park Service signs blocking the road. Spray-painted arrows guided us as we walked toward the sea, the lava flow thirty feet or so to our left. Scorched trees exploded into flame. Heat and acrid smoke swirled in a heavy black veil. We were extras in a disaster movie.

At the beach, a fresh wind blew in from the sea and a full moon hung beyond the breakers. Molten fire flowed from a lava tube mouth, seared the sand, rolled into the surf, and broke into flaming chunks roiled by waves. Earth, fire, water, wind, full moon myth and magic. Maybe I could live here. Maybe I'd found home.

THREE

GOING NATIVE

Jeanne's friend Emily Stark invited me to a weaving class—weaving a meditation, no thinking required. As my hands threaded long green ti leaves into patterns, all I had to do was watch. In North Kohala, the multi-ethnic community served up multi-experiences. We attended a harvest celebration at the Tong Wo Society and listened as an old priest chanted, accompanied by a soul-shivering reed flute. Jeanne introduced me to Susé Suarez, a small man whose knees knurled from years of hula, and who only charged twenty dollars a month for classes. When I asked him if I could take lessons, he said yes. The Hawi library, white clapboard under a chapel-peaked roof, fed my searching soul.

In Mexico City, I'd wandered the British Library, studied the history of my northern England name, and wondered at my Celtic warrior blood. After gathering armloads of books by writers I'd never heard of—Colin Wilson and Lethbridge and Lovecraft—I'd spread them on the floor of my apartment and sit cross-legged next to the coffee table, tea and journal at hand, as I searched for clues, alone in a city that did not know my name.

In Hawi, even the librarian knew me. "You're Jeanne's sister?" she said. "You look like her." Nothing by Colin Wilson or any of the writers I'd discovered in Mexico, but I found a shelf of Carlos Castaneda; John Irving's *A Prayer for Owen Meany*, an elegant little book; *A Tree in Bud*, by M.G. Bosseront d'Anglade, recounting a Frenchman's travels in Hawaii from a hundred years earlier; and Pinkola Estes's *Women Who Run with the Wolves*. Pinkola Estes reminded me to reread Carl Jung, as once more, I pondered questions I didn't know how to form.

"Come on!" Robert called as I read. And off we dashed to plant a vegetable garden beyond the house: sweet potatoes and cucumbers, melons, beans, shaded from the midday sun by an equally expansive kiawe tree. Another day, we foraged on the several acres he'd planted with palms, bananas, breadfruit, and mango trees. Our arms and baskets filled, we carried bounty home.

When no work demanded, I sat at my Smith Corona portable word processor, wrote letters, and worked on the manuscript, forever waiting, of my life in Mexico.

A treasure, this first ever computer-typewriter was bought during a trip to the States and carried back to Mexico through suspicious customs agents. Was I going to sell it? No, it was my personal typewriter. Is there anything inside? Only paper. They opened it anyway and finding nothing, waved at me, "*Vaya!*" meaning get going. I got.

It went to my Zona Rosa apartment over the travel agency where I worked, only to carry it to D.C., and Hawaii, and rooms with a view. As a kid on the farm, I'd inherited the one single-occupancy farmhouse bedroom when my sister left for college, an attic room, blue-painted wallboard rising to an overhead peak, an east window with a view of the lane down to the road, and records stacked on the portable player. Now my Hawaiian sanctuary was filled with the sound of sea, the rustle of kiawe branches, the scratched call of a mynah bird as I wrote letters and bits of poetry on my Smith Corona.

On a grocery trip with Jeanne to Kapaau, the next town past Hawi, Jeanne grabbed a cart and walked off. I dawdled, distracted by bright packaging and unfamiliar products. I heard Jeanne's voice and saw a man reach to a top shelf and hand her something. "Thank you!" she said. I followed around the end of the aisle to the meat counter. The butcher wrapped a parcel in brown paper. "Thank you!" Jeanne said when he handed it to her. At checkout, the woman at the register picked up the bag of groceries, walked to the end of her counter, and snuggled the bag securely into Jeanne's arms.

"Thank you!" Jeanne said, smiled, and walked out the door.

As if rooted by the proverbial light bulb, switched on, I watched my sister go out the door. I rarely said thank you. Back home, a retreat to my room gave me space to figure out this latest piece. Opening my journal, I wrote and with the same light-bulb realization, understood. My history said receiving meant pain, or it meant someone wanted something I wouldn't know how to refuse. My body, for example. I sighed. It seemed I'd had a rare, but expressive, visible signpost.

Self-consciously, I began to practice thank you, deliberately, stubbornly: thank you to the mail carrier, at the store, when the kids handed me a kitchen implement. Now I had two tools for practice: Ouide taught me to ask for what I wanted, and I could say thank you and receive.

Jeanne sensed my restlessness and prodded me to find a job. I dressed appropriately, drove down to the Mauna Loa Hotel, and filled out an application for a receptionist job. "Thank you," I said to the woman who took my form without glancing at me. I attended a meeting of the West

Hawaii Communicators and a woman invited me to a before-theater party. "Thank you."

In the local paper, I searched for an opening, a clue, as if I were playing poker with God. Sometimes I played recklessly. Reviewing my behavior/my life/my dreams sucked me into a whirlpool of self-reflection. Restlessness drove me from the house.

Walking the pastures was a familiar escape, my same escape as a farm kid. I skirted the grassy fields sliding from the highlands, stood at the field's edge, watched the waves, thirty feet below, crash onto rocks, and wondered at the chain of events that had deposited me like so much driftwood. I smelled sea as wind rocked my body and gusted hair across my face. I was too close to the edge. I kept writing about my trouble moving forward, yet all I seemed to do was move, restlessly, from one point, one experience to another, moving always moving. And yet everywhere I'd lived, eventually I came to this same place. A stop. Or a precipice. In this case a cliff. Knowing there was something that had to change, not knowing what it was, as I stood, toes hanging over, wondering if I'd grow wings. And the waiting! The long-drawn-out waiting.

I retraced my steps to the house.

That night, I woke from a dream. I'm packing to go on a trip. I'm tired. I cross a street but have trouble moving. This man, the dark-haired dream man, reaches out to help me. We go into a shop for coffee and he tells me it can be hard to move. He's cultured and I ask if he's from Europe and he tells me no, from near D.C. in union country. Union country?

My scribbled-out line on the preceding page faced the written-out dream: *How do I find the courage to do things my way. What is my way?*

I had neither courage nor a decision. And I sure couldn't find a direction. In effect, after searching and traveling and reading and even moving to Hawaii, I felt split, with no idea how to merge the parts of me. I had to find a job, but I couldn't find a job until I figured out what I was doing. The back-and-forth waiting rubbed sores on my soul.

Each morning, I opened my journal to pages written by a mad woman, scrawled with night-written pieces of dreams, short pieces of poetry—two or three lines, a stanza, bits of my ideas. *Your memory is a monster; you forget—it doesn't. It just files things somewhere you can't find.* Like a tornado's tail spinning in place, my attention drilled my interior life. Turmoil and chaos leaked from the notebook's pages while rage stalked my nights—rage, an old and too familiar friend. Pages filled with a kaleidoscope of dream images: fighting with past lovers, foundering at school, dark male figures chased or threatened or yelled. A lion, a huge lion, chased my car, jumped on it, stopped it, and I was afraid, but it transformed into a happy baby lion. A lion. Something about strength and courage chasing me? Was the baby lion a gift?

Paired typhoons in the Pacific sucked out air and vitality, the sky streaked and gray. The sea lay as heavy and greasy as the air. Bugs landed in the pool, not understanding the blue space so like the sky was their coffin and grave. I scooped their carcasses in the morning, scooped more before swimming in the afternoon. The family tottered about, slow and stupid; we picked at each other and bickered; we retreated to our separate rooms. Some of the crankiness was directed at the growing storm, but the rest was directed at my over-giving and fixing, as if doing could solve my poor relation status.

That same fixing created uproars with Bill. He said I tried to control everything. I thought I was keeping things safe. Except for packing up and moving to Los Angeles or finding the apartment in New York or typing his manuscripts, nothing I did was right. He complained I didn't make enough money, and he complained when I accepted a job on a film in Utah instead of traveling with him to Isla Mujeres.

Why was I blaming him? I was as absorbed in my own need for recognition as he was by his. And why was I re-whining all this like a fugitive peering through dead weeds of the past? What I needed to do was to figure out how to change something that didn't work into something that did. Like maybe offer? Like, let me know if you need my help? Or, do you want me to… well, whatever. Another signpost; another practice.

The director from the West Hawaii Communicators phoned. "We're doing a murder mystery at Parker Ranch for dinner theater. Are you interested in the mother role? We're paying five hundred for the week."

I was interested. And returned to re-live what had been, a woman passionate for acting. On the stage or in front of a camera, I could be someone brave or good or funny. How many years, how many years of community theater playing the maid on the tracks or the wild beauty luring the hero? In my childhood country schoolhouse, I'd played the mother in Christmas school productions; in Germany, I'd worked in Armed Forces Recreation theater and played complicated women; in college at K-State, Nora in a Doll's House suited my history. I tasted stardom, moved to Austin, earned a coveted Screen Actors Guild card, moved to Los Angeles and to New York. In New York, I worked off-off Broadway and some film jobs before the project that seduced me into Mexico.

Now I was the mother in a who-dunnit for audience participation between courses, roast beef and gravy smells wafting through the curtain.

The play ended. I said thank you. I picked up my check and returned to books.

More books. I needed more books to build my raft. I checked out mythology and reread stories of journeys and fear: Orpheus, who loved Eurydice, traveled to Hades to find her but lost her because of fear. Psyche feared and peeked at the sleeping Eros—he fled. Odysseus blocked from his journey home: fear and more fear. I understood fear, the great mythological terror stalking my nights. Where was the baby lion when I needed it?

At 2 a.m. I startled awake in a dream of my father John's voice on a speaker phone. He says he's been seeing a blond woman. He says he was involved with her several years ago and recently became re-involved. The dream shifts to a woman, sitting inside a safe. A man comes in and tries to kick her, but she's in the safe. I wrote out the dream and ended with: *my father? on a speaker phone???*

My father didn't leave a lot of history behind him. Nothing tangible but a few photos and one letter he wrote to my mother after he set off across the Pacific toward a war he couldn't enter because of flat feet. He did the next best thing and became a merchant marine, but after reaching Hawaii, he was put on another ship heading back to California. The history he left were his children. I looked like him. The oldest brother who died looked like him. I wondered if that's why Mother and I had fought so much. I wasn't Little Joe.

Two hours later, a chase dream, familiar, like I'd had it before. Dark men chase me. I run on a lava field. But instead of running straight as I'd done before, I zag left and crouch behind an up risen and frozen black wave.

On our morning walk, I recounted the chase dream for Jeanne. "Well, you have to decide," she said. "Either everything is safe or everything is dangerous. Which do you want?"

I wanted safe. In my next dream, I'm sitting on the ground as a hawk circles above me. A long, raw wound runs up my leg, but it's stitched and beginning to heal. Returning my stack of mythology to the library, I checked out books on Hawaiian history.

Hula class with Susé Suarez lifted my spirits, even when my knees and hips ached from the semi-crouched position. At least I was moving. I didn't have to be a perfect dancer; I had to dance. I practiced thank you. I monitored my over-giving. And my solar plexus, an always-tight spot, began to relax.

FOUR

NAVIGATING INTO TOMORROW

A passing wind-fit bobbed colored bulbs on palm tree fronds; strings of lights decorated the general store; a snowman with a lighted top hat sat in a yard, a trio of angels in another. The towering fir in the middle of the town square, inconspicuous most days other than being tall, erupted in a blaze of multi-colored glory one evening as I drove past. The abrupt illumination drew me off the road to park and stare. A poem rattled in my head, fat geckos wearing silver bells and dragonflies sporting red wings. It needed work. Misty rain shimmered in the lights.

When I was a kid in Kansas, wearing jeans, long johns, overshoes and mittens, and digging trails through drifts to the barn, Christmas cards came from Aunt Doris in Florida. She'd say she was decorating her tree while wearing shorts. Seemed odd and hardly Christmassy, but I remembered her as I wore shorts, trimming the tree at Puakea.

Mom arrived and resumed her usual winter life, including laundry.

A short newspaper article described a Wellness Program at a retreat center near Volcano and invited applicants. Participants would work at the center for room and board plus pay $200 a month to participate in the program. I pulled up my resume on the Smith Corona, removed the bartending, emphasized my years as an assistant in the Mexico City travel office, my years teaching at the ESL school and the Office of Personnel Management in D.C., and wrote a letter of introduction asking for office work and a stipend instead of paying the fee. I posted it in the mail with the same dash I'd done everything else. They did not reply with dash. I dawdled, vacuumed the pool, puttered with Mom, and helped her fold clothes.

"How's church? Is Lavern still alive?" Dad and Mom had moved into town a few years before he died. Lavern's husband, Virgil, was a friend of Dad's. They bowled together, served as elders at church, and died within months of each other.

"Oh, my yes. Ruthie picks her up every Sunday before she comes by for me," Mom said. "Young Virg and Marilyn sometimes. They live a couple houses down, you know." Young Virg would never graduate to his dead father's Virgil. She told me a story about kids coming up to her and measuring their growing heights against her 4'11" frame, which somehow evolved into a story about the preacher. Not the same preacher I'd argued with in my adolescent years. The current preacher was young. A friend to Mom. I nodded, said nothing.

Throughout my youth, I argued with church preachers and Sunday school teachers. "Jesus got angry," I'd say. But his anger was justified, they said. I was simply angry. That part was true. I spent years fighting with Mom. After I married, I fought with my husband. Maybe the residue of my father dying so young, but still. In Germany, after a fight, I ran through the woods bordering the housing compound, pounded myself into the path, salty sweat and salty tears dripping off my chin. Panting, I collapsed on a fallen tree trunk, head down, hands braced on my knees, grasping at air. I'd fought with someone for almost as long as I could remember, and had kept on fighting, angry at life. I lifted my head. Green-speckled sunbeams arrowed through the canopy. My life; my mother's life. I imagined her as a woman my age who lived with the death of both her first husband and first born, and a writer trapped in housework. The vision shocked me. She'd had none of my advantages. I had the women's movement and modern psychology. I'd found a way to stretch into possibilities she'd never known. Head down, ashamed of my rage, I forgave my mother for being my mother and picked up responsibility for my own life.

After I left my marriage and Germany for college and Kansas, I often drove to the farm for weekends in the old brown Chevy Dad bought me. Mom and I spent hours talking stories. One day I asked, "Why did Dad and I argue so much when I was a kid?" She glanced up from mending a shirt collar. "I suspect you looked too much like John Sunderland," she said. An old story: my father and my dad dated her at the same time; they'd disliked each other; after my father died, Mom and Dad met again and married.

Now we folded clothes and talked family and church.

A notice appeared in the newspaper for the First Annual Poetry Festival at Kalani Honua, the retreat center where I'd applied for a residency. Jeanne encouraged me. "It's in the jungle so take bug spray, but you'll like it. Mom can do the laundry." She drove me into Waimea to catch the Hilo bus.

Traveling down the windward side of the island, I held my journal in my lap and wrote one line: "We so seldom know each other—and inside families we know each other even less—or perhaps we know each other so well, the role we play within the core group remains the same; we slide into the same patterns, and it takes an effort to be ourselves."

I could be me for a weekend.

The landscape outside the bus window filled with lush, rainy-side vegetation. Volunteer sugar cane grew in abandoned fields; small, banana-tree-shaded towns stretched for a quick glance; a whiff of ripe fruit drifted in the open window. Tantalizing roads branched from the main highway, and signs pointed to towns or beaches with unpronounceable names: Honoka'a, Kukuihaele, Laupahoehoe, Kolekole. Learning Spanish in Mexico taught me to listen to the music of a language, and while I could hear the sea in Hawaiian, the multi-syllable vowels eluded me. The land became deeper, covered in vegetation. Overhanging trees shaded the road, so unlike the wide and open spaces of North Kohala.

As we entered Hilo, the city engulfed us in car fumes, noise, and flowering bushes. A crowd of people surged at a stoplight. I left the bus at Prince Kuhio Plaza and searched for the Kalani Honua van. At the front fender of a blue van, a man held a hand-lettered sign: Kalani Honua.

"I'm Janet," I said. "Am I riding with you?" He nodded. "Climb in."

The highway wound south through Pahoa, a small town of head shops and health food stores. The driver picked up boxed supplies and turned onto the Red Road, tunneled by overhanging, gnarled trees belonging only to myth. Leaves shadowed into black, and tantalizing glimpses of sun-drenched white-topped waves peeked between the trunks on ocean side. Turning off the road, the driver bumped up a lane past a field where horses grazed and stopped in front of a low, screened building. "That's the office. Go in there to register," he said. Four women sat around a picnic table, threading white flowers into leis. I retrieved my key and walked past a swimming pool to find the room: a single bed, screened windows with no glass, and resident geckos.

That evening, the festival, dedicated to the Beat poets, opened with *West Coast Beat and Beyond*, a film paean to Jack Kerouac, with Ginsberg, Ferlinghetti, and Gregory Corso reminiscing about Kerouac and reading poetry. In the film, Jan Kerouac read a passage from her mother's memoir about how she'd tried to leave Jack but he sat on his desk and the movers moved him with the desk. It was supposed to be funny. People laughed.

It's never easy to leave an outlaw.

I'd tried to leave Bill in New York but he followed me, not sitting on his desk but lugging papers and books in box after box into the new apartment with windows on West 85th. Windows in the front room, anyway. The one window in the bedroom looked out on an alley. I should have asked before building the loft bed and stationing his desk under it. That caused a huge fight. I couldn't remember if we discussed decisions. I made decisions; he made his. More loudly than words, our actions stated we couldn't trust each other to put the other first. My memory wandered through New York to some party when Ken Kesey came to town. The guys stood in a circle around the kitchen's butcher-block island, glasses and half-empty bottles littering the surface, and spun out stories of one great man or another. Bill and Kesey were close in age, both too young to be beatniks, both regretted their near miss. I waited behind Bill and listened, invisible.

As the film ended, our Kalani group began a general shuffling around with drinks and accolades to the generation of Beats. No mention of the rage that drove them. Rage rarely is a nice subject and everyone was nice. Drunk was the most outrageous anyone got. I headed to my room and bed.

The next morning at breakfast, Aelbert Aehegma, whom I'd met the evening before in passing, sat down at the table. "You're a writer?"

"I don't know. I write. I'm an actor."

"Really? I'm working on a video project." Pushing a hand through sandy hair, his fingers ruffled furrows. "I'm working on the Kumulipo. You know? The Hawaiian creation chant," he added when I shook my head. "I want to film first woman rising from the sea. You want to try it?"

"Sure. I guess. What are you thinking?" What I was thinking was how far into and out of and did he mean nude.

"I want to shoot where the lava flowed over the beach a few years back. You know that beach?"

I shook my head. "I've been on the North Shore for a couple of months. And down here for the first time."

He wrestled a script out of his bag and studied it.

"You have a pareo?"

"Pareo?"

"Like a sarong."

"I have one from Mexico, blue with flowers."

"Good." He studied the script. "This is what I'm thinking: the water up there's a little rough, so I wouldn't want you to go out too far. Up to your knees is okay . . . and walk out? Can you do that?" I nodded. "And then I'll have you run over the lava. It's pahoehoe so you can run barefoot. What are you doing today?"

"Uh . . . " there it was, love caught between plan and desire. "I planned on joining the morning walk to explore the land, but I can . . . what did you have in mind?"

"This afternoon? That would give me time to get stuff ready." I nodded. "I'll see you here for lunch," he said and shoved the script into his bag.

Odd coincidences seemed to be happening—or maybe magic—faster than anywhere since Mexico. At least on this wild side of Hawaii. I'd longed to do films again, but I didn't expect it here. I'd expected poets.

And there were poets. At the previous night's gathering, a man in a maple leaf T-shirt introduced himself as Will; he'd owned the bar in New Orleans where Bill Joyce and I read poetry. I tried to tell him the story of the Mardi Gras night we had a reading at his bar after drinking Captain Morgan all day, but he didn't listen. He talked. He'd come to Hawaii from teaching at Old Miss, but he was tired and wanted to get away from people. Really? So he'd come to a poetry reading? While not exactly magical, it was bizarre. My own Kerouacian thing, watching how his mind worked in the external world. I didn't make it a poem.

Magic, however, accompanied the walk. I hadn't been near a jungle since living on St. Lucia for a couple of months one winter. I'd followed Sabella, niece of the caretaker, into the valley of banana trees and up a jungle path to where she kept pigs. No pigs on this walk, rather miles of jungle and lava outcroppings, the caved-in mouth of an old lava tube, and screeching bird cries. The jungle's raw fierceness gave way to a clearing where a green pond, like a hidden emerald, lay undisturbed, glowing in sunlight.

At lunch, my tired legs stretched out, I wondered how often I'd have to run out of surf and across lava.

Often, as it turned out, movie-making being what it is. But the salt water washed away the ache, and Aelbert so encouraging and so full of praise, I forgot tired as I lifted handfuls of water and trickled iridescent streams through my fingers. The short runs on lava were just that. Short. And pahoehoe lava, I learned, was smooth.

"You're running from sea monsters," Aelbert said.

Now there's motivation.

I napped before evening festivities.

That evening, with jazz and poetry on the schedule, we gathered. Ray Besom hunched over a table, fiercely scribbling, while the guys, the ever present guys, gathered in homage to hunch with him. Their musty male scent formed a wall. Besom disentangled himself long enough to read a long rambling freshly composed poem. Lots of being led around by his cock and disjointed phrases I couldn't follow. All in a sing-song voice that grated on my ears. The guys laughed. I didn't.

About to call it a night, a poet who introduced himself as Kristan walked to my chair. "Do you have anything to read?" I did. So we read poetry to the accompaniment of a sax and raised-eyebrows-who-is-this-masked-woman-with-Kristan looks. On the way to my room, my memory wandered over the years of poetry readings with Bill, sometimes with a guitarist, and I thanked his tutelage. He taught me to give lines their natural space and rhythm.

The next morning, before taking the van to Hilo for the bus to North Kohala, I walked to the office and introduced myself to the program director, Howard Duncan. Healers were coming from all over the world. I wanted to be one of them. Was there an office job? He nodded.

"Letters of acceptance will go out in January," he said.

FIVE

STORMY WEATHER

I returned to North Kohala and two letters forwarded from my D.C. address from Bill. Given the past few days, they seemed a wry gift, as if I had pulled him in with my poetry jaunt. I held the letters and read the postmarks, one from Prague, the second from Virginia, as dusty scene after dusty scene wound through my memory. It still surprised me that in D.C., we had finally ended our life together after inching toward a breakup for years. Even after I'd moved to my studio apartment and he'd moved across town, we continued spending time together. Until we stopped.

He'd agreed to pick me up and take me to the repair shop where my Smith Corona was being cleaned. I watched in the direction I thought he'd come, not seeing he'd parked up the block behind me. Wheeling in a U-turn, he slammed to the curb. I could see he was angry through the starburst-patterned windshield.

"What happened?" I slid into the passenger side. My question unleashed a torrent.

"You spaced out again. You're always daydreaming. Look what's happened because you can't pay attention!" He jabbed his fist toward the starburst. "Who's going to pay for this? You?" Oh. He'd punched it. "We're always going to be failures, it doesn't matter what we do. This'll cost more than two hundred . . . "

My shoulders curved, sinking into myself. The voice commanded Stop!

As if a string attached to the top of my head pulled, I sat upright. We were coming to a stop sign. He stopped. I flipped the door handle, got out of the Renault, and carefully shut the door. "I'll take the metro," I said through the open window.

We didn't communicate for a long time. We did, unexpectedly, see each other a few months later, but communication wasn't what happened. Three-year-old grandson Michael had come to live with me for a few months, and he and I went to meet Dena, a friend from when I first moved onto P Street, at a local sidewalk café. She adored Michael and he loved sticking his hands into her dark, wavy hair, grabbing curls.

Michael and I joined Dena. Bill sat at a far table beside the wrought iron fence marking the restaurant's boundary, every inch the garrulous writer hunched under his hat, the same straw panama slanted over his eyes, the same suede jacket as in a photo I'd taken in Mexico. I handed Michael over to Dena and walked to Bill's table. He didn't look up when I sat down.

"Ron's coming any minute. That's for him," he said, glancing at the chair.

I stared at him, bowed over his soup, and willed him to look at me. He didn't. Or wouldn't. The conversation more a one-sided monologue, maybe a harangue. "If this relationship can be fixed, you have to do it. I'm done with fixing," I said.

He looked up, or rather swept a look around, "Everyone can hear you."

I didn't particularly care, but I ran out of words, collected Michael from Dena's table, and left. Michael's short legs struggled with the steps up to the sidewalk, but once there, he slipped his hand free, ready to see what lay ahead.

It didn't occur to me then, but I wondered if people thought me a wronged wife with son since Michael and Bill's dark hair and eyes were copy-shaded, as well as the shape of their eyes: an AmerAsian grandson and a Black Irish former lover who didn't fix. I regretted he'd never met Michael. We broke up before he got the chance. Bill was good with kids and with animals. Why or how we began communicating again lived in that part of my memory resistant to remembering, but we'd stayed in touch off and on. When I traveled west to Hawaii, Bill traveled east to Prague.

What bound us for ten years? Our passions, yes. I thought we were partner artists, but his true love was writing the story of Gorm, his alter-ego, or maybe his daemon. Why didn't we let go? Our separation was more a yo-yo game of drop/yank/drop/yank.

That's how the dream gondola traveled on its uneven ride, I now remembered. I hadn't paid attention.

Opening the Prague letter, dated late October, I learned his bronchitis, a left-over from Pittsburgh coal-dust air, was back. It was "raining little razors that carve the bones into Pleistocene remains." The man did have a way with words. He'd had success selling *For Women Who Moan*, his book of poetry sporting my photo on the cover. *Der Stern*, a German magazine, had interviewed him, which brought German tourists to line up for the book. "So now you are ensconced in many a Berlin apartment and Danish seaside town," he wrote, followed by a long paragraph of how the country had been sold to Coca Cola and Stockholm investors. The second letter from Virginia put him back in the States, hustling his books, working a poet gig at some college, and complaining about the slick suburbs. I sighed.

Love. I didn't even know what the word meant. Passion, pain, persistence. Bill's seduction added charm and intelligence. When Irish eyes are smiling, sure, they'll steal your heart away. My heart was stolen, and I kept hunting for that person I believed was the truth of him; but truth, by its very nature, is slippery. And I was easily seduced.

Winter Solstice arrived with Christmas following on its heel. We kept the solstice candles burning, cooked and laughed and retold stories. "Remember the winter Mom and Dad went to Florida, and it snowed so much we had to dig tunnels to the barn? Remember Kenny Dovorik trudging across fields to help us dig? Remember?" But Jeanne wouldn't have dug snow. She was too young. She remembered a photo of her and little sister Julia, sitting on top of a drift as high as the grain bin. Mom said, "Dad was allergic to trees. We put up an artificial one. I wonder what happened to it." We baked cookies and laughed. We wrapped presents and laughed. It was high season, so Jeanne dusted off her hands and dashed to the hotel more than she wanted. But we were all home Christmas Day.

On New Year's Eve, Robert took me to the newly opened Bamboo Restaurant in Hawi for a community party. Jeanne wasn't interested. I danced the year in, first with a good dancer who left for another party, and then with a second who danced with himself and complained about the band.

My next partner flirted and wanted to know why I was in town. He said he played guitar and had all these great ideas for doing something with music. He was charming. Could he be a lover for fun? Warning bells clanged. Another artist who needed a caretaker? I'd be hooked in no time. I quietly wound my way to the table where Robert sat in conversation.

We drove home in a storm that lasted five days.

I read, recorded more dreams: traveling fast to a new job; cooking with a whirring blender and feeding people; this man, kind and gentle, helping me. I dreamed of being as light as a feather, free of guilt, and remembered a dream from Mexico, a gray bird, caught in string. I'd climbed on a chair to cut it free. If I'd finally cut myself free from Bill, where would guilt-free lead? Too many questions, too few answers. Laboring to find a system, form, a way to hold the chaotic and disordered fragments in some pattern, I fumed and stomped and argued with God-of-many-names.

When Kona winds blow, they bring the big storms. Waves rolled fierce in the channel. Instead of a Kansas nor'easter, we had a Pacific sou'wester. We were cold. The house wide, no central heat, and the warm spot in front of the fireplace didn't reach far. Robert tied plastic bags over his shoes and waded water to the car. Rain came in waves, vertical waves, sheeting from the ocean, up the hill, blasting the patio doors into rattle. Tree branches whipped, tossed back on themselves. We dragged in the patio furniture, the cat bowls, and sopped up water on the floor.

At last, a morning rainbow built itself over the slate-colored sea. The winds died. Lives uprooted, family members staggered to their routines. Mom and I dragged patio furniture onto the patio and sent the cats outside. The pool looked as if a very large ship had foundered a cargo of palm fronds. I tugged and tossed fronds and set the pool vac running. The water too cold for swimming.

Cabin fever propelled me out of the house. I drove down to Kwaihae Harbor to see the storm damage, felt fury in my chest as if I were storm, crash and wave to consume me, as I walked among the old and giant trees, over-toppled, roots grasping at air. The pier twisted like a tangled wooden slat-bridge, and deep furrows led to boats shoved onto the beach, exhausted on their sides.

Crawling between the open roots of a fallen tree to sit on the sand, I hiccuped through sobs. I wanted to go home but had no home to go to. "What do you want with me?" I whispered. In Los Angeles and in New York, I'd had times of despair, retreating to bed, pulling covers over my head, resisting all solace except chocolate. I didn't do depression anymore; I did anger. And I was tired of being angry. How many times did I need to remind myself I was tired of being angry before I did something about it? Hunched over my drawn-up knees, I wrapped my arms tight around them as pain twisted a black drill into my solar plexus. Perhaps before birth, my soul sat in heaven on a soul tree and decided to come into this world and learn how to battle. That eclipsed any angels-on-a-white-cloud image. No doubt the tree branches were devoid of leaves, only little souls, bent over, peering down. There's a father who will die young. Yep. That's where I'll go. Or maybe a turtle soul, afraid for its neck. Perhaps I'd decided to learn how to be safe and battle became my vehicle. In January, in the detritus of storm, I didn't believe in anything, not my path, and certainly not God. I'd cried out so many times in so many settings. Did it mean anything anymore? Another empty question asked to an empty sky. No answer. There was never an answer . . . oh, sometimes "Wait." That was not helpful. All I did was wait while random events stacked lopsidedly against one another, and which I reshuffled, hoping to find the message.

Locked in my fury, a memory surfaced from my theater days: my arms are too short to box with God. Somebody already had that line. Sand on my hands, sand in my eyes from rubbing them. I'd probably go blind.

Then I wouldn't have to keep looking. I crawled from my sanctuary and shambled to the car.

Driving up to Mahukona, I sat on the rocks as surf crashed and saltwater washed my face. Salt water to wash sand tears. Restless, I drove on, past Puakea, past Hawi, until I turned onto a dirt road at the arrow sign for Koakea. Out of the car and walking, I found a tiny Japanese cemetery with small block headstones flat in the ground, their legends, names, dates marked in characters I couldn't read. But the little garden was peaceful. The air smelled clean, and I wasn't in the ground.

I sighed deeply. Another day to ponder.

Back home, I picked up Mom and drove down to the point for a close up view of the sea's rough white caps. My mother's Quaker heritage had lived at odds with her anger. Anger at her mother as she, the eldest daughter, toiled at tasks her mother didn't want to do: the washing up after meals, laundry, caring for younger siblings as her mother read. My mother had buried her firstborn and two husbands. Now she seemed at peace as we stared over the sea's wrath.

In a quiet voice, she began a story about Little Joe who first got her to eating Cheerios. He heard an ad on the radio, she showed him the ad in *Ladies' Home Journal*, and while shopping, she bought some. The baby was probably Judy since Little Joe was dead by the time Cheerios came out. But I didn't say anything. She liked her stories, and I liked hearing them. Listening to her, I wondered if she'd vowed to protect her children from fate, and so fate looked for us.

That night I dreamed of sorcerers healing themselves, reaching inside their bodies to heal themselves, and me packing a suitcase for a convention to learn how to be a healer.

A phone call from Kalani Honua interrupted my morning journaling. The director, Howard Duncan, said, "Janet, you've been accepted into the Wellness Program, but no scholarship. It's two hundred for the workshops." Two hundred! That'd be about the end of my money. "Do you want to come?" Yes.

But the anger resurfaced. Not good enough, obviously. Why wasn't I ever good enough to get what I wanted?

Night after night flooded with dreams: cleaning up a church; sweeping out cobwebs and dirt; going outside into the dark, but wanting to be inside. Had I locked myself out? No. I go inside until daylight. Mom calls me outside. This man, the dream man, sits on a log talking to Mother. He'd come to see me. Hang on, I said, let me get ready for school. Another dream where my back was to him, his arms around me, and then I was at his back, my arms around him. I was given his true name: Krasinski. I'd known a Joseph Krasinski at K-State. Why would I dream of him? The dreams continued, thick and furious, several a night, fighting, traveling in a car, being sent to Kansas for a job, bringing people to life, a ghoul chasing me and the spirit lover, as I began to name him, coming to rescue me. Great. I was one of those wacky women with dream lovers.

But I believed in love. In love and peace and balance. How could I find it? Where?

The whales returned for their yearly calving in the ocean beyond the house, breaching, splashing, and making a great show. Smaller backs curved through the water against the big backs. New birth. The turquoise swimming pool, the sky sky-blue, and the ocean layered in blue. Blue the color of the throat chakra. Ah. That's why singing was so important to Hawaiians and why chanting was a part of Huna healing. Several of the workshops at Kalani put an emphasis on sound as a healing tool. Gloria had chanted as she initiated me in Mexico, an *oracionista* (healer), healing with sound and energy.

Okay . . . okay. I was okay.

I pulled the wellness schedule Howard Duncan had sent from the pile of papers on my desk and studied it, marked the classes I wanted to take. A resident Tai Chi instructor. That for sure. I'd wanted to take Tai Chi in D.C. but the centers were all out in the suburbs. Tai chi and yoga, every other morning.

In a phone conversation, Howard Duncan said, "We've talked of adding a program director to the staff. If you fit down here and want to stay after the Wellness Program, you could probably have it." He said I could come early if I wanted.

I began packing. Jeanne would drive me to Kalani with my Smith Corona and my journals and my memories. I'd dabbled in hula, I'd keep that; used my hands to make art, good but not that important; I'd read and written, keep that; doing theater was okay, not necessary, I'd keep the film work; and I'd done a fair batch of self-discovery, I'd probably keep doing that.

Now it was time to move on.

SIX

ONCE THERE WAS A FARMER

After we unloaded the car, Jeanne began her journey back to North Kohala, and I visited Howard Duncan in his office as he sat behind a wide wooden desk stacked with papers.

"I'm glad you're here," he said. "Are you settled in?"

"Well, not settled, but my bags are in the room. I still need to unpack. It's a great room, but I wondered if there's a small desk I could use."

Howard's eyes darted from one pile to another as if he were looking through papers for his own desk. He shook his head. "I don't think so, but talk to Miles. He's the plant supervisor. He might know." Howard shot a thumb back over his shoulder. "Follow the gravel road and you'll see the plant. Can't miss it. Miles is a big Hawaiian. Can't miss him, either." His head bent over his current pile of papers, dismissing me. My neck tensed as the memory of Bill, dismissing me and bending over his soup, flashed in my memory.

But I said thank you and following the direction his thumb pointed, walked behind the office and found the road. The plant was, as Howard suggested, hard to miss. A big building. I found Miles inside, bent over what looked like a tractor motor. He looked up when I joined him.

"Miles?" He nodded. "I'm Janet. Just arrived. Howard said you might know of a small desk I could use."

Miles stood, pulled a rag from a back pocket, and wiped his hands. "How big?"

"I just need something small; maybe this big?" And spread my hands three feet apart.

"No. Nothing that small. I can build you a table. Would that work?"

"Thank you! That would work."

Miles nodded and resumed his battle with the motor.

Following the gravel road around the compound, I spotted my building and climbed the stairs. Hale Makani held the kitchen on the ground floor with a surrounding dining area. From my time in Hawaii,

I'd learned a hale is a large and open-aired Hawaiian building with various living spaces. Above the kitchen, our rooms bordered a polished wooden floor, space for yoga, Tai Chi, and dance. My room's hollow-core door rattled as it opened.

I liked this new home: walls cedar plank, open at the rafters where geckos slept and probably laugh me awake each morning; screen-covered windows filled the wall opposite the door. Two single beds sat ready with blankets and sheets folded at the bottom, one bed beneath the windows and one on the right hand wall. A small closet was built into a corner near the door. I'd chosen the bed beneath the windows. My suitcases and two boxes lay on top. I unpacked.

For now, the rickety straw and wood chair at the end of my bed could serve as a makeshift desk. Setting the Smith Corona on the fragile seat, I looked out at the second story view of gardens and jungle. And sky.

The soft slap of sandals announced arrivals. No one needed my attention. No drumming rap on my door. Rather an easy sliding slap, going or not going, as evening walked in. My roommate, Barbara Cameron, entered with two suitcases. She came from Australia to teach Chinese medicine. A fine Aussie woman, brash, always ready to laugh. I liked her on sight as she bent over a suitcase, unpacking T-shirts and khaki shorts, tucking a wedge of chestnut hair behind her ear to get it out of the way.

"Are you okay with that? I can trade if you'd rather have the bed at the window," I said.

"Nope," she said. "I'd rather have a wall to back me up." Barbara grinned.

For how long had I wanted to live in a commune? Since I'd first read *Don't Push the River*. Then I had two little boys and a husband. Now I had me. And Barbara. We wandered down the stairs to the lanai.

An elegant woman, a Norse Artemis with white-blond curls feathering her face, slid from a table and stood. "I'm Krysta," she said. "I came from Findhorn to warm up!" She laughed a deep, throaty laugh, and I realized we were close to the same age. "There's a beach not too far down the road. Let's go."

When we returned, two new women sat on the lanai. They introduced themselves: Sharon Scow, New Zealand, an energy healer and a mystic. She'd chosen to live alone in a tiny A-frame against the jungle wall. Her red-gold hair snapped fire in the late-afternoon sun and belied her gentle nature. Marion DeNeice, born in Sir Lanka, emigrant to Australia, and newly pregnant, came to teach yoga. An exotic beauty with burnished hair, almond eyes, golden-brown skin, and a palpable, radiating spirit as if she were wiser and older than her years. We ate dinner together and talked until nearly eleven when the generator shut down and darkness reigned.

As I drifted to sleep in the jungle's night whispers, I hoped we'd be each other's circle and support.

The next morning, I checked in with Howard Duncan. He suggested I work in the gift shop, so I puttered, cleaned a little on things that didn't need cleaning, shifted a few items to show them off. Ran out of things to do. No customers came in. Bored, I stepped outside.

A man trimmed a tree beyond the door. "Can I help?" I said. He nodded. "Take this." He picked up a leaf-covered branch. "You can use it to brush away cobwebs. They aren't poisonous," he added, nodding at a huge spider in the middle of a large web. "Cane spiders."

We worked in silence, he pruning and clipping, me dusting with a leafy branch. "They catch the dew," he said. I presumed he meant the giant cobwebs. "Come out here early some morning; you'll see them glitter."

Brushing the tree, I was a bride wreathed in spider webs on the turning-not-yet-knowing path across the threshold.

A phone rang in the office, people entered and left. No one came to the gift shop. I stayed where I was, brushing cobwebs. "Do you live here?" I said, searching for some slivered opening into conversation.

He shook his head and lifted one shoulder to rub at his bearded chin. After a long pause, he said, "I have a tent at a friend's place. I do the grounds." He tossed his head sideways, indicating the land. A bird trilled, sharp and insistent, beyond the yard's cleared edge.

"Do you need help?"

"I don't know. We have a full crew, but you can ask."

I nodded.

The silvery strands from the giant web trailed down my arms, my back. Even after brushing them off, more floated from the branches, silken as a kiss. The heady scent from the plumeria grove, paces away, wound around me as my branch swept the air. Something new was happening, something new and peaceful. I wanted to hold it, to stand in that place of transformation.

At the end of my shift, I found Howard Duncan in his office. "Howard, would it be a problem if I transferred to outdoor work instead of the office?" He lifted his attention from a pile of papers and gazed absently over my left shoulder. "José wants someone to work in the vegetable garden. Go talk to him." Duncan resumed his paper battle. My shoulders relaxed. "Thank you," I said to his bent-over head. He nodded.

Behind the dining lanai, I found José hoeing between rows of lettuce. He was easy to recognize: a sturdy Mexican, dark curly hair, flirting eyes. "I'm Janet. Howard Duncan said come talk to you about working in the garden."

He wiped his forehead on his sleeve and leaned on his hoe. That characteristic behavior so like Dad's might have warned me, but it didn't. Instead, I saw the same face I'd known in Mexico, a face that laughed and teased. Putting energy into convincing him what he needed was a farmer's daughter, specifically me. I said I'd grown up on a farm, gardening, planting, and tending, and I'd lived in Mexico. He nodded and grinned. And just that easy, our arduous friendship began.

That night I dreamed of Dad in a shadowy room, a room for making things happen. I had to send him away, get him to let go and do what he needed to do. Enigmatic, often ponderous, dreams rarely revealed secrets in the moment. We'd butted heads often, Dad and I, both growing up and again when I returned to Kansas for college. Whatever the topic, we'd find a way to argue. Never about politics. For a Kansas farmer, he was liberal in his views and always voted Democrat. But religion? The poor you will always have with you, he'd remind me when I argued in favor of expanding food stamps or wages as if our family was somewhere beyond the poor stage. And in reality, we were. We never had luxuries but we always had food, the animals had food, and he worked hard to make sure of it. We always had books. Maybe he'd taught me to be as hard-headed as he was. Or maybe it was who I was and the best candidate in the family for a good argument.

The best part of Dad was his sense of humor and his stories. Stories were an excuse for stopping, resting, getting a second wind. I couldn't even count the many times I'd heard his story of Lawrence Welk and the dance platform Dad built in a pasture at the end of the lane. How he had loved to dance a polka. Dance had, as family stories go, brought him to Mother after my father died. A year or so into mourning, Uncle Kenny and his wife, Wanda, told Mom she needed to get out. They took her to Kahon's Ballroom in Marysville, a notorious Polka hall. She sat demurely drinking a Coke when Dad walked in. Recognizing each other from their early years of dating, they sat and talked, and six weeks later, married "between the milo harvest and corn harvest," as Mother told it. And we five kids with my mother moved to the farm. Although Dad and I often argued, I had to admire a middle-aged bachelor, willing to take on a widow with five kids. And he loved my mom. A year later, she gave birth to my youngest sister, Jolene.

Dawn tipped the jungle beyond my screened window, whispering me awake. One bird hiccuped and then another in the fringe of trees lining the compound; deeper, where trees crowded close, a single call answered, okay . . . okay. It reminded me of the years Mom called up the stairs to wake me for chores, and I'd drop a leg over the side of the bed to hit the floor with my heel as if I were up. "Okay," I said. She must have known as five minutes later, she'd call again. The jungle rustled; I lay on my side and watched out the screened window as the sky trailed paint through the morning. Before long, a cacophony of bird calls ricocheted across the clearing, reached a crescendo, and stopped. I guessed they'd left their nests in search of food.

Time to pull on sweats and hit the hardwood floor beyond my door.

Tai Chi became an extension of hula, slower and without music. The music rose from our breath and the muted squeak of feet shifting on the floor as we followed Ken Wright's lead. I felt the strength hula had built in my thighs and knees. The slow, steady rhythm suited me; my arms moved as if on their own volition and the energy grew in my hands. Old images shifted as my legs shifted: K-State ballet class with Roni Mahler; dance class at Zilker Park in Austin; class at the Alvin Ailey studios in New York; the shine of floor, the shift of weight. My left handed body struggled with choreography, but I could follow Ken.

After breakfast, I headed to the garden, eager for my new job, and found José, a shovel balanced on his shoulder. He stared at the tangle of vegetation at his feet, but when he saw me, he grinned. "We need a bigger garden." A wheelbarrow, deep scratches in the red paint, sat beside him. He tapped the rim with the shovel. "I'll dig. You dump it in the trees." A quick chin point indicated the jungle wall.

I nodded. Emptying a wheelbarrow easy. I guessed it was weeds and vines he was digging out. Ah, ye of little knowing. José dug, and he did, indeed, pull up a clump of weeds, but attached to the weeds hung a chunk of lava. He plunked it in the wheelbarrow and returned to digging. So proceeded the morning, work familiar from farm work with Dad: the man did the heavy part, the side-kick did the walking. José leaned on his shovel and rested during my trundle beyond the service road and into the jungle. I tipped out the chunks and waited as he dug. We were both grateful for the lunch bell.

When I stood up from lunch, my legs complained. Tai chi and wheelbarrow duty. I climbed the stairs and rested on my bed for a brief fifteen minutes. Once more in the garden, I was surprised to see José raking dirt. We'd actually cleared a strip three by six feet and he wanted to plant. Okay, then. Bending over and planting would stretch my hamstrings. At the end of the shift, I slowly climbed the stairs. Dirty, all of me dirty. Grabbing a muumuu, I retraced my steps, showered, and climbed the stairs once more, longing for a nap.

Barbara sat cross-legged on her bed, a spread of medicine cards in front of her. "How's the garden?"

"Growing," I said, and she laughed. Barbara had passed through earlier to see if there was anything to harvest for the kitchen. Not yet, but soon.

"We planted more lettuce," I said. "Wha'cha doing?"

"Looking. Same thing I talked about last night. I guess we'll both be wiser by the time this is over."

The previous night as we'd drifted in the darkness near sleep, we'd traded parts of our stories. We both wanted love. I'd told her about scars so deep I didn't know if I'd ever trust love, or even be lovable. Barbara had her own stories and didn't know if she'd ever find anyone she wanted to love. She came to teach Chinese medicine but wasn't sure it was her life path. I doubted I had a path.

"Want me to read for you?" She scooped up the cards and began shuffling.

"Here's your power animal." She flipped a card. A porcupine. "Tough on the outside, dangerous when threatened, but soft on the inside." She continued to lay out cards. "See this? There's a connecting link between you and your father. This is the dreaming/letting go card. You need to somehow visualize this whole grief thing and send it to the light."

"How do I do that?"

"I don't know. Maybe that's what you came to find out."

Maybe.

Her hair scooped over her cheek, shading her eyes as she reshuffled the cards and fanned them for herself. I sat at the end of my bed and flipped open the Smith Corona, stared at the narrow, green screen, picked up my journal and riffled through pages. Fighting dreams, struggle dreams, driving a car that needed work, a few scattered phrases: the negative voice will respond positively to recognition by lowering its volume. If my negative voice lowered its volume, I might not have anything in my head at all.

Let die the values within the psyche which no longer sustain.

Ouch. Where did that come from?

I FOUND WHAT I WAS LOOKING FOR. A FEW DAYS BEFORE MOVING TO Kalani, Jeanne and I drove to Waimea for a reading with Kam Night Chase, a Lakota medicine man. He'd flipped the porcupine card, too, and said it was my power animal. He'd said the little prickly animal was innocence and joy. I could see why: porcupines waddled along, taking whatever came, one step at a time. Below that, I'd written, "The Dreaming One is the hard one—the place of sacrifice."

Apart from underlining, it would help if I'd be a little less obscure in my sudden revelatory notes to myself.

ONE NEW YORK AFTERNOON, DAYDREAMING MY WAY HOME ALONG 85th Street, Bill saw me coming and hid behind a row of garbage cans. When I was a few steps away, he reared up and scared me. I jumped; he laughed. And then he lectured. "You've got to pay attention! Toughen up! You can't be daydreaming. You're going to get hurt." Maybe his way of protecting me. I learned to scan the street ahead and carry my biggest key jutting from between clenched fingers; at night on the subway, I rode in the first car next to the conductor's door. Never got hurt, but I stayed prickly. Most of my headshots from New York showed the same fierce eyes.

The years in Mexico softened me, washed off the toughness and gave me gauzy, ruffled skirts to wear. I'd laughed more. But the quills grew in D.C. Seemed I'd spent a lifetime trying to protect myself.

DAYS FOLLOWED EACH OTHER IN REGULARITY. AFTER TAI CHI OR yoga and breakfast, José waited. We dug and hauled lava until noon, planted in the afternoon, and indulged ourselves with breaks on plastic chairs we'd placed under shade. One day at lunch, the kitchen served fresh pineapple. José collected the cut-off tops and we planted them in a row along a pathway. If a southern California Mexican and a Kansas farmer's daughter could have a chop wood/carry water Zen experience, this garden was it.

One afternoon as I started to change from garden clothes, Miles proudly carried in a small table he'd built from scrap wood and set it at the end of my bed. I had a desk, a smaller version of the wooden table I once bought at a Mexico street market and carried home upside down, balanced on my head. They both wobbled. I tore out an empty journal page and folded it tight to slip under one leg for ballast.

The next morning, a soft rustle of rain woke me instead of bird calls. Rain! I wouldn't have to water the garden. Downstairs, I grabbed a raincoat from the rack and walked to the point. Rough waves crashed on the rocks below. The hooded raincoat made me feel like *The French Lieutenant's Woman* standing at the end of a pier, watching for his ship. The sea was rough, the rain was not, and I pushed off the hood to feel misty breath on my face.

The sun ventured out at lunch; we went to the garden. Too wet to dig, so José marked plots and built lattice string webs as if he were a cane spider, weaving territory.

With me as a free and willing helper, we laid out ambitious plans to feed the community. I pulled weeds, planted lettuce and peas, and wondered at putting myself on the land as if searching for Dad, or maybe searching for me. Each day, there was more, and every afternoon, I climbed the stairs, one weary step at a time.

SEVEN

ELUSIVE MYSTERIES

As I left garden work at the end of a shift, I saw Ben on the one small knoll in the expansive grounds. He and I had met one evening at dinner while he was sitting with Leon Kalili. Leon and I had become friends immediately, recognizing something in the other, as I had recognized Barbara and Sharon and Krysta. The bridge-son of an African American and a Hawaiian, Leon was big and solid and filled with laughter, a masseuse in the old Hawaiian tradition of Lomi Lomi. Ben, also a masseuse, was browned and lanky, as quiet and contained as Leon was ebullient. When Leon had introduced us, Ben looked at me, his head tipped as if to capture the spirit-voice pushing me forward. He'd trained in Native American traditions and would lead sweat lodges each new and full moon.

I walked onto the knoll where he was anchoring the sweat lodge poles. "Need some help?"

He nodded, eyes smiling. "The frame's almost done, but I could use some help with the blankets." His head tip indicated the pile.

I braced poles as he tied leather thongs, and we shifted to the next. Every few steps he jiggled at the frame to judge its sturdiness. When he was satisfied, we lifted the blankets, thick with warm wool smell, one at a time, crisscrossing and tying, beginning around the hole at the top before continuing down the sides. He checked the strength of the frame every two or three blankets with a quick jog from the heel of his palm as he told me about the medicine man he'd worked with. I told him about meeting Kam Night Chase. The dinner bell rang and we looked up surprised. Shadow fingers sketched the lawn as the sun dipped toward its jungle bed.

"Well," Ben said. And stretched. "We got most of it. I can finish in the morning." A full moon was coming and the first sweat for the community. I nodded. Working with him was easy and time slid by softly.

Ten of us gathered for a sweat two nights later. A pit outside the lodge opening, layered in logs and rocks, had burned into coals through the afternoon. Heat shimmered off the rocks. I'd never participated in a sweat and felt unsure, nervous, but I trusted Ben.

"We'll start these rituals easy," he said. "For now, crawl inside and find a place to sit around the outside edge. I'll load the rocks after you're in. Just so you know, it's cooler near the door, hotter on the far wall. These are the four directions."

He stood with his back to the opening. "This is the east, the direction of new beginnings, of spring, birth, and spirit. This," he turned a quarter-turn, "is south, the direction of youth, of summer and learning, of air, and growing emotions." He turned. "The west is the adult, water, fall, and intellect." He made one last turn. "And the north is winter, the sacred place of the White Buffalo, earth and death and the physical."

Ben faced us. "You may sit where`ever you want and you may leave the sweat whenever you need to. Trust yourself to know when to leave. I'll not make it too hot this first time. The rocks will go in the central pit. Be careful around it." He nodded and we crawled one by one through the opening. Ben loaded rocks into the center pit, closed the blanket flap, and sprinkled water onto the rocks. A blanket of steam rose.

We sat through a round, Ben chanting, before he lifted the flap and allowed a rush of cool air to enter. A few crawled out, but I stayed. I'd chosen to sit on the north wall, not too far in, close enough to escape if I had to. I drew the cooler air deep and remembered Banti Kamalasiri, the Buddhist monk in D.C. who'd taught me to sit and breathe. I sat. I breathed.

Ben flipped the blanket closed for the next round. Steam rose. I kept my eyes closed and swayed to the sound of his opening chant. "You are the grandmother," I heard him say. My eyes flew open. He nodded once and resumed chanting. Krysta sat across the fire pit from me. Her blond curls floated in the steam. Her eyes were closed. She, too, was grandmother, the fairy godmother of stars and legends while I the grandmother of rock and earth.

In the final round, Ben sprinkled less water, the steam less intense. He began chanting and I hummed. My throat broke free and a chant rose, releasing itself from some place I didn't know, answering some thread from Ben's. And then we were silent, breathing in the rustle of heat.

Leon and I had scheduled an appointment, so after the sweat, I wandered down to the massage room, half-dazed, the cool night air drying my body and airing my sarong. The moon rose over the wall of trees and hit me in the face; dew-freshened grass tickled my bare feet. Moon Crazy. That would be easy. I chuckled. That already was. Leon held up a white sheet as I untied my sarong and lay face-down on the table. I liked him but he was big and powerful, and I felt vulnerable. The powdered scent of flowers drifted over me as he spread the sheet across my lower body.

He stood at my head and pressed his hands along the sides of my spine, forcing out air I didn't know I was holding. "Breathe," he said. I breathed. Again, he pressed air from my lungs. I didn't have to be reminded. I breathed.

"We are majesty," he said, as he swept thick forearms over my back, "We are all of us majesty and we forget." I heard deep haaaaaaa breaths as he worked. My body sagged into the table as fear dissolved.

When he asked me to turn over, he had to help me, tucking the sheet under my side and rolling me. "The old Kahunas of Lomi Lomi worked on the royalty every day so they'd have clarity," he said. I opened my eyes and as they swam into focus, I saw a gentle face smiling at me, eyes polished onyx. "You are royalty," he said, and began the steady sweep of arms and breath on my torso, my belly, my legs. I sank into my breathing body. Time had no clock, no meaning. Rubbing his hands together into heat, he placed them over my eyes, rubbed again, placed them on my belly. His breath blew fire into the third eye chakra between my brows, fire into my throat chakra. He rubbed his hands into heat and placed them over my ovaries, wounded by a hysterectomy. "Speak through her, Spirit."

How had he known about my ovaries, I briefly wondered as he tapped my forehead, and in a great whirlwind, a vision bloomed. I'm walking into a sacred room, a pyramid or temple, the walls slant inward. I reach up... a hook, a key... escape... run away... not afraid, but running... to someone I'm forbidden to love. As I visioned lifting my hand for the key, a crackling bolt of light shot down each side of my body, parallel lines of searing heat through my groin, exploding down the inside of my legs, out my feet. Surprised, I lost the vision, but a voice spoke: *celibate... killed many children... you are forgiven*. A flashing memory of surgery: a hysterectomy because of endometriosis years past.

In near-hysteria, I struggled to sit, shaking from the electric current. Leon lifted my shoulders and wrapped gentle arms around me as I sobbed out the vision. My throat choked on the word key... a key. He wiped my tears with his palm and wrapped me into my sarong. A branch rustled somewhere beyond the service road. The glow from a single bulb above our heads held us in a cone of light. Never had I felt so totally loved, especially by a man, in a completely non-sexual way. No. My father... fishing day, a riverbank, rinsing out a beer can for the sunflowers I'd picked. Leon placed his hands on my shoulders and bent his head, commanded me to look at him.

"Your soul was a temple keeper or in some part of the priesthood and forced to be celibate. Now that part is healed." I abruptly laughed and he laughed with me.

We went outside, climbed into the Jacuzzi, sank into hot water, stars blazing above, and the tail ends of my sarong floating. Another dimension touched, another time. Starlight glittered in Leon's dark eyes as if he were an ancient, not bounded by rules. My body felt light-filled and clean. The water anchored, calmed, and allowed me to settle into wide-spaced openness. I didn't want anyone else to see me or talk to me. We sat late into the night, casually talking, as the Milky Way revolved above our heads and light danced in the water. At last, the generator shut down and Kalani settled. I crept to my room, barefoot, brushing the grass lightly to leave no footprint.

Lying in bed, I remembered visiting a friend in California after I'd left Germany and trying psilocybin mushrooms. Staring into the bathroom mirror, hands braced on the cold white sink, white walls, white light, I'd watched my face change, as if centuries of lives passed through my reflection. Once a cat, white face framed in black. Where did they come from? The same place as the dreams or the visions? What synoptic switch had been triggered . . . or broken . . . or refined . . . or . . . boundless?

I drifted into sleep.

The next morning, I woke to jungle, my body filled with the sound of bird song. Turning my head, I looked at Barbara's bed. Saturday, but she was up and out. I regretted falling asleep the night before instead of staying in the space of no boundaries. Rolling onto my side, I picked up my journal from the floor and read notes I didn't remember making: "Walking down a path I hear my name and I turn and see him, see his true face, a good-looking, pleasant face. Younger than I am. I was told he would 'come soon.' Come in dreams or in the material world?"

If I hadn't fallen asleep, maybe this dream wouldn't have come. Whoever this man was, real or imagined, comfort wove itself through bird song, a path to somewhere I could follow without knowing.

EIGHT

BABIES IN THE GARDEN

Monday, as I stirred to the jungle's waking, the reality of schedules and demands crashed on top of the weekend's full moon sweat, the massage with Leon, and a Sunday afternoon beach trip. Barbara, Krysta, and I had walked the road to Kehena, its black sand beach at the foot of a long path, an idyllic view from the side of the road with families picnicking, naked bodies sunning, and waves rolling onto shore. Climbing down became the reality of jagged footing and shifting lava rocks. Beyond the surf break, dolphins played, and everyone wanted to swim with the dolphins. I wanted to swim with the dolphins, feel their sleek, arching bodies, and hear their chittering amusement. I understood the Caribbean's soft waves, but regardless of how I entered or returned from the Pacific, my body was fair game for dashing waves, even as a good swimmer. Vowing to move with the waves, I swam out to where my toes found a sudden drop-off to deeper water, the dolphins yet further out. I'd dog-paddled, scanned the waves for shark fins, but the imagined shape chased the want from me. Watching for a wave curling soft, I swam to shore, but it tossed me onto the beach, sand rough against my skin. At dinner, Ross had told me about a local man swimming at night with whales, but that was so outside my abilities, I could only wonder. On the Kansas farm, I'd learned to live with the possibility of rattlesnakes, a familiar danger and easy to avoid by making noise. Whales and dolphins and silent deep water? Couldn't do it.

I rolled over and picked up my journal from its station on the floor. "Each new adventure has the same conflicted vision," I wrote, got up and dressed for Tai Chi. Barbara was asleep. I shook her shoulder gently. "Tai chi." She nodded groggily and stretched. A week in residence, two, counting the week we'd come early. Maybe I'd have time to sit in front of the Smith Corona in the afternoon, before dinner, before the evening workshop.

Ken waited on the polished floor. Others trickled in. Precisely at

7:30, Ken took position with legs spread, knees bent, arms extended; we followed like a wave commanded by his hand. Tai chi built an energy I could shape and hold between my hands, when, at the end of class, we anchored in qigong. We bowed to Ken and silently scattered to begin the day's work.

José was not in the garden. Michael Koob came through, and when I asked if he'd seen José, Michael said he was probably fishing. "The ocean's quiet today. That's usually when he goes." Whew. No hauling lava.

I sat in a shady row and weeded, pulling small leaves apart to peer into the heart of a lettuce. The plants too small for hoeing, so I pulled and scooted, pulled and scooted. I have to tell Dad about this. My heart contracted. Dad was dead. I remembered childhood slights, his angry voice when I did something wrong or had an accident. Maybe his angry voice was the scared voice for an impetuous child. He taught me to care for the land, how life flows from our hands, even hands guiding a tractor's steering wheel. When I lived in Mexico, I wrote him about the Mexican farmers, birds following as the farmer turned furrows with a one-bladed plow behind a horse. My tangle of emotions reflected the tangle of my journeys. Tears grew hot in my eyes. Each time I thought I had things sorted out, they'd swing with the force of a dragon's tail to lash me as I looked back on myself looking back on myself, dancing on a fulcrum point, riding some story that might fling me into yesterday or tomorrow or into a room filled with fun-house mirrors, every reflection reflecting deeper and deeper until I was unsure where I began.

I'd become maudlin. And probably in error since fitting a dragon's appendages, even a young dragon, into a fun house, might be more than even my imagination could manage.

Tears blurred my vision. I'd probably uprooted lettuces instead of weeds. Swiping the back of one wrist across each eye, I shook my head clear. A tiny, emerald-green grasshopper sat on my hand braced in the dirt. Maybe a half-inch long, fragile as a wish and tentative in new life. *You gotta get out of your head if you want to see*, I scolded myself as I inched my hand toward the closest lettuce. The baby grasshopper quivered as it gathered itself for a great baby leap into baby lettuce. What had happened to my wildness, to the Mardi Gras life of the gypsy? Instead, I sat in garden dirt and watched a baby grasshopper peek between lettuce leaves. And who are you trying to convince? A grasshopper? My single Mardi Gras in New Orleans, bartending at Molly's at the Market, when I wore a black taffeta dance hall dress, priming the pump by sticking dollars under the red ruffle across my bosom. I went home papered in dollar bills.

Earth smell hung in the air as if it were fresh from the laundry, a constant, waiting.

How would I describe the smell of earth? Rich and loamy, but that presupposed knowing the smell of loam. I picked up a handful to let the fine, cool dirt trickle through my fingers. The grasshopper waited, translucent in a sliver of sunlight. I'd smelled earth for most of my life. What would you tell someone who hadn't stuck their nose in dirt?

I pulled my 3 x 5-inch sketch book from my back pocket. One corner of a Willy postcard fell out, tiny writing in green ink: "Having a wonderful time, wish I were here." I grinned. A Willy line if ever there was one. Tucking it into a crevice between pages, I settled, cross-legged, and searched for the drawing Deborah made shortly after we'd arrived, a loving, colored pencil sketch of a woman garbed in a sky-blue gown, kerchief on her head, curved over a plant, new leaves shining between her hands. A fine script bordered the kneeling figure: "There is a time to plant, a time to harvest, and a time to meditate. All are part of life." The woman was round and soft. Had Deborah drawn me or herself? I wanted to believe it was me, the gentle, nurturing me, not the edgy, conflicted me.

After the evening's meal, we gathered on the second floor of the library hale for the first of six weekly classes with Saki Lee, a guide in the Sufi order. The room wonderful: dark plank walls, pillows, filled bookcases, and wide windows. Between two windows, a huge Oxford Dictionary sat open on its stand while a white rug filled the center of the room, the circular weave sprouting soft tufts. Saki had arrived over the weekend. She was beautiful. Long hair framed an Asian face, her hands fragile as leaves dancing, and a voice much younger than her soul. As we entered, she motioned for us to sit with her around the rug.

"It's nice to be here," she said and picked up her guitar to sing a song of centering and peace. We ended the class with qigong, a meditational pose to ready us for sleep.

José waited in the garden the next morning, a little surly from a fruitless fishing trip. We resumed the ritual of him chopping lava, me hauling it to the jungle, and us planting new rows in the afternoon. Toward the end of the week, and in a better mood, he called me to the row of pineapple heads we'd planted. "Smell that," he said, pointing into the spreading depths of the center leaves. A baby pineapple thrust up its tiny pointed head. It smelled soft and sweet, a baby-smell. "They'll make?" I said. José grinned and nodded.

I didn't need to move far inside the rim of overhanging trees to feel alone and separate from activity. After dumping a load, I waited, quiet, and listened as a breeze brushed branches. A brief scurry cocked my head to decipher some small animal's hunting story. I could never linger. Behind me a shatter as José tossed chunks of lava into a pile, but for a moment, I breathed. Eh Laka Eh ... as the light shifted in the breeze. E Laka E ... queen of voice, giver of gifts, giver of bounty. Queen of jungle and ferns and hula, and a sister to Pelé.

Kalani Honua sat on the far eastern edge of the island, a land where Goddess Laka's bounty and Goddess Pelé's lava twined in a symbiosis of destruction and creation, where rains came, seeds sprouted, and roots extended between cracks, breaking the hard lava into dirt. The dirt, imbued with lava's deep energy, the plentiful water, and the more or less constant temperatures, created a cornucopia.

I'd heard talk of Pelé since arriving. Kilauea, the active volcano in our Kalani backyard, her home. The rock I'd found at Pololu a gift from Pelé. The full moon over the lava flow with Jeanne and Robert another gift. The volcano's toxic breath of gases and steamy ocean brine, vog—volcano smog—Pelé's displeasure when it rolled upwind into Kona.

As the story goes, Pelé built her first fire pit on the island farthest to the west, but the sea seeped in and put out her fire. She traveled to the next island and the next and the next, in each building a fire pit, until arriving on Hawaii Island. There she found a place deep enough to dig a pit the sea could not reach. Thus was birthed Kilauea. That's the island story, complete with love and anger, betrayal and siblings.

Geologists and volcanologists have a different version: Hawaii's islands to the west are older than Hawaii Island, each built from the same undersea volcanic mountain range, and in time, each island shifted to cooler water. Kilauea is a teenager in geologic years, and its caldera, Pelé's cauldron, five-hundred feet deep, produces enough magma to keep Hawaii Island, already the largest, growing as Hawaii shifts to the northwest. The elder Mauna Kea, high and sacred near the Kohala side, has aged into sleepy dormancy. But the scientists' story is as fantastical as the Hawaiian. Underwater volcanoes? 'Splain that one! Oh, yeah, Earth's core. The lady Pelé, on the other hand, more relatable.

I'd expected living at Kalani would bring up power issues, but I was unprepared for how fast the garden grew. Each mid-morning on a break from lava hauling, I'd fetch a huge aluminum bowl from the kitchen and fill it with lettuce, peas, green beans, and herbs from rows José planted before my arrival. In another week or so, there'd be eggplant to harvest.

During the program's first week, we'd had a workshop on Progoff's journal writing. I found a copy of *At a Journal Workshop* in the library, left behind, perhaps, by some other writer searching for direction. The first prompt—writing how we got to where we were—was easy. I knew that. I just didn't know where I was going; maybe writing would show me. At the gift shop, I bought a thick, deep-blue binder and taped the card I'd drawn in Saki's first workshop to the cover. Practicality, it read, as yet unclear whether my nature or my quest.

One afternoon, the compound grew quiet after work. Bari, who worked in the kitchen, said Miles was driving them to another beach and asked if I wanted to go. I didn't. Laughing voices walked past my door

NINE

FORGIVEN

The new moon sweat arrived fast. Seemed shorter than two weeks since the full moon sweat. How did steam and heat create an altered reality? The purity part made sense, the cleaning out, but why reaching limits of endurance might open into visions, I didn't understand. Yet crawling into the lodge felt safe.

In the first round, the energy was quiet, more inward-turning than at the full moon. The steam rose, the breathing synchronized in a wave. I whispered an invitation to my father's spirit. The second round began with more steam but silent, still inward-turning. Ben offered a prayer to the wind, to the wisdom of growth. In the third round, the round of the west, of adulthood, Ben prayed for peace. And in the fourth round, the round of the ancestors and the white buffalo, the sound of humming rose, round and round the circle. Bodies swayed. The humming grew louder, lengthened my torso, stretched my neck, lifted my chin....

I look into my father's eyes, feel the group's energy circling the lodge. The chant holds us, pulling in a cone of light. The light is safe. You are free. Held by the white light, my father's energy lifted ... up and out of the sweat lodge.

When Ben flung open the blanket, a cool rush of air swept our sweaty bodies. Gingerly, one by one, we crawled out of the sweat lodge. No light showed in the compound; the generator's constant throb silenced. Overhead stars quivered. The others who emerged before me drifted like shadow figures and scattered. How many years had I recounted my grief, to counselors, lovers, body workers, to friends. Why had no one said that to heal wounds of the soul I needed to work in spirit? Perhaps there is a time for all things: a time to plant, a time to harvest, a time to wound, and a time to heal. All take their own time and their own journey.

Beyond the tree line, the North Star hung steady, the star of my childhood nights. In Mexico, making the movie, I'd searched for the North Star after Gloria's initiation when she lay hands on me and summoned energy I didn't know I had. How many times would renewal need to come, my contours shifting, dissolving, before I became who I was? Such a long journey to a new path—maybe the same path, different crossroad. Was physical stress and discomfort a requisite for all transformations?

I glanced over my shoulder at the sweat lodge. The left-over rocks in the pit no longer glowed. Tossing the towel over my shoulder, I walked in the direction of the North Star, back to my hale where I slept without turning, beneath a window filled with sky.

The week passed in a blur, not because the days moved fast but because I moved slow. At Eighteen Buddha Hands, we practiced qigong, and I dropped so deeply into myself, all was energy, no thought. In Tai Chi, Ken shifted on his feet, a poem in motion; breath fed my movements. On Wednesday, I pushed myself to go to a past-lives regression workshop, but the experience in the sweat lodge precluded any deep work. I visioned a house—gardens, a pumpkin, braided rugs—a voice said, *wait*. A horse-drawn carriage came up the road carrying what . . . my higher self in tulle skirts? Maybe I'm Cinderella turning into a pumpkin, I mused, or maybe the witch, reformed.

TEN

A MOTHER'S HAND

José and I inched the garden larger. Together we built a sanctuary. Plastic chairs appeared beneath a palm and in the shade cast by José's trellised beans. In the early mornings, beyond my bedside window, I'd see blond-headed Michael Koob watering the garden before joining Miles at the plant shop. I discovered a circle of stones under a palm tree and cleared the debris from an earlier, unknown worker's sacred space. We mulched walkways between vegetable patches. Kitchen workers harvested beans, eggplant, herbs, and lettuce.

On Friday afternoon, I rode the van into Hilo while Mother rode the bus down from North Kohala for a weekend before she returned mainland. She stepped down from the bus, one careful step at a time, accepting the driver's proffered hand, and wearing her customary travel clothes: red pants, red shirt. Even if small, she intended to be seen through crowds in airports or buses.

"Ma!" She glanced up, her smile wide, before focusing on that last long step down. Hugging her was a little like hugging a ten-year-old—you had to be careful not to squish. "I am so happy to see you," I said into her white curls. "Are you hungry?" I leaned back to look at her and she patted my cheek.

"Jeanne packed a sandwich. I'm fine. But I need to find a shorty muumuu. And a bathroom. Jeanne said go to Hilo Hattie's." She finger-combed her bangs in place, hiding the tell-tale dent in her forehead where doctors had removed a piece of skull after her car accident with Little Joe. Her own Harry Potter-like mark.

"Hilo Hattie's, it is. We have an hour before the van leaves to Kalani. Where's your bag?"

She pointed to the driver unloading suitcases from the luggage compartment. "It has red yarn on the handle."

"Yeah. I remember." I collected her bag and slid my hand under her elbow.

The Hilo Hattie's sign beckoned from the end of the block. As we walked, Mom caught me up on family news: Jeanne worked long shifts at the hotel; Lia rehearsed a play at school; Robert hired a new office worker at the clinic; Daemion was learning to sail an outrigger canoe.

We searched through several racks before finding a muumuu short enough for her, a twining pattern of green vines with pink and red flowers. "Look at that!" I said as a childhood memory surfaced: me walking down the narrow, dark, enclosed farmhouse stairs, proud of my colorful choice of red pants and pink shirt.

"Remember when you wouldn't let me wear red and pink to school?" As if wearing red and pink to a one-room schoolhouse would somehow break decorum.

"That was before I lived in Hawaii," she said, holding the dress in front of her and turning back and forth in front of the full-length mirror. "It's not too bright, is it?"

"Nah. On you, it's perfect." She laughed like a little girl who'd found a princess dress.

We returned to Kalani in time to settle before the evening meal. Barbara moved into a small A-frame for the weekend so Mom could have her bed. I hung up clothes in the closet while she cut tags from her new dress and slipped it on. The thing about Mom, she was adaptable. Wherever she was, and especially with one of her children, she'd adapt. Her ocean cruise around the islands was nice, she said. She sat in a sun-washed deck chair and watched the sea. "But we were never out of sight of land!" More than anything, Mom wanted to sail far enough to feel suspended between sea and sky. Once a newspaper columnist, her writing now confined itself to letters, but her writer sensibilities remained: at peace with her own thoughts and able to tell a story to any ear ready to listen.

She became an instant hit. She, the quintessential white-haired grandmother, who loved and laughed and told stories. Being the center of attention in a group where her one-liner wit drew applause suited her fine, and listening to her, I heard the source of my own one-liners, wondered how I hadn't seen it before. We laughed through a helicon evening of stories, surrounding her like a tiny lighthouse from home, beaming on each of us in turn. At eleven, the silencing of the generator sent us to bed.

Saturday morning, Mom went downstairs to strike up a conversation over breakfast while I answered letters on my Smith Corona. Barbara opened the door. "I'm taking your mom for a walk around the grounds," she said. I nodded and returned to writing a letter to Willy. His letters came in colored-pencil-doodled envelopes with special stamps, and I wanted him to know how happy they made me feel in the muddle of sometimes feeling out of time. After lunch, where Mom was prodded into more stories—farm stories and writing stories and family stories, all of which needed little prodding—she napped while I walked to the pool for a swim. Marion, Barbara, and I floated after a few laps and told mom stories. We could have swapped mothers and lived the same outcome they were so similar, at least in the telling.

Mom and I dressed for dinner. Halfway down the stairs we heard a loud babble.

Bari, Alison, and Victoria clustered, gesturing, voices high pitched. Rar, Kevin, and Russ stood by the buffet line, plates in hand, talking over each other. I saw Barbara behind the buffet.

"What's happened?"

"A woman from down the road was raped this afternoon."

Ben nudged Russ from the buffet line. "Let's go lock the gate," he said.

Our corner of Puna sparse, fairly wild, a scattered population, and few of us acquainted with the neighbors, but the rape sent palpable shivers through the community. When the men returned, they set up security patrols. Dinner conversation had none of the musing, questing focus, but instead pointed to danger: lock your room; stay secure; be wary.

No one stayed up late for stories.

Mom and I ate Sunday brunch and shared the Hilo paper. In the early afternoon, we walked to the point and sat on the grass, gentled in afternoon light, and looked out over sea. I told Mom the sweat lodge story of looking into my father's eyes and lifting him up and out. She nodded, tears bright in her eyes.

We walked up the lane past grazing horses.

"I guess the circus arrives tomorrow," I said. "They'll camp in this field. Wonder where the horses go."

"A circus?" Mom's eyebrows lifted in wings when surprise and judgment faced her at the same time.

"Well, not quite a circus, I guess. The worksheet says Vaudeville Conference and someone said jugglers and acrobats. They have a performance at the end of the week. Seems an odd place for a jugglers' gathering."

"Unless they're Tarzan's children," Mom quipped, dodging under a hanging vine.

Several people huddled around a table as we walked onto the lanai. Mom wanted to nap, so she went upstairs. I walked to the table.

"Hey, guys."

Krysta glanced up, her usual clear, Swedish cheeks splotched with angry red patches. "That guy raped Denise this afternoon." Denise a quiet and gentle woman, a resident worker at Kalani.

Krysta scheduled a women's meeting, a sexual abuse survivors' meeting. After dinner, we met in the writers' hale. Angry voices trailed over the books and hung in the corners. One voice wailed about innocence raped, and Joy said, "Men should . . . " but the rest lost in an uproar of anger and grief and shame. Was that a given for so many? At the top of the stairs, I rested on the floor beside Barbara. My body tensed. I didn't want to be angry. "Maybe we need to learn to be more assertive," I blurted. Several women talked at once. Deborah, who never raised her voice, shouted, "So you're saying it was my fault I got raped?"

"No! That's not what I meant . . . I'm sorry . . . " but the talk skewed in another direction . . . a man/uncle/friend who'd . . . now I was angry at myself for not saying what I meant to say. What had I meant to say? Krysta put her arm around Deborah who was crying; Joy got up to talk to Christine, also crying. Barbara tipped her head toward the stairs. I inched sideways on crossed legs, Barbara behind me. The steps gritty and even with my legs extended, each bump down jarred my spine. We carefully opened the screen door and carefully closed it to prevent squeaks.

"Want to go swim?" Barbara said.

I shook my head. "I'll find Mom."

Mom wasn't in the room. I picked up my journal but couldn't write, blocked by the clenched fist in my chest. I remembered seeing dark shadowy air around Denise . . . when . . . last week? I'd asked her if she was okay, and she said she was, a customary smile inched at her mouth. But I'd seen darkness. What was I supposed to say? There's a dark shadow thing around you?

Mom came in. She must have seen my tension. "I went to sit with Denise and hold her hand," she said.

That was the thing to do, not fume and speak stupidly. My fights with men came from them wanting to control me. And I'd been hit plenty of times. Was it the same or different?

No José in the morning. I picked green beans, the fuzzy pods sunlight-warm and tickly in my hands, and tossed them into an aluminum bowl. My anger impotent. I wanted to pass on how important to speak boundaries and be heard. But maybe boundaries didn't always work. I'd spoken stupidly. Deborah entered the garden and turned onto an outside path.

"Deborah! Wait. Please." She waited.

"I don't know how to be helpful," I said when I caught up with her. "I'm sorry. I'm really sorry if I hurt your feelings." Deborah nodded but her face stayed stony. Mom sat on the lanai with Denise's boyfriend, a young man from the wider community. I saw her leaning in, holding his hands as he talked, his face screwed up against tears.

The Vaudeville Festival arrived for its residency and the lawn filled with noise and jugglers and flying circus rings and clubs.

At dinner, I overate, returning for rocky road cheesecake, not once but twice, sneaking out to the garden to eat. Junkie behavior. Crumbling the last few bites, I tossed them into the garden, climbed the stairs, and flipped open the Smith Corona.

"Why this anger? What's it about," I wrote, eyes closed, letting my fingers record.

"Look clearly, do not build walls, see things as they are, be aware. Least resistance means not fighting. This is not a pathway for all but for you. Watch. Observe."

I stared at the words on the tiny screen, read them over and over, hoping to find the key. Salt tears, as useless as icicles in a desert, tracked my cheeks.

Mom came upstairs and we readied for bed. Loud music from the circus amplifiers flooded through open windows. Twisting in my sheets, I pulled the pillow over my head. All of Kalani was chaos and noise.

I dreamed big waves crashed toward me but didn't sweep me away.

Gecko chatter woke me into a misty dawn. Clinging to the screen above my head, a four-inch gecko, tail twitching furiously, challenged a bigger praying mantis on the opposite and impossible-to-attack side of the screen. The mantis reared on its hind legs, motionless, its head cocked as if listening to the gecko. Maybe that's what I needed to do— sit quiet and listen—a cloistered nun, maybe, with a screening veil to serve as a gag.

Mom and I left mid-morning on the Hilo van-run for her to catch the bus to North Kohala. We didn't say much, both of us weary after a fractured night, both of us staring past the windows to watch the sea. She clasped my hand in her lap. At the bus stop, she hugged me and brushed hair off my face. "Just be nice," she said. Tears smarted in my eyes and she brushed them away, pulled my head down to kiss me on the cheek. I helped her up the steps and settled her into a seat, climbed off, and waited below her window. We smiled at each other. The bus lurched. I returned her wave and wondered when I'd see her again. She was nearing eighty and returning stateside to an empty house. I could have crumpled on the pavement and bawled. But I didn't.

On the drive back to Kalani, I stared, unseeing, out the van window. A cacophony of discord had loosened as if someone or something had died; perhaps it had, perhaps the sense of spirit as protection. There lay the betrayal, the fatted calf upon the altar. If offering ourselves, our work to something greater, to spirit, wouldn't protect, what could be trusted?

I hadn't considered how tribal we were until the other tribe, the jugglers and vaudevillian players, arrived with noise and laughter, loud circus music during the day, loud rock and roll at the nighttime bonfires. Our tribe wounded, theirs sprouting all the aggressive good health of youth. What was the young man's name who'd been talking to Mom? Tom

Foolery. The Kalani community sulked, crept around corners, surprised each other in improbable spots coming or going from mysterious missions. What was mysterious about rage? Barbara sat by the juggler's nighttime fire to listen to music. That was her path of least resistance. What would be mine? Could I grow into my mother's kindness?

ELEVEN

CHAOS AND RAGE

Morning found me as exhausted as the day before, but yoga called. Marion walked among us, guiding with her rich, gentle voice. I felt old, so old. The cold wooden floor hard and unyielding. For so long, since-when in a now-forgotten past, I'd rested on my back with hands over my pubic bone, finger tips touching, as if guarding some secret wasteland. Marion straddled my legs, leaned over, lifted my hands, and placed them on the floor alongside each leg. I was exposed, vulnerable. My body cracked into sobbing tears.

Marion lay her fingertips on my heart. The sobbing stopped. Tears continued to leak from the corners of my eyes, but my chest softened and I drew in a deep, shuddering breath. Marion brought herself to standing, levering her lower back to help lift her pregnant belly.

"Pull your knees up to your chest," she said. We followed her voice into a shoulder stand. Her free hand rested against the pillar of my upraised legs. When I remained steady, Marion dropped her hand and walked on. Blood flowed into my heart, my legs strong, my toes pointed to the rafters. I'd stopped crying.

That evening, we gathered on the same floor for a two-hour workshop with Tony Selvage, the space more isolated, and a closed door to the stairwell blocked sound. The music he'd play for us, Tony said, was Healing Mother Earth. I folded the blanket from my bed and lay down, the blue notebook and a pen at the ready.

If there are other lives and times, how many must I live to make sense of me? The cries and whispers of play, and doors pushed aside. How many lives? No wonder I have wide hips. I need them to accommodate all my lives banging around.

Children laughing. The lightheartedness of fireflies at dusk. May baskets and hidden trails along railroad tracks. I forgot too soon, too soon moved to revolt. All that's needed, really, is the laughter of childhood, catching fireflies.

The tenor and color of childhood memories change if pre-John's death or post. Pre is softer, greener. Past drier.

At the end of the workshop, I bought a copy of the music from Tony.

That night, alone, Barbara in the A-frame, I put on the headphones and dropped so deep the clicking-off didn't register. A violent dream woke me. A dark man follows me; another dark man gets in a car with me but I push him away, try to drive while pushing him away. We struggle. I bite a piece out of his cheek, spit it out, and hear, *your anger is keeping you from moving to the light.*

I searched the dream for a trail, a pattern. I wanted to move forward but violence kept blocking me. My own violence? My need to control, to stay safe? My anger, old anger, kept me from . . . what? Who was I without anger? What was holding on to me; what was I holding on to?

José stayed gone. I puttered in the garden. Once the jugglers left, he'd be back to hauling lava. In the afternoon, beside the pool, I lay on a lounge, waiting for Ben to finish a massage, and drifted off. When Ben sat down, my eyes blinked open, startled. Ben smiled. "You ready?" I followed him into the massage room.

"There's some old grief I need to release," I said. "At a cellular level."

He nodded and began along my spine, his long fingers spreading and thumbs probing. I flinched as he found a deep pocket, his pressure lightened, rotated deeper until the pain dissolved. His hands searched out another pocket. *This is only a body,* I heard somewhere in the back of my mind, treat it kindly. Ben was no longer Ben, rather pressure . . . pain . . . release . . . pain . . . release. The moving pressure arrived at my shoulders with the same rotating command, release, pressure, release. A hawk, soaring, flew through my mind.

That evening, my shoulders tender, I didn't want to move off my bed. Not exactly soaring, are you? Food didn't appeal, but I went downstairs, ate some salad, avoided conversation, and climbed the stairs to my room where I lit a candle rather than turn on the overhead light.

Marion knocked on my door. "Do you have time to listen to a dream?" I always had time for dreams.

We sat cross-legged, facing each other on my bed-chair-sofa. Her fingers drew idle circles across her belly. "I dreamed this child would be a boy and would carve a path without me. I don't know what that means. What does carve a path mean? Will he go live with his father? Will he just go? I don't know what this is supposed to mean or what I'm supposed to do." Her eyes, when she looked up, pooled into brown puddles.

"Boys leave," I said. "My sons and I are close, but as older teenagers, they both distanced themselves. I didn't see Nathan for more than two years while he was in Korea. But as young adults, they returned. If you let him fly, he'll come back, Marion."

The worry crease softened between her eyes. "Are you sure?"

"No, nothing is sure. But I think it's what young males need to do. They have to leave the nest and prove themselves. I think trusting my sons to do what they needed to do is what allowed them to come back. It was hard, but I didn't judge and I didn't complain."

A knock interrupted our conversation. Raven stood at the door, peering down from his lanky height to see my face in the shadowed room. "Do you have an extra blanket? I've been cold at night."

"Sure." I opened the closet door and grabbed a blanket off the shelf. It smelled of heat and too-long storage.

"Thanks!" He wrapped both arms around the blanket, hugging it to his chest, before turning away.

"That was interesting," I said to Marion. "I wasn't feeling very good about how I spoke at the survivors meeting, but at least I can help the boys."

Marion's laugh, like her voice, was warm love. She stood up and hugged me. "Remember," she said. "When we channel information, we'll also be blamed for any pain birthed by our words. Perhaps that's why I teach yoga. No words. The body can either do or not do, stretch or tighten. If you listen to the body, you only have yourself to blame!" We hugged again at the door and she left for her own bed.

That night, my dream put me in a car, alone, zooming backward, up a hill, around corners. The vehicle seemed to have its own mind. When I struggled to drive forward, I couldn't find my way. The road ended. I parked the car and walked, saw an old school being repaired, and went inside. On the blackboard: "You are at a crossroad. Wait for direction."

My eyes flew open and I stared at the dark space of rafters, a lighter dark where dawn began. *How long will I stay at this crossroad?*

The voice in my head answered: *You may be at this crossroad for a while.*

I needed a weekend off from soul searching. The grounds were quiet, either everyone out somewhere or in the Exercise Technology workshop. I swam laps, sat in the sauna, and skipped lunchtime people to take a nap. After the chatter died into another stretching silence, I left my room for the writers' hale and lifted the dictionary from its stand. Holding it in my lap, I turned onion-skin pages, light as if fabricated by silkworms, too fragile to hold the word I wanted to understand. "Rape: The refuse of grapes left after the extraction of the juice in winemaking; from Old French, *rasper*, to scrape off. Really? From Indo-European rep; to snatch: rape, rapacious, rapid, rapt, raven, ravish. The crime of forcing a female to submit to sexual intercourse; the act of seizing and carrying off by force; abduction; abuse; violation. Refuse left behind. Violation. Rasped by force, greedy, ravenous."

None of them expressed in an adequate way the emotions raised. The word had no emotion of its own, rather reaction to and from oozing wounds and old stories. So maybe I hadn't learned anything. I'd certainly not learned to keep my mouth shut. Maybe that's why I'd kept getting hit. I wouldn't keep my mouth shut. I'd raged against injustice all my life. What a tangle. But keeping or not keeping my mouth shut didn't deserve hitting, saying or not saying didn't deserve rape. There was no justification. My jaw clenched, chewing remorse. And at the same time, hard up against that truth, was the one that said I had to recognize my boundaries, really listen to my body so that I didn't need to keep my mouth shut. Not fix or be nice or reason. I'd stopped clenching my jaws but my chin jutted out. And how many times do you need reminding to breathe? Obviously, soul searching wasn't over.

My head was tired. It was my son's birthday. I'd call him. He'd make me laugh.

Only he didn't.

"Mom, we need you. If you don't have a job, come here. We've got two businesses and Michael needs to get to kindergarten. We have an extra bedroom. You could do whatever you want during the day after he goes to school."

"But what will I do in Georgia even if I have time?" The afternoon sun drilled my shoulders, our pay phone stationed on the wall outside the office. The receiver felt sticky on my ear. "I'll think about it. But I need to get off now. There's someone waiting." I hung up the phone and stared at the rough planks in front of me. Scent from the plumeria bushes circled my head in a dizzying drift. Living in Georgia was not what I wanted to do. He'd begged me to live with them since Michael was born. Every time I visited . . . *Mom, he needs you . . . Mom, we need you.* Maybe it didn't seem I accomplished much on my own. Nobody needed the phone . . . need need need. I probably needed to look up that word too.

On Sunday night, the vaudeville group invited Kalani to a final performance: three rings, music, jokes, and audience participation. When Bari asked if I wanted to visit Volcano instead, I said yes. Immediately. We climbed into the Russ Truck, as we'd named it, and under an almost-full moon, Russ drove to Volcano. Lava poured from the rifts in rivers of fire, rushed into the sea, water boiled, and shiny new black silica chips rode the waves to shore. Crackling sounds ricocheted through my head.

Off the beach, we walked on the cooled flow, the pahoehoe lava shining black satin in the moonlight. The flow had destroyed a cinder block home but left a battered trashcan stuck to a battered wall. The fury of the volcano matched the fury at Kalani, destruction into renewal, as if the passage had no other way than through the valley of death. Some fifty yards farther, where the lava crossed the road, it had stopped six inches from an intact red stop sign. Earth's message: Stop! As if we knew how.

With the jugglers packed up, the tents, the balls and hoops and loudspeakers all gone, José showed up again on Monday morning and we worked at chopping and hauling lava, but we worked slow and joked through most of it. He'd brought new gloves to replace the ones I'd torn and snagged on jagged lava. We didn't talk about the previous week. Miles had watered, so the garden smelled of clean dirt and shiny leaves. I'd worn my bright blue T-shirt with "Toto, I don't think we're in Kansas anymore" across the front in big white letters. When Barbara came into the garden carrying an aluminum bowl, she erupted, laughing. "I gotta get a shot of this!" She dropped the bowl and pulled her camera from a rear pocket.

"Stand together," she commanded. We posed as if for a newly-married photo, José with an arm protectively around my shoulders and the other crossing his chest to fold my hand to his heart. Click.

Maybe Kalani was returning to something that passed as normal.

Or maybe not. The next morning at breakfast, and after a peaceful and centering yoga class, we gathered for a meeting. Everyone but José— he'd disappeared. Howard Duncan carried his clipboard and read off new rules: security, watchfulness, no one to walk alone on the road. He left with his clipboard and angry conversations replaced his read-off list. I left for the garden and kept to the back rows of lettuce, out of sight. I hadn't said anything because I didn't know how to trust the right words would come out of my mouth; instead, in my head, I fussed and fretted. None of which was particularly effective. Sitting in the cool dirt between rows of new plants, I tried to see the crossroad; move on, even if I didn't know the direction. *Change your attitude,* I heard. Great. More enigmatic lessons. I left the garden and the messages and helped Ben put up the sweat lodge.

Crawling into the lodge that evening, I circled the stone pit and settled myself opposite the door. During the first round, I prayed to see the crossroad and the path in front of me. The steam rose in thick clouds. Ben had said the west side was the hottest. What had I done? Could I find space to lie down where it was cooler? The dirt under my hands rough and hot. My searching fingers found a stone and curled it into my palm. The smooth stone anchored me, held a solid center in all the drifting steam and hope and dreams. Hold on . . . hold on. Shadowed figures sat close on each side.

When Ben lifted the blanket flap, I crawled out and let the nighttime air dry my shoulders and neck. I could breathe again, and my heart slowed its rushing. A light mist turned into sprinkles, promising more. We returned to the sweat, and in the second round, I saw my father playing with me . . . a happy childhood. In the last round, the light expanded, and I understood that light, joy, innocence was mine. Follow the path. Stay joyful. The rest would follow. Ben began a chant to the skies, to clouds for rain to wash all of Kalani from the energy of the previous week. The rains came.

The week filled with gardening and more gardening as if José did penance for his time away. My new gloves blossomed new snags. Regardless of how many times, or in how many ways I explained I was wearing down, he met each remark with cold silence. But I wouldn't give in, wouldn't give up, and my stubbornness drove me to keep going. Wheelbarrow after wheelbarrow of lava chunks erupted from the earth; I carted them into the jungle, crashed into bed when I could.

Some nights I attended classes or workshops, always Eighteen Buddha Hands with Saki Lee, on another day an impulsive late-afternoon trip with Sharon, Marion, Barbara, Krysta, and Isobel to Kapoho. Kilauea's lava flows formed most of Puna's coast line, and at Kapoho, the warm tide pools bubbled up within lava walls, heated by the underwater volcano that fed Kilauea. We practiced watsu water massage, rocking each other in the rhythm of the sea. My body relaxed, undulating in the warm waves.

Rested and shining clean, we returned to a wellness party in full swing. But instead of ukuleles and hula, repetitious gripes danced in the air.

The administration had asked an eight-month pregnant young woman, Amber, who had camped in the field during the jugglers' stay but who hadn't left when they left, to move on. The young woman went into labor. Someone phoned for an ambulance. Faith, a resident worker, moved herself and Amber into a Kalani bungalow when Amber returned, still pregnant, from the hospital. After the grief and anger of the rape, this new grief, a destitute mother-to-be in her hour of need, raised dissonance. But by the end of the week, Faith and Amber had left Kalani Honua, and Denise—who'd kept a low profile, not working, not talking much—had moved in with her boyfriend several miles down the road toward Kalapana.

On Friday Ben walked through the garden. "Your neck looks tight." He brought over a chair and gestured for me to sit. Putting his hands on each side of my head and cupping my ears, he lifted my head until all the vertebrate separated in soft, popping sounds. I was a baby turtle, sticking its head into an unpredictable world. Barbara left for a week of vacation on the other side of the island, and the room was mine and quiet.

TWELVE

Taking the Wild Path

At a leisurely Saturday brunch, a young man, Nick, sat across the table from me. He grinned and nodded. Nick appeared and disappeared with some regularity, sometimes staying for a meal, sometimes for conversation. We'd named him Nick-Who-Swims-With-the-Dolphins to differentiate from Nick on the grounds crew. "I went swimming with the dolphins last night," he said, his smile wreathed in a soft, three-day growth of beard. I wondered if he cut it with scissors since it always seemed about the same peach-fuzz length; his body slightly built as if it could slide into silent places, unseen, part of the elvish folk. Michael Koob sat down with us and pushed his blond and unruly forelock from his eyes. Michael had watered the garden often enough to make me his forever-friend.

"I'm going up the King's Highway to the Royal Palms. Do you want to come?" Nick's smile included us both. Michael looked at me, a question forming in his eyes: a Don Quixote moment when shoving my fist in the air and shouting "More adventure!" might be appropriate. But I didn't. I smiled and nodded. And so, throwing all caution, to say nothing of wisdom to the winds, and following this path of impulsive joy, I took off through the jungle with Michael and Nick-Who-Swims-With-the-Dolphins.

Nick led us along the edge of the jagged cliff wall and pointed out pieces of the old road, faded, but still visible. "King Kamehameha built this all the way around the island. Most of it's gone now." Nick looked saddened by the wavering marks at his feet. He lifted his head to look out to the sea and his eyes narrowed as if wondering whether the enemy were people, or sea, or time, but he caught himself, his almost-always smile back in place. A salt tang drifted on an errant breeze, while below, the waves murmured history. After about thirty minutes on the King's Highway, Nick abruptly made a turn into the jungle, and we walked on spongy ground under old and gnarled trees. Nick pointed. "That's an Ohi'a. If you get caught in a tsunami, climb into one of them." So that was the Ohi'a of legend, twisted and strong. I laughed. "They're strong with deep roots," Nick said, a tone of insistence in his voice. But I hadn't laughed at his advice; I'd laughed at imagining myself a scarlet flower in the lofty branches during a hurricane.

Nick led us on into rows of towering royal coconut palms. "This used to be a plantation. You can see the coconuts, see? Under the branches? Like the tree has balls!"

His remark was more raucous than might be expected from someone related to the elves, but I believed his plantation remark. He had an unending supply of history about Puna, and my farmer eyes could recognize a plot of straight rows, although the trees were so tall that seeing coconuts—next to the trunk and overshadowed by long, arching fronds—took some pointing on Nick's part.

We smelled smoke. Nick tipped his head and frowned. We followed the smell to a sweat lodge nestled between large boulders and fallen tree trunks: two women, three men. One of the men wore a bandanna around his forehead. "I'm Charlie Day," he said and we shook hands. He'd come from Mt. Shasta, he said. It seemed a far piece to come for a sweat lodge, but oddness had a way of popping up in Puna.

My usual reserve around strangers dissolved in the presence of fellow sweat lodge travelers. "We have sweats at Kalani Honua," I said. "New and full moon. I'm Janet. This is Michael and Nick." Mentioning Kalani created a passport of sorts. We were no longer suspicious. The young women scooted aside so I'd have a place to sit on their tree trunk. The woman on my left passed a coconut shell half-filled with sweet coconut water. Sweat pooled in the crook of her elbow. Nick and Michael edged away to sit on a nearby boulder.

I saw myself both being and watching the fire, the people around it, Nick and Michael as they sat apart, me inside the circle of vision seekers. I'd stepped into my journey as elder, that was clear, but the journey so new, so anchored in life at Kalani, I didn't know how to see myself as these young people might see me. What did they see? I'd always been an outsider, and this sudden leapfrog to insider rank surprised me. No one talked. The space of waiting was recovery time, not story-time.

Charlie Day sipped from the coconut water and placed the shell on the ground. "It is time. We invite you to enter with us." His shadowed eyes were hard to read, but I heard respect in his voice.

"Thank you, but I need to return to Kalani. You are very kind to include me," I said and stood, my knees complaining. As they filed into the small, round lodge, I walked over to Michael and Nick. "I'm ready to go." Michael nodded. We walked to the road.

"If a car comes along, I'll hitch a ride," I said. I'd entered the ranks of elder, and elders could make their own decisions. Besides, I was tired.

"Is that smart?" Michael asked. "You don't know who's driving out here."

"But I know to trust my instincts. If someone isn't safe for me, I'll know."

Michael glanced at the overhanging trees. The sun inched itself below the jungle treetops and shadows deepened. We heard the sound of a car behind us on the Red Road. I flagged it. Hitching a ride in Puna was a common and easy experience and my sense of power a mantle of protection. Michael followed Nick as he slid into the jungle.

The car's driver was an old Hawaiian. He didn't say much, had nodded briefly when I said I lived at Kalani. It wasn't far. I gazed out the window and wondered at Michael and Nick's discomfort. I recalled an old Hawaiian legend Jeanne told me, how at birth, children were given a bowl of light. If they tended the light, it grew, but if the child became fearful or envious or angry, a stone dropped into the bowl of light. Enough stones and the child became a stone, unmovable. But in order to change, the child simply needed to turn the bowl over and dump out the stones. The light would return. Had I emptied my bowl of stones? I'd often felt needy—needing love, needing support—and goodness knew I'd been angry, but not so much at Kalani. In the community, I'd grown to . . . to what?

The driver dropped me at the gate, we nodded our goodbyes, and I walked up the lane. Ben worked at the sweat lodge, preparing it for a visiting group's ceremony. He smiled as I joined him. "Want to assist me tonight?"

The group arrived and jostled themselves around the fire pit. Fifteen women: a full house. Ben and I scrunched into spaces on each side of the door. The first rounds were calm, but in the third round, one woman began an impassioned prayer, her voice rising in a disjointed singsong. More voices joined, each more determined to out-passion others, pushing the energy toward hysterics. I heard Ben say, "Okay." I echoed his okay, and we tossed open the door. A rush of cool air swept the ragged energy into a dissolving ball. The fourth round settled into silence and calm. Ben on one side of the door, me on the other.

I showered, the water soft in the soapy smell of flowers, and descended the stairs dressed in my green-leafed muumuu. "You're glowing," Raven said. No dreams disturbed my sleep.

On Sunday morning, as I walked to the washing shed to move my things from washer to dryer, I saw Ben removing blankets from the sweat lodge. "Give me a minute and I'll help you," I called. Ben raised his arm.

"Good job last night," I said as we untied and folded blankets into a pile.

Ben shrugged. "Well. Maybe. Duncan said they came in and complained."

"About what? Did you tell him how crazy it was?"

"Yeah. Sort of. Not sure he heard me. The guests said I'd interrupted a vision quest."

"Some vision."

He laughed. "What are you doing? Want to spend the day with us?"

Would I ever! "Let me get stuff out of the dryer."

"Bring your suit," Ben called as I raced across the yard. "And flip-flops."

We picked up Sarah and their son Chris and drove to Kapoho to play in the warm tide pools, drove back to the house for afternoon mimosas. Chris showed me his drawings, boy drawings of spacemen and space ships. I gave him my little black sketchbook to draw in, and he drew a spaceman. I thought of my grandson, a couple of years younger than Chris, and wondered if he drew spacemen. This family setting so comforting, no longings or tales of the search, rather a quiet family afternoon. When Sarah rustled in the kitchen, I joined her. We cooked and ate dinner, drank more wine, puttered around cleaning up. Chris headed off to bed. Sarah, Ben, and I settled into the living room.

"Oh, my gosh!" I said, suddenly realizing the time and jumping up. The wine in my glass sloshed but little enough remained to spill. "It's 10:30! I'm scheduled for generator duty. I've got to get there!"

The up-late-duty to shut off the generator at eleven each night was listed on a clipboard sheet in the office. Once shut down, the compound settled into a silent, dark space of jungle-filled-with-unknown-dangers. At least in my mind. I was in trouble. I hated being in trouble! I had dreaded the duty, afraid of the dark, still, at my age, but I didn't say that.

"Someone will shut it off. It's happened before. Don't worry," Sarah said from her curled up position in an armchair. "You can stay here tonight."

"But who'll do it? No one knows I'm gone!" My voice held an edge of hysteria.

"I'll take you, if you want," Ben said. "But really, it'll be okay."

His words settled me. "Okay," I said. Maybe I could be a little unpredictable? Maybe I always was.

Early the next morning, Ben drove me to Kalani. I wrote a note, thanking whoever shut down the generator, pinned it to the office note board, and walked toward the dining lanai.

Howard Duncan walked toward me, his clipboard under an arm. "Did you know you had generator duty last night?" he said.

"Yeah, I know. I was at Sarah and Ben's and it got late, so I decided to stay. I put a thank you note on the list for whoever turned it off."

"I did when I came in last night," he said. "No problem. You can do it for me sometime." Howard walked toward the office.

"Thanks," I called after him. And of course it was Duncan. He shut down the generator and was tolerant of my lapse. I walked up the gravel path, head down, trying to remember another time when forgiveness came to my mistake. I couldn't remember. No, that wasn't true. My sons forgave me.

Whoops of laughter greeted me as I walked onto the lanai. Marion, Isobel, and Sharon sat over the remnants of breakfast. "Where were you? We thought maybe you stayed with Nick and spent the night!" Marion said.

"I was with Ben and Sarah. Why would I stay with Nick?"

Marion laughed again and prodded me in the side as I settled beside her. "Nick's very charming," she said. "And young. And energetic."

"I'm not sleeping with Nick," I said, catching on.

Michael Koob walked over. Too much interest, way too much, in my absence. "You okay? You weren't here last night. Howard shut down the generator."

"I know. I was at Ben and Sarah's and fell down on my responsibilities!" I wanted to make a joke, but it sounded flat.

"Oh. Okay," he said and leaned down to kiss me on the cheek before walking away.

Koob didn't kiss anyone. And he kissed me for making a mistake? I watched him walk into the garden. The last he'd seen me was on the road when I'd hitchhiked. Maybe he was glad I wasn't raped or dead somewhere. It hadn't occurred to me that someone might actually worry about me.

The week progressed: garden, yoga, Tai Chi, swimming, Taoist yoga, and Eighteen Buddha Hands. Tuesday night, I stayed up to shut off the generator before collapsing into bed.

"You're late," José snapped as I joined him beside a pile of disrupted lava. It wouldn't pay to respond. My share of forgiveness had been used up. Bending to the task, I lifted chunks of lava, tossed them into the nearby wheelbarrow, filled the wheelbarrow, pushed it past the edge of the jungle, dumped it, returned to the pile, loaded another, and on and on and on. José attacked the lava with a pickaxe as if he had a grudge. I wondered who he'd fought with. After every third or fourth dumping, concealed by jungle, I'd stand, stretch my back, listen to distant bird song—jungle music. Lunchtime came and went. José stayed surly. I stayed quiet.

Another massage with Ben was in order for the afternoon. I asked him to particularly work on my bad hip because it had ached for days, but as he finished, it felt as if he lifted a shell off my back. Lightly lifted it off. Along with being a turtle with my neck sticking out, I was a turtle without a shell. I could barely get off the table. Ben cupped my elbow and walked beside me. "Are you okay?" he said, tipping his head to look at my face. I couldn't stop crying and shook my head. I was . . . what? Frightened? No. Vulnerable. Several people sat on the lanai.

Ben put his arm around my shoulders and guided me toward a

bench until I managed to collect myself enough to walk to my room. I considered skipping the Trager Massage class that evening, but I went and asked Victoria to partner with me. "I can't handle it on my back, but I can do yours." She smiled the sweetest smile, forgiving and generous.

In the night, I woke with my arms lifting above me as if I were praying.

I rolled over and picked up my pen and journal.

"You are restructuring. The pain is the shifting of hardness you no longer need. You must trust even though you don't understand. Slowly you will find a new way to stand. You stagger now because all is new and you are unsure where balance lies. Rejoice in the changes. Pain will teach you tolerance. You will restructure this shell you live in. But it is a shell, flesh, not permanent. It is the shell you call I. That shell will change; the I remains. Love moves in you, and while not making you young again, it will make you free."

Light-threads shifted through the screen as dawn slid in. I remembered my arms reaching up on another night but hadn't registered, fell back asleep. Now I was awake. Soft twitters, tree rustles. The jungle's morning smell—musty, earthy—breathed through the screen. A random call. Deeper and farther away, a song answered, then another. Light widened into pink feathers. What was guiding me? Love would make me free? When had love ever freed me? What would make that happen? How do you build a love that frees you? I didn't know. And yet, whatever it was, this love, this yearning opened a crack, and spirit had taken root. Maybe in the same way lava cupped water to nourish seeds and allow roots to crack tough layers. I stretched, long and slow.

Ooooowwww. Body had not taken kindly to having its shell removed. Maybe yoga would help. And maybe José would be more interested in planting seeds than chopping lava.

THIRTEEN

Lifting My Arms

José wasn't in the garden. I harvested lettuce and beans and eggplant and carried three full aluminum bowls to the kitchen. "Oh," Bari said, taking the bowls, stacked on top of each other, "I didn't know there was so much." Nor did I. Not a lot of head-lifting-looking around when pushing a wheelbarrow. I weeded the new lettuce, my neck and shoulders tense and stiff. A headache tracked the top of my head. Even my eyes protested by scratching at their lids. My hip wasn't hurting but my knees were. Shifting position, I sat and stretched my legs down the row.

"You okay?" I heard Ben's voice behind me and shook my head. He knelt behind me and began working on my neck. "I met with Duncan. He's removing me from the Wellness Program after our final sweat."

"Why?" I tried to turn and look at him but he steadied me with a hand on my shoulder.

I lost track of what he was saying, but it seemed connected to the complaints from the women's sweat lodge chaos. His hands moved up my neck to my head, pulling and lifting. My neck relaxed as if the top of my head were an upside down funnel, pouring out.

Ben patted my shoulder. "It'll be okay." He unfolded from his knees and I heard his receding footsteps. Rolling from sitting to prone, I lay beside the lettuce, a trellis of beans shading me, and curled my fingers into the cool dirt. I let myself dissolve into earth. Tension slid away. I dozed. The sound of the dinner bell, hanging steps away, jangled loud and long. Startled, I opened my eyes. I'd slept in the garden in the dirt. My hands, curled into the soil, lifted and flexed. A long sigh rippled through my body. Turning on my side, I stared at the lettuces in front of my face, hoping the magical grasshopper would make an appearance. What would Ben do after the program? I forgot to ask. I got up, dusted myself off, and washed for lunch.

In late afternoon, I climbed the stairs again, slowly, to my room. I couldn't get past being tired. All the time. I'd have to give up something, obviously not the garden. Classes? I often missed the Wellness classes anyway, but I wasn't giving up yoga or Tai Chi or meditations for sleep. I shed my garden clothes and slid a muumuu over my head.

Someone knocked at my door. I groaned but not loud enough for anyone to hear and opened it. Krysta waited, holding her hand, her eyes scrunched at the edges.

"I have a blister!" she said, holding up a finger. "It keeps hurting. It's bad. Tootsie just said put some Bacitracin ointment on it."

I took her hand and turned it to examine the finger. A blister. "That'll work. You'll be okay. Put some Bacitracin on it." Krysta was Nordic and invincible, so I wasn't prepared for the sad wail in her voice as she turned.

"Krysta. Wait. I have some in my box." Jeanne had sent a small first-aid kit with me, saying if I lived in the jungle, I better be prepared. I was. Bacitracin, Band-Aids, and gauze pads, plus some antiseptic cleaner. "Sit down on the bed and I'll clean it for you." If someone asked, I could give.

Holding her hand in my lap, I examined it closely, cleaned it gently, applied salve and a Band-Aid, murmured responses as she related how she'd burned herself on the clothes dryer. She was tired of doing laundry. She missed Scotland. She missed mountains. It would be spring soon. She'd miss spring.

"So are you leaving?"

"I like Hawaii. I haven't seen North Kohala yet. Maybe we could go up there together." She inspected her finger, not noticing the apparent contradictions. It didn't matter. "Thank you. It doesn't hurt now."

She was ready to leave so I walked her to the door and we hugged. It took so little to be kind; why couldn't I remember that? But I had to quit beating myself up for my mistakes.

Pulling the shoebox from under the bed, I dug through and found a Lynn Anderson meditation, lay down, and drifted in the sound of her voice. If your picture were on the cover of *Time*, what would you want the legend to say?

Bolting upright, I grabbed my journal and sat staring beyond the screened window. Unclipping the pen, I wrote Shaman/Healer/Teacher and stared at the words, kept writing:

Life Arrow (things to do)| Death Arrow (give away)
continue to study | blockages in my body
open myself to love | eating to replace love
live in trust | fear
trust vulnerability | intolerance
be open | insecurity
learn compassion | judging

If I was rebuilding myself, recreating my life, and redefining, who or what would I be? If I could learn compassion for others, maybe I could learn compassion for myself. Well . . . soul digging, obviously, wasn't over.

At dinner time, racket met me as I walked down the stairs. Marion and Sharon sat at a far table and I joined them. "What's happening?" It could have been anything.

"Spring Equinox," Marion said, as if that explained everything. I looked around. Everyone seemed okay, hyper, but okay.

"When? Today?"

Marion sighed. "Day after tomorrow."

"What's tomorrow . . . I mean, what day is it?"

"Tomorrow? Friday."

Friday? How did it get to be the end of the week? "Do we have a workshop tonight? Or is it tomorrow?"

"Herbal Medicine. But I can miss that," Sharon said. Marian and I nodded in unison. Rar and Gary play-wrestled at the end of the lanai, banged into the corner of a table, rattled chairs. The guys whooped and laughed. Sharon shifted, lightly, a twitch, as if something itched at her customary gentle humor. "I wonder how late they'll be up."

"Can I stay in your room until Barbara comes back?" Marion stared straight ahead. "Sure," I said as Bari came out of the kitchen and clanged the dinner bell. A general sort of rushing headed for the food line, boy/girl/boy/girl it seemed to go. Spring definitely in the air. After dinner, Sharon headed for her A-frame and Marion and I upstairs. We closed the rattley door behind us and both of us sighed. "Thanks," Marion said.

I made up Barbara's bed with fresh sheets. We were asleep before the generator shut off.

My roller-coaster life with José stepped up its pace the next morning. He was already hacking away at a thick layer of lava. I pulled on my gloves and began filling the wheelbarrow. Impatient with my pace, José picked up several big chunks and dropped each into the wheelbarrow with a clanging splatter of fragments.

"Let me go dump this before it gets too heavy," I said and grabbed the handles to shove the wheelbarrow toward the jungle edge. José turned to lift the pick ax. I dumped the load and returned to the garden.

"You're too slow," José snapped. He lifted chunks difficult for me to handle and toppled them into the wheelbarrow. I trundled across the road, tipped the wheelbarrow, returned; he lifted bigger chunks, I staggered to the jungle, returned. Lunch came. After eating, I rested fifteen minutes on my bed. At the garden, I found the wheelbarrow full, a heap of chunks waiting beside it. José hadn't stopped. I dumped the wheelbarrow, returned, filled it, dumped it, returned . . . this was crazy. We already had more garden than we could handle. "José, we don't need all this garden!"

His eyes glittered like shards. "You don't make decisions. I do. You do what I tell you."

"I'm really tired, José. You had some days off. I didn't."

"You're lazy!"

I felt the spray of words on my face and something more: an old and familiar clap of rage gave me no time to reconsider.

"Fuck off, José! Chill out!"

He flung the pickaxe across the garden, striking a bean trellis and crumpling its side pole. He glanced at the broken pole and strode from the garden.

My legs crumpled and I sat in the dirt next to the lava pile, head bowed. My rage erupted from my own story: belittled when I didn't work hard enough or daydreamed instead of hustling; a lack of understanding or caring about who or what I was. My thoughts tumbled. Maybe if I'd tried less to impress José at the beginning. Maybe if I quit putting men in the protector category, expecting them to be my father, and then turn on them when they aren't. Maybe if I'd learn to communicate instead of whine, if I'd said I'm going to take a fifteen minute break and I'll be back, or you've been working hard, too, let's go sit for a few minutes and tell stories. Maybe if I practiced a little compassion. Instead, I fought back.

I sighed and stood up, lifted the half-load of lava, dumped it in the jungle, put the empty wheelbarrow in the shed. Another lesson to learn.

MARION AND I LAY IN OUR BEDS SATURDAY MORNING. TIME, THAT most precious gift of the protogenos gods, given and stretched, wrapped us in glorious freedom. Rain, pocking through the jungle, woke me briefly during the night, but morning wore a sapphire gown ruffled with bird song. The garden below our window glittered green, the wet lava chunks varnished to a high black gloss. Breakfast smells rose from the kitchen: coffee, pancakes, eggs. I pulled a muumuu over my nightshirt and walked downstairs to fill a tray. We ate in the room. If there's one thing a nomadic life teaches, it's how to make a comfortable home wherever the stopping happens to be. We sat cross-legged on the bed, my writing table, emptied of notes and Smith Corona, our dining table.

"I wish I could see where all this was heading, this whatever-we're-doing-here thing," I said. "You'll go home to a family and a new baby. I don't even know a direction."

"Where do you want to go?" She popped the stem of a banana.

"That's just it. If I knew where I wanted to go, I'd be there. It doesn't appear I'm staying in Hawaii. I want to. It feels like home. But I don't think it is. My dreams were showing me . . . maybe places. Maybe people. But I haven't dreamed lately."

She peeled the banana skin and tossed it onto the tray; a soft ripe smell hung in the air. "What kind of dreams?"

I picked up the discarded peel, stalling for time, unsure how much to reveal. "Did you know banana trees talk? I lived above a banana plantation once, up on a mountain-side. Well, visited. On St. Lucia. We lived there one winter between semesters, one of those happy times. I'd sit on the patio to watch the sun come over the mountains and listen to the banana trees talk. I told you about Bill." Marion nodded.

"Is that what you're dreaming about?"

"No. I'm not dreaming about Bill. Or St. Lucia." Marion looked at me. I looked down, tossed the banana peel onto the plate. "Things I'm running from—like scary men and monsters. Things I'm walking toward—a home in various stages of construction, lots of those; churches. Mom was in some of them—the dreams, not the churches. I'm entering the churches. I was dreaming of a man, brownish hair, sorta my size, for several months." I shrugged. "He's usually in the house dreams. Sometimes there's white all around him. He's rescued me a few times. Not lately, but I'm not having monster or chase dreams anymore, so maybe I don't need rescuing. Maybe I'm just a crazy lady in the jungle minus spirit lover." Marion smiled at my half-hearted attempt at humor but didn't shift her gaze. Her eyes pinned me like a moth in a display case. "The other night, I woke and my arms were above my head, like this." I lifted my arms, head back. "I was praying. That's what I mean when I say I wish I could see where this is heading. What am I supposed to be doing? Or going, as the case may be."

My own voice surprised me. It wasn't tough or strong or questioning. Only quiet.

Marion smiled that slow, wise smile she wore during yoga. "Maybe we have to give up measuring by any yardstick or any road or any doing. Maybe we have to accept. The greatest power lies in accepting. Accept the gifts and the challenges. Give up judging our lives in order to stop judging others." She broke off a piece of banana and handed it to me. "Not knowing is probably the biggest gift of all. If you were sure what was coming, maybe you'd think too hard and decide not to do it." She laughed. "Look around you—friends, smiling faces, peace. People who love you. What's so wrong with that?"

I blinked. "Bhante Kamalasiri said that. He was my teacher in D.C.—a Buddhist teacher. I loved his name. Bhante Kamalasiri." The syllables' sweetness rolled off my tongue. "From Sri Lanka." He barely came up to my shoulder. About twenty minutes into sitting meditation when our arms and legs were aching, he'd say, 'Lift the corners of your mouth.' And we all did. At least I did. I expect everyone did . . . and smile.

"One day, I asked to talk to him . . . a bunch of stuff happening in my life; I was worried about my son. Bhante fixed tea and we sat in the library. He listened patiently to my litany of worries. When I ran out of words, he said, 'But Janet. You are with a friend. You have a warm cup of tea in your hands. What is so very wrong right now?'"

Marion laughed suddenly and rocked, arms wrapped below her stomach. "That . . . is so . . . monk-like." She stopped, inhaling as deep a breath as she could. "They say the best things. He's right, you know."

Yeah. I knew.

We finished breakfast and lay down to read, our voices low when we talked at all, or when we read aloud from our respective books. Outside the door, we heard footsteps scurry past, calls to Bari and Stephanie to hurry. A truck growled to life, gravel crunched beneath tires. Sudden quiet. The jungle sighed, the palm frond tattered, birds twitted at each other, as intermittent as our voices.

In the middle of the afternoon, tired of reading, we wandered to the pool. We swam, practiced the watsu massage we'd learned in the hot pools at Kapoho. A cloudless sky watched itself in the waters of the pool as we lay suspended, floating, Marion's belly mounded up like a crown jewel in the bracelet of the world. We walked to the lanai, hoping to find some fruit on the counter and found, instead, tall, willowy Dharma, backing out of the kitchen door, her hands cupping several pieces of fruit.

"Danny and I are driving into Pahoa for a Santana concert. Want to come?" *Santana? In the jungle? Absolutely.*

"I have some things," Marion said. In her room, she unearthed wildly colored scarves, beads, soft cotton pants. "I used to wear these all the time," she said. "I brought them because . . . well, I guess because it's Hawaii and I always wanted to visit Hawaii. Now I can barely get into any of them." She patted her baby-belly.

Laughing at our desultory mode of hip-chick/hippie-cool/jungle-ease, we dressed for a rock 'n roll concert. Dharma worked for the office, so she'd managed the use of the van and had gathered up Rar and Claudia as well as Danny. In the car, she handed around fruit. We were a party.

The restaurant-turned-club in Pahoa wasn't large. The crowd was. I stood in the middle of the dancers, swept by swirling lights—red and green and yellow—and danced to Santana. The music pounded. Twenty years dropped from my body as I danced, arms above my head, for my youth, for Marion, sitting, too far along in her pregnancy to dance, for new life and old life, for surrender to whatever was coming for both of us.

FOURTEEN

SURRENDER TO THE ROAD

B arbara was due back, so after our late-morning breakfast, Marion and
I gathered up the multi-colored scarves and beads and clothes from
the night before. "I'll miss you being here. You anchor me," I said and
laughed at her raised eyebrows you-were-the-wild-woman look.

"Really, I mean it. You understand when I talk this Hecate/Crone/
threshold/ not knowing transition I'm doing. Not many can wander
through those weeds with me. You do."

She smiled and looked at me as if burrowing me into her memory. We
carried her things downstairs where I left her to nap.

I swam alone in the pool, the afternoon quiet. When I climbed out,
I saw a dark-haired woman sitting at the end of the pool. Toweling off, I
walked over to say hello. "Hi. Did you just arrive?"

She accepted my proffered hand, her handshake firm. "I'm Monique
Pasternak. I'm here to do a reading, but I live down the road."

"I didn't see that on the schedule."

"It's for the outer community, but you can come. We're in that big
room off the office. It begins at five. You'd be welcome."

"Thank you. I will."

I hadn't checked for mail in a few days. Beside the mail slots in the
office, I saw her flier on the notice board. "Teacher and Poet Monique
Pasternak: The poet of truth is a lover anointed by Spirit. Such an
anointment turns the world upside down and allows us to explore the
alternate worlds that can best be discovered when the task of leading the
search is entrusted to the heart."

My temper created more warrior than lover . . . whew . . . trust my
heart? Trusting my heart sent me off on this journey to Hawaii . . . a year
ago? I counted on my fingers: October, November, December, January,
February, March . . . April. Seven months?

I'd been in Hawaii seven months? That's all?

A letter from Mom waited in my slot. Along with her letter, she enclosed a newspaper clipping showing the jugglers. "I cut it out for you," she wrote, "so you could maybe enclose it in your daily log. I love their assumed names." She'd drawn a line to the names in the caption, Tom Foolery and Tom Renegade, and written "Indeed!" She'd laughed with both and they'd adored her. "Janet, I did enjoy so much spending time with you and seeing your garden. It's laid out so neatly and evenly. Surely wish Dad could have seen it. And lots of other things." Quick tears burned and I blinked. Yeah. I wished he could have seen it too. At the end of the letter, she wrote, "Tell everyone I said hello."

I showered and dressed, thought I'd have time to talk to Monique, but the room was full of people I didn't know. Monique was sitting at the front, her hand wrapping the neck of a guitar propped on her leg. No sooner had I found a chair than she began to speak. "Do not seek to see, let the eyes rest inside and you will see with your heart. As you know, Passover begins next week. Now is the time to prepare our hearts." She strummed the guitar strings. She introduced a man I hadn't noticed. He wore a yarmulke. "I'd like to call up Rabbi Hanan," she said. He joined her and they sang.

The songs were Jewish songs, but a literal understanding unnecessary. I listened in my heart. Voices joined until everyone was singing, my own chanted version included.

Monique read several of her poems, and in closing, said, "Offer yourself as a vehicle for the universe. Use your past to infuse your present. Your body is a temple; pray in it every day."

Passover was coming; Easter would follow.

Too many people crowded around her for us to talk, but I managed a thank you. "If you want, I can come here tomorrow afternoon," she said.

"We don't finish work until four." She nodded.

As I wandered to the lanai, the dinner gong rang, more loudly than necessary since everyone seemed to be already milling about. I found Sharon at an empty table. "May I sit with you?" She smiled. I sat. We waited until the buffet line narrowed, filled our plates, and returned to the table. She and I attended the same workshops, but she didn't talk much, listened and absorbed, rarely called attention to herself. We often ate together, and while she always smiled, she left quickly after meals for her A-frame solitude. When she walked through the garden, she smiled, unhurried, each step placed in concentrated precision. The dining lanai emptied quickly; three guys remained at a far table, bent over a board game.

"Do you want to work tonight?" she said. We'd talked of working together, she leading me in a deep meditation, but we hadn't set a time.

I nodded. We carried our dishes to the kitchen and walked to her A-frame. Sharon crawled in, lit a candle, and motioned me inside. Soft fabrics, shawls it looked, hung over one beam of the wooden frame, beaded necklaces hung from nails on another. Her clothes were folded neatly into an open suitcase. A bedroll stretched along the front screen and a pile of cushions in an opposite corner. A simple and comforting home in the jungle.

"You can lie on the bedroll," she said. "I'll sit here."

Sharon gathered cushions into a nest, set the candle by her knee, and picked up a yellow legal pad. "I'll write whatever you say." I stretched out on the bedroll.

Her hair glinted coppery-gold in the flickering light, and sparks flashed in her eyes: dark light dark light. Night pressed the screens. "Close your eyes," she said.

From somewhere, a breeze whispered.

I dropped down, down into my body, her guiding words lost, a murmur, a wind. More urgent, I heard her say, "What is the puzzle piece you need now?"

My voice, speaking vision, whispered. "I follow a woman down a hallway. She's dressed in blue. A kind face. 'You're choosing the places to stop,' she says. 'This is the room of old dreams.' I back away and see a round drum, leather, feathers hang from it. I pick it up. I want to make music drumming, but I don't know how. I put it down. 'Your impatience keeps you from learning,' she says.

"'You don't understand,' she says, 'this is your home.' Not an imaginary place. A home that's waiting. A house where I can write, where people will come.

"'What is the bridge, the vehicle to get me there?' I ask her. My mate has been coming to me for nearly a year.

"'Remember the dream when you shook your head no?' she says.

"The first time I dreamed of him, I was watching a cathedral procession to Mother God. I saw him; he had his back to me, facing a mirror. We saw each other's reflection. He nodded yes; I shook my head no." The faint scratch of a pen stopped as I stopped talking, resumed when I spoke.

"She wants to speak to you, Sharon.

"'She is opening to receive a partner,' she says. 'It means one is coming. They will have fun together. She must wait. I am the barrier between them. They yearn for each other. They need to yearn for God so they will understand that loving the God within is what they need, not to become obsessed with longing. They will walk in laughter. They will be teachers together. They will teach how to live in joy. Their love will be a refuge, but they must learn the value of their separate corners before they live together; otherwise, they will live together in one chair, one pot. In one pot, you don't have separate flavors, you have mush.'

"Now she is laughing. She speaks to me. 'Don't waste your time on playmates. You don't need a lover. He will come, your husband. Do your work; you know what it is. When you do your work well, you'll be allowed to play.'

"She is talking to you again, dictating," I said.

"'There is no set time frame,' she says, 'they must both learn to live in hopelessness, to live in the now and not wait for tomorrow. She must get up in the morning for meditation. She must not work so hard in the garden. She must take the time to rest. The most important work is her dreams and meditations. If she writes to contact me, I will talk to her.

"'She has channeled me now. I am the puzzle piece. She did not know she could do this. My name is Sarah. When she needs to find me, she only need ask.'"

"It's time to return," Sharon said. Her soft command said "Breathe," and I breathed deep into my belly. Sharon guided me along the path, lifted me out of the meditation.

Whatever spirit lover meant or was or was not, I wouldn't physically meet him soon. My heart filled with relief and sadness: relief in the promise, sad at not knowing when or where or the outcome. The promised love was consigned to choices I hadn't made, didn't know, or how to choose when they appeared.

I thanked Sharon and returned to my room. Sometime after midnight, I heard Barbara come in and rolled over long enough to grunt a hello. In the morning, quiet not to wake her, I dressed for Tai Chi. She rolled to greet me when I returned, one eye open. "Do I need to get up?"

"Probably. If you want breakfast."

She nodded. Closed her eyes again. "Have a good time?" I said. She grinned and nodded.

When I left, Barbara was staring at the ceiling as if it held answers.

José was in a miraculous mood. We worked easy, joking, making new rows of beans; after lunch we planted squash. He left at 3:30, so I cleaned up and put away the tools. Krysta had returned from her vacation, and during lunch, I told her and Marion about Monique and that she was coming this afternoon. We walked down together. Monique sat on a grassy patch near the office and smiled when she saw us. Rabbi Hanan was with her. We formed a circle on the grass.

She picked up her book, *The New Siddur*, and began reading.

"As we progress on the road of co-creative evolution, we learn to let go of control over our destiny and empower ourselves in the knowledge that a Greater Energy guides us. Knowing we are perfect beings walking the perfect path, we surrender to the road rather than seek it. To seek indicates that one is off the path, to seek is to be lost."

"Shalom," she said. "Peace be with you. Peace teaches us love. If we would love, we wouldn't need to call God by any name. When we love, we are able to be. In that space, we might call God Beloved. We might just breathe."

She smiled at the book in her lap. "Breathe. As you breathe in, breathe the blessing of the day; as you breathe out, bless all that you see. The path of inner discovery is as much a dedication to Spirit as any service formally performed in church."

Her words rang true. Inner discovery meant learning to listen with my heart instead of my head. My reactions too hasty, disconnected from who I wanted to be. Practice. I knew the answer and needed to remember I knew. I also knew fear lived in my heart, fear of not-good-enough, fear the spirit lover would remain a dream, fear I'd fail again. My heart tightened and I breathed to release it. My heart said fear is always worse than the reality. A long, slow breath filled my body.

She and Rabbi Hanan sang. At last, she brought our gathering to a close. "Jacob wrestled with the dark side of God when he wrestled the angel. Jacob was renamed Israel, and Israel means, 'He who wrestles with God.' We are all Israel."

We are all Israel. My body released in a long sigh.

That night, I woke with my arms lifted, and heard, *She ordered her world the way she wanted it and then let go.*

Letting go was my task.

By midweek, José was being José and angry I'd left the garden on Tuesday to drive to Hilo. He hadn't been there but maybe he came by later or Donna told him. Howard Duncan had walked through the garden, asked if I had a driver's license, and could I drive the van to Pahoa for supplies. I said yes. Sitting in the padded van seat reminded me how tired my body felt.

"José, you don't understand how tired I am." That was not the thing to say. He chopped furiously at the edge of the lava and piled chunks into the wheelbarrow.

The dinner bell clanged and I walked to the lanai, filled a plate with salad, carried it up the stairs to my room, and opened the Smith Corona. Sarah said to ask. I'd ask.

Closing my eyes, my fingers asked, "What should I do about working in the garden?"

My fingers responded. "The garden is not important. No work here is all that important. You already know the answer. Go to Duncan and talk to him. It is important that you continue your true work. Do not let others tell you the right path. You have learned endurance. Now you must learn trust. The way will be made clear. Trust."

I wasn't ready to go to Duncan. I'd be quiet. Simply not fight with José.

He must have decided the same thing because he didn't appear the rest of the afternoon, or the next day. Alone, the garden empty of visitors and distractions, I pondered my Georgia decision. There wasn't much point to being a healer if I couldn't help my own kids. I'd fly to D.C. in June. Maybe hustle up some work at the Office of Personnel Management. I didn't know what I'd do with my apartment but I'd figure it out. Maybe put everything into storage. I could get to Nathan's by August. My body didn't twist up or shout no. I sighed. Georgia.

That night, two dreams in quick succession woke me. The sky dark. Barbara asleep. Patting the floor under my bed, I found my flashlight and journal. Dream One: A pathway between low trees. Cobwebs hang between the trees. On the right, another path, clear. I don't remember starting, but I chose the clear path.

Second dream: I'm trying to get away from a "monster," monster in the sense of future space types like a boy would draw. So this space man (future man??) chases me. I keep ending up at a big house on the corner where the space man lives. I go another direction and turn another corner and there is the same house. I can't escape. The monster comes out but he's not a monster. He's that same man. I can't see him clearly; it's as if he's blurred in white. He stands on the steps, looking for me.

The other side of me? My masculine side that wishes to integrate? Accepting and blessing the angry side of me? The aggressive, masculine energy—the yang? Or the future man who is coming? From whom I can't get away?

Shutting off the flashlight, I lay and watched the sky inch toward dawn. Marion was leaving, a pillar yanked out. I'd never had many close friends except for my sisters. Friends, yes. Few close friends. Cynthia was my close friend. We did Texas politics and women's groups together. Late night talking over wine. And Kate, Kate who came to Mexico on sabbatical, braved adventures with me, climbed a pyramid, climbed Popocatepetl, drove to Puebla so we could search out the mythical chilies en nogada. Kate was a close friend. So many people, so few pillars. A bird woke in the jungle. Streaks of dawn slid in like a tattered flag. I heard Barbara stir and turn over as I dressed for Marion's final yoga class.

After yoga, Krista, Barbara, and I breakfasted in the garden. We ringed three plastic chairs beside the circle of stones, shaded by a bean trellis, our plates on our laps. They'd both traveled to Kona side and both had stories. I half-listened, half-watched the sunlight prodding at the garden. It sounded like Barbara and Keven had met up along the way.

"I want to live with him before I go," Barbara said.

"How soon are you leaving?" That was Krysta. She was trying to plan her own future.

"I don't know when I'm leaving. I know I want to live with Keven before that." Her voice had an edge to it, grief building for a future she couldn't see.

I was heading to Georgia.

I'd phoned Nathan before breakfast, said I'd come. He was happy. I asked about the new video store they were opening next to the restaurant. "Open before you get here! Thanks, Mom." I'd said you're welcome, suppressed the big sigh living in my chest.

Marion joined us. Barbara got up to give her a chair. "I gotta get busy. I'm way behind." Along with work in the kitchen, Barbara was slated to begin a weekly class, Traditional Chinese Medicine. Krista said she needed to check in with Tootsie and picked up my plate as she left. I was already in the garden.

And Marion. She was here. After our silent retreat, she would leave and return to Australia for the birth of this coming child.

"Want to meet at the pool after work?" she said.

"Sure."

"I'll meet you down there."

She lifted herself from the chair with both hands on the arm rests and planted her feet. I remembered being pregnant, huge, a young man whistling at me as I parked the car. He stopped, grinning. When I levered myself out of the car, he did a double-take at my belly and drove away.

José never showed up, so I did the routine I always did when he was absent. The lettuce looked wilted, so I watered, and while I was at it, watered the squash trellis and the beans. After lunch, I harvested.

As I changed from garden clothes, I slid my supplies box from under the bed, and at the bottom, found my little baggie of jewelry, none of which I'd worn in Hawaii. Special pieces: a narrow, braided silver necklace from Mexico; silver wire earrings, also Mexican, with bits of turquoise in tiny silver flowers; three favorite pins: an oval of blue Wedgewood with diminutive white cupids; a purple rose carved into plastic like my Uncle Kenny used to make; and a broach my mother once gave me, or someone did, dark green faceted stones in a cast silver base. I picked up the silver earrings. Against Marion's dark hair, the silver would shine.

I found her in a shaded deck chair beside the pool. "I brought you something," I said, and opened my palm. "These are from when I lived in Mexico." She found the holes in her ears and slid them on. "How do they look?" She shook her hair, her eyes dancing laughter, the tiny flowers dancing on silver stems.

"Here. I have something for you." She dug in her towel and handed me a pair of cat's-eye earrings. "I put them on when I want to see." I glanced from the stones to her. The brown stones matched her eyes. I swam laps while Marion floated on her back, propelling herself along with her arms. We watsu massaged each other. Barbara joined us, livened up the gathering, and we played.

FIFTEEN

THE SONG OF GOODBYE

That evening we began a three-day women's silent retreat with Saki. We'd discussed the retreat with longing: a weekend of silence—no need to justify or explain, no need to counsel or entertain, no responsibility except to ourselves.

As dusk settled over the compound, we gathered in the upper room of the writers' hale and settled around Saki's large white rug, soft, comforting, woven perhaps from mohair, thick strands, wound round and around, with silken tufts sprouting through the coils. Saki lit incense. I examined each face in our circle and wondered if others were as uneasy as I was, as unsure of what they sought. They shifted, glanced up, looked down, a determined slant to a jaw, a forehead furrowed. I longed for a mirror to see us, together, apart in silence, heroes all on this journey, stripped to an essential nature and strength, each with a separate path into the enchanted forest, our sword a pen.

"Ask yourself these questions," Saki said. "What are you looking for? What guidance do you need? What transformation? What realization?"

In unison, we leaned forward to write. The hand on my left, braced on the floor, delicate, the fingernails trimmed, the cuticles neat. I looked at my hands. Garden hands, strong, square, my grandmother's hands. I'd watched her knead bread, roll out sugar cookies, tell the story of how the tips of her two middle fingers were whacked off by an errant hatchet when young. Pulling myself to the present, I picked up my pen.

What am I looking for? Home. Peace. A purpose to my life. I've been a good mom, but my sons are grown.

What guidance, transformation, realization? To understand how to be a channel of peace instead of anger.

"Listen to your inner voice and learn the meaning of surrender. Ask yourself if you've let anyone down. If you can't answer now, write down the question and perhaps something will come later."

Have I let anyone down? Cynthia. I'm always leaving for the next adventure.

"Is there an attachment that draws you away from connecting to your Higher Self?"

My fearful ego that has to be in control.

I didn't have an answer to the next question: did I carry grudges? Bill? Not really. Not my folks.

"Do you discount anyone?"

Me. I discount myself.

"What is the land of your soul? What is going home? What is returning?"

Too many possibilities for that question.

"What is your prayer for this week?"

May I learn discipline and spontaneity. May I learn the answers to the above questions.

"What is your Higher Self's goal for this weekend? What is your spiritual goal?"

To be observant, to meditate, to remember. A shaman healer must make her magic, blend diverse elements of herself into a new form. Her strength and integrity heals herself and others. You are your art form; your life is your canvas.

I stared at those last words. You are your art form; your life is your canvas. What kind of art has jagged edges and missing pieces? How could I smooth out the jags and connect the pieces across empty space? A sigh built in my body and I let it out slowly to make no sound. How could I have known, then, that my journal writing would lead me to being a full time writer of memoir, my life as my canvas?

We sat in meditation and closed with silent qigong, walked to our rooms in silence. In the morning, we rose in silence, ate in silence, picked up notebooks and walked to the upper room in silence, entered in silence, sat silent in a room filled with bookcases and small tables and a round white rug with flowers and stones scattered in the center. In the opening invocation, I invited Anael, an angel—what else to call such a presence?—who'd communicated with me during D.C. meditations. I heard: *I have stayed away so you could see me in others. You have seen me in Raven, in Ben. You were allowed to love non-sexually. You are learning to love in a new way. Rest in that. Your husband will come soon.*

I'd not connected to that voice since before the business plan failure when I'd filled my life with doing. Silent tears leaked down my cheeks.

"Come." Saki said. "We'll dance." She led us out to the grass where she sang a song of peace. I didn't hear specific words as much as heard their vibration. Barefoot, we walked in wide circles, one circle inside the other, in opposite directions. Saki said, "Turn and walk the other way." We turned and walked the other way, greeting each other. My silent tears became gulping tears: for the world, for me, for the women in the circle as we prayed for peace. At the end of the song, Saki said, "Rest and come here after lunch."

I slipped into my sandals, walked to the sweat lodge, and sat with my back against the frame, facing the jungle and its cap of blue. The tears wouldn't stop. They ran rivers down my face and dripped onto my muumuu. What was this? I breathed and watched the wind ruffle tree tops. A dot bobbed and tracked. A gray hawk wove its way toward me, freedom in its wings. My heart soared with it as it circled, once, above my head.

Take the joy from your solitude to heal whatever sadness in the world you can heal.

The words stopped the tears. Heal the world? That was my answer? No problem! Laughter erupted from my belly. I laughed and laughed. No problem. The hawk swerved and soared, flew away.

You are tested and found worthy.

I recalled dreams of hawks, visions of hawks, and one that flew through my mind during the massage with Ben. A hawk with freedom in its wings would be my *aumakua*, my totem.

The little black sketchbook now lived inside a pocket of the big blue notebook, and I pulled it out. Create your world, Sarah said, so I created: drew lines, a stick-figure me, dancing, and rubbed it with bits of grass, green stains etching my fingers as some bits gave more juice than others.

I didn't judge the grass . . . or plants, or animals; even plants of the same species had differences. Why did I judge humans?

We ate lunch on the dining lanai in silence, the men of the community itching in their chairs. Ben came to sit across from me; I showed him the drawing but didn't speak. He tipped his head, looked at me with steady eyes. I smiled, climbed the stairs to my room. Rested briefly before walking to the writers' hale and climbing the stairs. Saki offered an invocation to any spirits who wished to join us. I invited the angel Anael and Sarah. I asked to understand humility, to feel what it meant. *You asked to understand humility, and every time you invoke your angels, we come. How much more humble do you wish to be?* I stopped myself from laughing.

"Ego is not obliterated; it's lifted up by lifting the spirit," Saki said. "Divinity doesn't have to prove or demand. The more your self-confidence grows, the closer you are to your ego's truth. Judging others means judging self. Discover your Divine Sovereign and you discover yourself."

She sent us out to walk, to meditate. What would it mean to raise my spirit and release judgments—against others, myself—release money fears or job fears. Out on the truck path beyond the compound, I forced myself to focus on one step at a time and feel each foot-roll from heel to toe. Some puff of breeze brushed leaves into ruffle. All of me moved like a slow-motion movie. For a brief moment, I felt the earth revolve under my feet.

Gravel ruts ran down each side of the humped middle; grass and small plants grew in the protected space tires seldom pressed.

On the farm, brome grass grew tall along our quarter-mile lane as well as down the middle. Dad mowed it with a tractor-pulled scythe, the tractor running slantwise in the ditches. He kept the rest of us away. The blades sliced grasses and everything else, a careless hand, a misplaced foot. He'd spent hours teaching me to plow wide fields, and yet I tangled the tractor and plow in a fence on a too-sharp turn and tipped over. I could have died many times: turning over the truck driving too fast on a gravel road, turning over the tractor, tossing ninety-pound hay bales above my head onto a trailer. Any of those could have broken my neck.

Turning back to the compound, I slipped off my sandals and curled my toes into grass. I could have died in childbirth or on one of my witless dashes to freedom. But I hadn't. Was that Divine Sovereign protection or was that luck? I'd never thought of myself as lucky. I walked to a recently trimmed tree. It felt sad about its new haircut. I jerked myself up short. I was feeling what trees were feeling? I stared at the tree and ran my hand down the trunk, the bark smooth and warm. If I didn't judge the tree for looking ragged, why judge people for actions that had nothing to do with me? What if I spoke no judgment?

We gathered in the room. Saki asked us to choose a crystal from the many on the rug. I studied the crystals, picked one nearest me, and cupped it in my palm. "Go somewhere quiet," she said. "Hold the crystal to the light and ask what is keeping you from a closer connection to the Divine."

In between the day's moments of clarity, my mind had fretted about my decision to move to Georgia. As I walked the lane and sat on the cliff overlooking the sea, head-chatter upped its volume, the words jostling each other in a race across my scrunched forehead. What am I going to do? Go to Nathan's and take care of Michael. Why doesn't anyone take care of me? Why do I have to do everything myself? A little tower of stones, flower lei draped over the top like a crown sat a few feet away. A carpet of sunlight spread across my grassy patch. High-tide waves pounded the rocks below and tossed up spumes of spray. Lifting the crystal in my upraised palm, I asked aloud, "What is keeping me from a closer connection to the divine? What is keeping me from a closer connection to the divine?" over and over, a good girl mimicking the lesson. My forehead fretted: No one ever takes care of me. "What is keeping me from a closer connection to the divine?" Who'll take care of me? I'm never safe. "What is keeping me from a closer connection?" I always have to do everything myself. "What is keeping me from a closer connection to the divine?"

Trust! thundered through my head.

Stunned, my hand dropped to my lap and I looked at the land, the sky, the sea.

I sat in the sun, in Hawaii, waves tossing the smell of sea, a flower-covered altar beside me, and living on no money.

I laughed. I laughed and laughed as the salt spray washed my face and my fingers curled around a crystal.

To begin the evening ritual, we evoked the angels, walked around the rug, guided each other as we passed, keeping each other steady. Hands held me with such love, such security. We had, each of us, in our own way, put down fear.

"The spiritual journey," Saki said as she bid us to bed, "is about making God a reality."

I stumbled across the grass, pulled myself up the stairs by the banister, and sprawled across bed, too exhausted to undress.

Our silence disrupted the Sunday morning ritual of spread papers and shared news, so I carried breakfast to our room. Barbara rolled over as I opened the door but said nothing. I sat on the floor, my back against the bed, surrounded by books and journal and notes and fruit. Barbara unwrapped herself from the sheet, took the banana I proffered, picked up a towel, and left. To shower, I presumed. I was wearing the muumuu from yesterday. A shower would be good. When she returned, I left, and when I returned, she was gone.

We gathered from our various corners, walking solitary and silent to the upper room, and settled ourselves, the restlessness gone. Saki began teaching. "Yesterday, you rose and detached. Now is the time to bring spirit into matter and reconcile the opposites. Today is the day of descent. Call forth the qualities of your seedlings. Today you will nurture them."

Tolerance, trust, surrender, co-creator, non-judgment, peace, security, humility—such tiny seedlings.

An opening door downstairs rattled. We all looked up. Voices of several people, steps on the stairs. Heads appeared at the railing. Strangers. They saw us, backed down the stairs, banged around in leaving. Frustration and anger boiled. How dare they disturb our holy space? Saki lifted her guitar and led us as a shepherd leads sheep. The intruders left. Annoyed, I wanted them to hear our sacred song and realize what they'd interrupted.

It is not enough to have humility when things are smooth. Humility comes in not getting angry at others for small offenses. The angels don't get angry at your large ones.

The perpetual teaching voice in my head wouldn't let me get away with anything. I didn't laugh out loud, but I did duck my head to hide a grin. Maybe my lesson was to keep a sense of humor.

Saki lay her guitar on its case top. "This is your writing assignment.

Go someplace quiet and meditate on stepping out of your prison. Notice any yearnings. They are divine messages."

I walked to the road leading into the jungle. Birds chattered, insects buzzed, and sunlight warmed my skin. Trees, bushes, and tangled vines crowded both sides of the road. A longing welled for Kansas, to live on the hill, see the distant horizons. As if my journey home could be as simple as clicking my heels and chanting "There's no place like home." What's the likelihood of that, Dorothy? All my life when people learned I was from Kansas, they said, "Do you know Dorothy?" My response, always, "I am Dorothy."

I'd talked to Dad about building a retreat, an artists' colony on the farm. He'd laughed. "Who'll come out here?" he'd said, the farm six miles from the nearest paved road.

I sat on the grassy hump and leaned over to the small clump of purple flowers at my knee. A faint scent of violets. Like Kansas wild violets.

I straightened my spine and dropped into meditation to vision the prison I was leaving: a dark cell, the floor covered with rubbish and dust. Dark, cobwebby things on the walls. I toured the room, thanked it for contributing to my life, stepped outside, and closed the door. I unrolled a canvas to cover the cell, a painting of fields and green and sunlight and peace. That part of my life, the dirty cell, had a new image.

I opened my eyes. Attune to nature, Saki said. I could do that. Of all the tasks given me or that I'd given myself, attuning to nature was a given. I picked the small bouquet of wildflowers at my knee and carried them back to the room's altar. My newfound qualities of tolerance, trust, and humility were as fragile. Delores Joy brought a stick with a beautiful orange fan fungi growing on it and set it beside my bouquet.

We danced our closing ceremonies on the grass outside, danced the queen in us, and danced our heart's emotion. When I danced the queen, I felt joyful, almost flying; when I danced my heart, there lay sadness and compassion. "Practice seeing with the eyes of God," Saki said. See everyone with detached compassion. "By trusting the divine beauty in every person, we see beauty in ourselves. Be in love with God; that is the ultimate reality."

Deeply tired, I skipped the evening meal for bed.

In the early morning, Barbara and I walked to the screened porch outside the massage room. We sat on the floor for meditation: Howard Duncan, Beatrice, Sharon, Joseph, Isabel, Krista, Barbara, Saki, and Marion. A soft breeze, the early welling scent of plumeria, sun rays stabbing little spears through the screen. A chant swelled in my body, sadness and joy rose. *What if it sounds weird?* my mind fretted. I opened my mouth and the chant-of-no-words rolled from my chest, vibrated up my throat, lifted free, wobbly, at first, on its wings. When it stopped, tears ran down Marion's cheeks.

But how easily peace slipped away. José left the garden at lunchtime. I remained, irritation roiling at my having to stay as I huddled in shade and harvested basil. A tiny grasshopper, brilliant, perhaps a sister to the baby of . . . what . . . how many weeks ago . . . landed on my arm. It danced, cleaned its front legs, hopped away. Barbara walked down the path. "Come on," she said. "Pool time." We played. Barbara challenged me to jump off the edge of the pool onto an air mattress, and when I dove, missing the air mattress, I emerged sputtering and laughing. Barbara and I climbed into the hot tub, naked, dove into the pool to cool off, rejoiced in the water sliding off our skin, returned to the hot tub, our bodies in the warm water, melting. Mauve shadows stretched into evening. We showered, naked and strong, shared a towel, and as we dressed, Russ passed by after a week's absence of driving the island in his truck. We hugged him, and gathering slippers and books and dropped flowers, we walked together to the lanai.

Saki and Marion brought out baggage; Michal Koob stored it in the van. We clustered to say goodbye. Sharon and Barbara were riding along to see them off, but I couldn't. I couldn't see Marion leave. When I hugged her, she slipped her jade beads in my hand. "They're your color," she said. I put them on, warm comfort on my skin. Tears again. I was always crying. I laughed, hugged her again, and she was gone, the van's tail lights receding down the lane.

SIXTEEN

PRACTICING TRUST

I sleepwalked through the following day.

In two days, I'd catch a bus and go home to North Kohala for my week's break. Home. The words layered: Kalani, Kohala, Kansas. I wondered if I was running away or retreating to gather strength. José's absence grew conspicuous as if the women's power had eclipsed his. And yet, his own inherent feminine-force defined him as much as his masculine. Or perhaps, I thought, as I sat in the shade, separating each small weed from a cluster and pulling it free of the black dirt, he stayed away because nothing now rose to his bait. Why bother provoking if you can't spear the fish? Picking lettuce, a band of sunlight outlined my hands, and they seemed as if they belonged to someone else—not my grandmother— someone I didn't know. I was heading to Georgia, a litany I'd repeated so often to myself it was worn out. I'd have my own room. But what would I do for money? Live off my kids? Bartend? Not likely. I had a grandson to raise. My mind was chattering. It had chattered far too long without me noticing. Berating myself for carelessness, for lack of vigilance, and heaping rebuke onto the fear that fed the chatter, I remembered: Trust! My mind slid into silence. I carried the aluminum bowl into the kitchen and handed it to Bari. "I didn't know there was so much!" she said.

It needed practice.

Wednesday afternoon, I rode the van to Hilo. No trace of Marion's smell. The handkerchief trapped in the backseat's fold wasn't hers, but I wore her jade beads. Climbing onto the late afternoon bus to Kohala felt like I'd joined a family reunion from the happy chatter of workers as they left their necessary paid work for their life of family and land. People stepped off at indecipherable paths and faded into jungle. We climbed toward Kohala and at last the scenery opened onto grasslands. Lia and Daemion met me in Waimea, and we drove down the familiar mountain road bordered by ironwoods and grasslands, into Hawi, and finally to Puakea. I was back in my room facing the wide Pacific.

Lia called out from the living room. "I recorded the Academy Awards for you." I joined her on the sofa. In years past, the Oscars show left me yearning to be part of it, but now I detached. No yearning. No regrets. Lia talked about a Los Angeles acting coach she'd met while working on a Hollywood movie at Kwaihae Harbor, and she wanted to move to California after high school. Jeanne came home and we fixed dinner. This the comfort bus riders looked forward to each day: home, family, stories. As I built a big salad, I told Kalani stories, or at least the general outline since so many of my changes were like summer lightening bugs—elusive, and no handy glass jar with holes in the lid to store them for display.

My visit home to North Kohala was to serve a double purpose: to rest and give my legs recovery time, and to attend a weekend workshop at the house with Kam Night Chase, the Lakota medicine man Jeanne and I met in Waimea months before. Mom was gone, the house empty without her, so I caught up on family laundry, finished preparations for the guests, rested at pool side in a torpor of sweat and sun with cooling dips into water. Late afternoon, I drove to Pololu to visit Kinde, but he wasn't home. I sat on the rock wall at the edge of the lookout and watched the sea, wondered if I had the energy to walk down to the beach; making it down was possible, but making it back up more work than I wanted to do.

A truck pulled up and Sonny Solomon climbed out, a straw hat shading his eyes. "You watching sea?" he said.

"Yeah. Kinde's not home. I'm watching."

Sonny jerked his head mountainside. "Come on," he said. "I'll take you to see better." We climbed into his truck. He drove the mountainside in low gear, bumping over ruts and cattle-filled pastures to a gate and the beginning of a trail. Sonny stopped the truck and pointed to the waterfall beyond, a long, narrow slash of gilded light, dropping into leafy silence. Overhead, a hawk circled, dropped closer for a look. Sonny laughed. "Io," he said, pointing, "Sacred messenger."

I told him the story of the hawk circling my head at Kalani and the message I'd heard. I'd not told anyone that story, but Sonny was an Hawaiian elder steeped in the magic of Hawaii. He nodded and climbed out of the truck, walked a few paces to a tree and pulled off a piece of hanging fruit. "Rose apple," he said, cupping a small, reddish, pear-shaped fruit in his palm. I took it, smelled the faint breath of roses. "What is it?" Sonny's gesture, a light flick of his fingers, belied the rough and calloused skin. "Eat," he said. I bit into a flesh cool and crisp and sweet as if this holy reliquary were a gift to bless my words with joy.

Sonny turned to drive the pastures, the truck tilting sideways downhill. His arm waved through the open truck window. "The first Parker Ranch, here to there." His arm swept forward and he pointed to a five-foot-tall stone with a ragged top like old cardboard. "That small?" I said. Sonny nodded. More a sharp head bob, the kind Dad made when I'd asked some superfluous and obvious question. Parker Ranch, founded in the 1850s, had grown to over 800,000 acres of North Kohala. Sonny pointed out a tumble of leftover stones, Father Damien's first church, also from the mid-1800s: land history, a quiet retelling of wind, rocks, water, and their fragile human marks. When he left me at the car, his gift of land mana lay as an ineffaceable mark on my skin.

Jeanne and I sat at the breakfast bar after the kids left the next day. "Kalani tossed me into a gorge so deep I might never climb out," I said. And my sister, wise woman as she was, said, "We must learn to process in the process because the changes will be coming so fast there will be no time to take time to process." That seemed right: no "will be" to it, more like is now. She left for the hotel. I swam and napped. As people began to arrive for Kam's Sacred Garment Workshop, Jeanne came home and handed me a chart to assign rooms and camping spots. She and Robert had tickets for the Tokyo ballet in Kona. They'd be home late. Lia had play rehearsals. Life here moved more quickly than it did at Kalani.

In the morning, Jeanne and I led the women through pastures down to the sea. We stopped at a three-foot column of stone beside a rock wall. "This was the original Puakea village. It disappeared over a hundred years ago." Jeanne's arm swept in an arc. The old wall was mostly intact, a few stones tumbled free. She rested her hand on the column. "This was Mama Kealia's healing stone. She was the village Kahuna. The depression in the top was where she ground herbs and roots." Jeanne and I had come here, the two of us, when I'd first arrived on the island, and she'd told me the story of Mama Kealia and how she heard the voice of the long-gone healer, offering guidance. One of the women placed a flower blossom in the healing stone's depression. Jeanne led us on to where two ancient pools stretched from the rocky beach into ocean water, bound and divided by rock walls: one the women's pool and one the men's.

"This first pool is the men's, but it has eels in it now. The next is the women's pool," she said. The women gingerly inched over rocks to enter the pool, Jeanne and I last. We chanted, offered flowers to the waves. Jeanne and I both scraped ourselves as we inched out backward, and the sea received its offering of blood. Accidental but appropriate.

We walked back to the house through the pastures to a gate. Jeanne and I pulled it open the same way we'd opened gates on the Kansas farm and stood at each end, one at the gate hook, the other at the hinge. "An image of strong sisters," a woman said as she passed. Others nodded. I wondered what they saw, what archetypal guardians, which sisters of fate or time. Maybe just strong farm women. I saw Jeanne smile; I smiled at her. Sea smell on my skin, a trickle of blood down my calf, and I felt strong, standing strong, as if the gift of self-respect I'd gathered over the months had transformed into a shaft of power down my spine. Together we became an image for others, a time-portal into the next stage of wherever they, and we, were going.

Kam's workshop continued the deep work from Kalani: the portal, once opened, must be fed. He said, "The Shamanic Death Ritual is to burn away the old life you were born into. Your body will be a new garment."

I sat in meditation for the infant's death and saw a baby in a circle of bones as it gasped its first breath, and I understood each birth is a birth into death. In the round of the parent death, I saw my father die in a hospital bed and the sheet pulled over his face. I walked to the bed and drew back the sheet to uncover his bones. I gathered them, put them in a beautiful carved wooden box, and carried it to the top of a hill where I gently ground the bones in a mortar and scattered the ash across the hill. I would not grind up the skull so set it in a place of honor at the hill's summit. Each grief, each loss marked me, some marks deeper than others. How could I take up the task to be reborn, to avoid acting out grief? How might life have been different, what other road might I have taken?

But perhaps there was no fault, no mistake in the choices I'd made, or my father made. He sang, "I didn't know God made honky-tonk angels," but he'd married a Quaker girl and took her to a farm. Some choices are more effective than others, or maybe they take you to the same place.

Stories never end. Stories as ancient as people: a shaman-in-training sent into the wilderness, sometimes buried in the ground, returned transformed; Osiris, dismembered, so Isis gathered his fragments and restored him; Jesus, crucified and resurrected. The stories all pointed to realities, life, death, resurrection, dismemberment, and reconnection. We change from one mode to another and transform, the future unknown.

On Sunday Kam led a sweat. Most of the people attending were new to the sweat lodge so it wasn't hot-hot. The rounds proceeded. Kam offered prayers and began chanting in Lakota. Sweat streaked the eagle claw scars on his chest. I opened my mouth and allowed emotion to transform into sound. The two, Kam's Lakota and my chant-without-language, wound into one song, one praise, one invocation.

The next day, after the visitors, the sweat tent, and the sacred songs left for somewhere else, I lay beside the pool and drifted into doze, only to be startled awake by a vision of me on a ski jump, sailing through the air with arms and ski poles jutting behind. I grinned and rolled my head from side to side. I hoped the landing would be soft, hoped this momentary sense of humor would remain. The abrupt out-loud laugh at discoveries wasn't quite the same as a wry humor to laugh at foibles. My own, particularly.

We drove to Kalani together, Jeanne and I, to attend a workshop in Holotropic Breathwork. Drumming and panting breaths became the vehicle for our journey into the extrasensory world. We paired, she keeping watch as I traveled; me keeping watch for her.

My panting timed itself to the steady sound of drumbeats as they pounded faster and faster. I asked Anael if I could see him, and a huge winged creature landed in front of me, brilliant, white, and swooped me onto its shoulders between wings. We rode in a terrific wind, whether from the beat of wings or some other source, the light blinding my eyes into squinches. Anael set me down in light, and a shimmering yet familiar man-shape said, *give up your apartment for storage.* Relief washed through me. As the drum beats slowed, my breathing slowed, but my mind slid from its mystic moment into worry. *Yeah, but then what? What about after I've been Grandma for a while, where do I go then?*

I had not learned patience.

The chatter stopped as I focused on my sister and watched her drop past conscious consciousness. My thoughts returned to hover at the edge of her clear space. It would work out somehow . . . a hard task to say goodbye to D.C. . . . always hard to say goodbye. Next stop Georgia . . . take my bicycle . . . perfectly Oz-like. Jeanne laughed and pulled my attention. She lifted her arms, the same way I had in dreams. I knelt, hand on her shoulder, and laughed with her.

For two days, Jeanne and I breathed through drumming and into the power of our lives as a part of all that was holy. On the last day, the drums led me to a stream, Jeanne beside me. Identical twins, we walked a flower-filled alpine meadow toward a cabin, our arms twined, fair hair swinging down identical backs. Inside the cabin, the twins are old, the cabin smoke-stained and dark. In a bed, one is dying. My eyes opened, found Jeanne's face. "I died. I left you behind. I'm sorry." Her smile offered forgiveness.

And then, abruptly, the workshop ended. Jeanne drove home to North Kohala without me, and I was alone, absorbing miracles.

I'd ridden on Anael's wings, saw my sister as myself, and heard a message to give up the apartment. Was the shimmering man-shape the spirit lover? Was our life fated? Was energy pushing us as if we were one storm front meeting another? What was leading . . . or pushing? Was I some loose piece in his puzzle that lacked essential pieces for a whole? Was there a whole? I longed for Jeanne or Marion to help me understand.

Lying on my side, the pillow bunched up under my neck and head, I watched another dawn inch itself across the sky beyond my screen. Easter Sunday. In the night, the smell of rain had forecast its walk through the jungle to the garden. Would I ever hear rain again without remembering this window and this garden?

SEVENTEEN

RESURRECTION

The Kalani community gathered for a long Easter Sunday brunch, dressed in our best, which, given our lives and circumstances, varied from person to person. Beads and soft shawls came out, and the men wore their best T-shirts. Oona set up her harp and sang, accompanied by a community man with a flute and jaunty red knit cap on his curls. The kitchen outdid itself: each table graced with a jar of flowers and extra paper napkins. We feasted. Fresh pastries, a variety of fruits, scrambled eggs, pancakes, French toast, and a bottle of real maple syrup. The espresso machine worked overtime. We listened to the harp and flute's ethereal sounds weave into the jungle. I remembered getting new shoes at Easter, and one chilly, damp Easter sunrise service in town, but couldn't remember how that had happened since we always had morning chores. We had lived with daily displays: sunrises, sunsets, clouds, and storms. Primeval symbols.

Krysta left Kalani after breakfast the next morning to wander the island, a backpack and a small multi-colored bag as her companions. Soon we'd all bid farewell as we stepped into a world that had forgotten us or managed to boggle along without us. I went to the garden.

Full of weeds, it mourned my absence. José must have taken a week off too. I weeded a patch and scooted to another, stopping to rest in the middle of a row or in a white plastic chair under shade. It appeared the kitchen crew had continued to harvest. That was good. Deb wound her way along maze of paths. "Did anyone tell you José threw you out of the garden while you were gone? He said you were lazy and never watered or weeded."

I laughed. "Sounds like he had a mommy tantrum."

"That's what I thought. No one seemed to take it very seriously. Thought you'd want to know." She smiled and wound her way out again, her peaceful self restored, the rape crisis left behind.

After work, I stretched out in my room to read Natalie Goldberg's

Writing the Wild Mind, one of the books I'd brought from New York and had left behind on my shelf at Puakea. I appreciated how she encouraged writing by any means, whether we remembered or didn't remember.

Mercy. What I didn't remember could fill a library.

I DON'T REMEMBER IF I CRIED AT MY FATHER'S FUNERAL. I DON'T remember my third-grade teacher's name. The year after my father's death is a blank. Did the boys tease me, call me fatty? Did that stop? Did Johnny Hogue still pump me high on the swings? Did I do well or poorly in school? Did I go to school? I must have. After the funeral I remember visiting new baby Jack and Mother in the hospital, but I don't remember anything more until a year and a half or so later. Looking through the kitchen doorway to the living room during our first farm visit, I saw Dad kiss my mother. It made me happy. The year before lies in a void. A suspended time. No memories. No, I have two: Mother sitting on the edge of my bed and telling me she could no longer afford my piano lessons; and the monster nightmares that even now feed my fear of the dark.

The fear of the dark—a lifelong companion. The unexpected, unexplained, unformed. Nightmares, right after my father died, brought monsters who chased me, who'd shred me to a pebble if they caught me, a pebble falling silently into a void so empty and unreachable, there was no snatching back to safety. But if I had forgiven, had lifted him to light, if dreams and memories held my fear, why couldn't I let it go?

I had to face the fear.

SHARON AND I SAT TOGETHER AT DINNER. WE WERE ALL WE HAD now, the others dispersed. We didn't say much and hugged each other goodnight as we parted. Barbara sat with Kevin. They'd moved into an A-frame together while I was in North Kohala.

Now there was only me in the room.

Waiting for midnight, I prodded myself to remain vigilant, fought the impulse to set aside the task for another day, life, eon. My pacing, waiting, stretching disturbed no one. Below me, the empty kitchen. The compound settled; the generator's roar slid into silence. I couldn't formulate a plan to distract me.

At 11:45, I couldn't wait any longer. I'd battled the impulse for bed, battled fear of walking outside alone, battled wanting to go and wanting to stay. I had to go. Now. Opening the door enough to slide through, not enough to hit the squealing snag, I inched to the stairs and began my descent into night.

Starlight filled the lawn. No moon. The jungle curved in silence. No lights, not even candlelight, flickered at cracks. I walked across the empty, dark lawn and sat, my back pressed against the Peace Pole, arms wrapped around my drawn-up knees. The pole, carved and painted, loomed a dark shadow above me. I did not feel peace. I told myself the cold light was beautiful, forced my attention to the shadows of bushes. Had I ever noticed shadows cast by starlight? Had I seen them on the farm? The tightness around my heart belied my thoughts. It wasn't working; I couldn't think myself to peace. Fear, loosed from its moorings, bloomed.

Breathe. If nothing else, sit and breathe.

I breathed. My tightly wrapped knees blocked my belly, so I released them, stretched out my legs, relaxed my arms, and placed my palms on the earth. Off to the right, a twig snapped in the jungle. My body reacted as if to a high-power rifle shot and compacted into a ball. Another crack. A rustle of leaves. My mind exploded: a man behind that trunk, there...no...an animal? No large animals here...a snake, a snake large enough or venomous enough...no, no snakes in Hawaii. A man?

Dark...no starlight spread into the trees. Dark. My throat contracted. My heart, a caged animal, slammed against my ribs.

STOP! Stop. Stop.

I breathed. Shoulders dropped. Arms relaxed. I straightened my legs. Sat. Put down the fear. It had sounded doable. Not impossible. Breathe. I breathed. This was far more work than I had ever thought possible.

The next cracked twig made me flinch, but not contract. I breathed. A rustle of leaves whipped my head to the right. Breathe.

I saw how blaming my father's death for my fear created more fear; how the nightmares of a child's grief belonged in childhood.

Why hadn't I seen this sooner?

I had lived life in fear: fear of abandonment, fear of love, fear of the dark, fear of pain. My anger, my fighting—it all grew from fear. I was the dark shadow in the jungle, carrying a sharpened machete, ready to strike at any provocation.

The unexplained night sounds were no longer unexpected. By tipping my head to listen, wonder entered into breath, and my throat no longer threatened to choke me.

Eyes drooped and I rested with them closed. I breathed. At last, after my nodding head jerked me awake, I allowed myself to rise and walk through the night's mystery to a silent bed blanketed with stars.

Classes at Kalani shifted from healing to hula in conjunction with Hilo's yearly Merry Monarch Festival: hula, chants, and lei making. Come

Sunday, we'd have our own festival and perform for the community. Leon Kalili led a workshop in the Hawaiian language. His task, he said, was to teach majesty. Whenever he saw me, he'd say, "Hello, majestic being." He greeted the class the same way, "Hello, majestic beings; good evening, royal friends."

Leon pronounced Hawaiian words and told us their meaning. We recited them, over and over, like first-graders reading *Run Spot Run*, the only book title I remember from all my years of schooling.

"Use words to create your being and clarify your language," Leon said. "Take the negative words from your vocabulary—can't, don't, hard, won't— because the lower body, the *unihipilli*, can only understand words that take you toward something. If you say, 'I don't want any more bad jobs,' the *unihipilli* understands 'more bad jobs.' So you get more!" His whole body laughed as he sat cross-legged on the floor, a curly-headed Hawaiian Buddha.

I'd voiced unworded chants, but Leon gave me words, words I could curl my tongue around. As we left Leon's class, he touched my arm and said, "Come with me to the festival's opening night. It's in Hilo. I borrowed a car."

We created quite a picture: he a big Hawaiian, curly dark hair, dark skin, and wide smile, a gold feather lei on his head, white kukui nuts around his neck; I'd braided a green ti leaf lei, wore Marion's jade beads and my jungle print muumuu. Our strides matched and heads turned as we strode past clumps of people to our seats. Temple drums rolled *bambambambababa*, and in the silence that followed, three soul-shivering conch shell blasts, one call following as the other faded, echoed across the auditorium. The hairs along my arms rose on end and a chill tattooed my shoulders. Leon tipped his head toward me. "*O kala kala nui* chicken-skin-shivers big-time," he whispered.

Standard bearers, men carrying tall, flat bats covered in red feathers, walked down the aisle; behind them, a man, a woman, chanting. Leon and I sat beside the aisle, and when the woman chanter passed, my heart thudded and my breath caught in my throat. Leon wrapped my hand in his. His whole face—eyes, lips, cheeks, eyebrows—smiled. Behind the chanters were the king and queen, and behind them the court. The standard bearers led the procession to high-backed wooden chairs draped in red silk at the foot of the stage.

Another conch shell blast echoed and out came a huge man, flowing red robes, followed by a young man carrying a tall bat with a yellow silk banner. The loud speaker boomed an introduction, "Uncle John Kaimikaua and Halau Moloka'i." Leon had told me Uncle John was a powerful *kumu*, a teacher who taught the ancient and sacred temple dances. He sat, spread his robes, and cupped his legs around a drum nearly four feet in diameter. The standard bearer stood behind, the banner rippled by random air currents. Uncle John's dancers followed in a sandy sound of bare feet, rustling ti leaf skirts, ti leaves banding ankles, wrists, crowning dark hair. They crouched, bent at the knees, waited. Uncle John lifted one huge arm and let it fall, *FROOOUM! O kala kala nui* big-time! The women stepped forward, and the men, fists planted on hips, lined the wall. Uncle John told a story of the ancient and giant lizards of Moloka'i who had threatened villages. Hula birthed itself on Moloka'i, he said. Moloka'i, the fiercest of the islands, the island King Kamehameha could not conquer.

Uncle John lifted his arm again. It fell with a thundering boom. He chanted. The women crouched low, their arms extended, sweeping back and forth as if they were huge lizards swinging their heads; the dancers hissed, bared their teeth, and slithered with outstretched claws. The applause thundered. And then more stories, more chants. I sat on the edge of my seat, leaning forward. Uncle John chanted the guard dogs of Moloka'i and howled as the women lifted their heads, arched their backs, and howled. So this was the beginning of hula. The men stomped and thrust spears and made the most horrible grimaces.

I released my held breath as the dances ended. Uncle John rumbled on his drum and a group of *tutus*—the grandmothers—came out. They danced a *me'i*, an elegant and subdued dance to sexual power. Men from the audience walked forward, threw money at their feet. Women revered for their age and wisdom and beauty, a lesson in my journey toward that invisible line. When I'd knelt in the Mexican desert and Gloria anointed me in a ritual as old as humans, was it a recognition of what was . . . or what would be?

THE NEXT MORNING, I PRAYED FOR A CHILL-OUT DAY IN THE GARDEN, no new teachings, no new epiphanies. A little six-year-old silliness and ribaldry would be good, I mused, as I harvested basil, José nowhere to be seen. Too many teachings of some sort, even if another of surrender. SURRENDER DOROTHY. I grinned at the image of the flying witch tracing words in black smoke above the Emerald City, picked up the aluminum bowl, and carried it to the kitchen.

Bari's eyes lit up. "I'll make pesto!" she said.

Kalani created its own festival on Sunday afternoon. We'd practiced with a local *kumu* who cradled her long gourd drum, planted her feet, and summoned with the same fierce authority and one-armed *kaaaboom* as Uncle John's while I chanted dance into being, the sheet of words in my hand, spelled out phonetically. I could hear authority in my voice, and even more, joy.

As I began my last weeks at Kalani, my writing focused on conversations with the energy I addressed as Sarah or Higher Self. Some classes interested me: Barbara's class on Chinese medicine, a dance workshop, Tai Chi with Ken, but the other classes slid away in a desire to live totally in the final days of retreat and listen to the voice awakened in me. For years, when life became too complicated or I was doing too much, being too busy, I'd longed to be a cloistered nun with a vow of silence, a Juana or a Hildegarde with her books and letters. Now mostly I was. In a world where all things are possible, all things are possible.

Discipline is the key. Discipline in the way you work, in the way you breathe, in the way you love, in the way you walk. No one can do all the practices all the time, but mindfulness will take you to the level where you want to go.

Forgiving self leads to self-responsibility leads to healing. The heavenly beings do not wish to cause humans trouble. They wish you to be happy. The difficulties lie in not moving with whatever is happening at the time. The universe is one cycle within even bigger cycles, but humans, bound to earth, can hardly comprehend the cycle of their own universe let alone the cycles of even greater heavens. As if making a garden, you must make a place in your mind where the silence flows. You allow lonely to be a reality instead of a passing moment. Do not hold on. No-thing is better than some-thing with no spirit.

EIGHTEEN

EXPULSION FROM THE GARDEN

Lonely and longing and leaving tangled through my head, my chest, my keyboard, and I remembered judging Barbara for these same feelings when she wanted time with Kevin, grieving a future she couldn't see. My future lay too close, or at least the future I could see: leaving Kalani's womb, a brief time with my sister, leaving Hawaii, leaving D.C. for Georgia. Big and clunky and grief-filled. And no one to talk to except the voice in my head. I'd come to Kalani for precisely this access to a deeper knowing; it was a lonely journey but there wasn't anything more I needed to do. I wasn't the crazy lady in the jungle anymore; I was the kid in need of comforting.

Do nothing before its time.

Yeah. I know. I got it. But couldn't I whine a little? I didn't even have to ask.

I remembered Xochicalco, a pre-Columbian site in Mexico, the odd suspension of time when I'd wandered off to sit on the hill above a restored ball court and heard faint but unmistakable sounds drifting up the hill: crowd cheers, the thump of a ball against stone, shouts. The sounds came in waves as if tossed on a breeze. Now there was Sarah or Higher Self or whatever it was dictating my . . . my what? My life? Could I choose?

I sighed. Choose what? A companion, a partner. If we weren't to yearn for a human touch, why be in a human body? Why go through the pain of feeling, struggling, letting go of struggling if I had to be alone? Submission was the hardest lesson.

There is much you have to learn from this time alone.

Another signpost destined to remain unreadable for an unspecified number of whatevers. Closing the Smith Corona, I returned to the garden and weeding.

I practiced patience with my chittering head. I practiced listening with my heart. I practiced compassion. I practiced and I practiced.

And then a day came when my practice failed me, as all practice does from time to time, and I got fired. Again.

After a week's absence, José came to the garden in a furious mood. He threw a shovel; I remained quiet, weeding. He began to shout, berating me, saying I was lazy and worthless. Forgetting my practice, I rose to his challenge and swore at him.

"You're fired!" he shouted as if he'd already prepared for this scene, already planned the words he'd use. "Get the hell out of my garden."

I got.

I walked to the office, told Howard Duncan what had happened, and asked if he wanted me to take up another job. He smiled and shook his head.

"Not right now. If I think of something, I'll let you know."

"Okay. Thanks," I said.

Less than a week remained of my time at Kalani, but I mourned the loss of my garden in the same way I mourned Marian's leaving. The garden had anchored me, given me a quiet place to absorb transformation, allowed me to be alone with thoughts when José was absent, and he'd often been absent. Sometimes, he was even fun.

I climbed the stairs to my room. José had disappeared from the garden, so I sat at the window and looked on our handiwork bordered by jungle: a still-life painted in sunlight. How long would it continue; how long would it feed the community? Had it been like a sand painting? Its value in the process, a process destroyed once complete? I replayed moments in my mind: the wheelbarrow full of lava chunks, the laughter, sweat, aching legs, the new gloves from José. Pineapple crowns putting on fruit. I remembered kneeling, curved over young plants. I leafed through the little sketchbook to Deborah's drawing: "There is a time to plant, a time to harvest, a time to meditate. All are part of life." Time curled. Mid-afternoon quiet lay over the community, a no-time of silence. If Krysta, Saki, Marian hadn't left, if Barbara hadn't moved in with Kevin, I'd be talking to one of them instead of staring out a window, talking to a deserted garden.

Leaving the room, I met no one on the way down the stairs, crossed the lawn and sat against the sweat lodge frame, facing the tree line. No Io to comfort me. I'd laughed out loud at the message. How was I to fulfill any of this? How was I to give up anger, eating too much from stress? Discipline. Discipline. The same message over and over. How to integrate freedom and discipline? I wished for a hawk to come, tell me what more I needed to know. Maybe something easier than heal the world. But I'd been told the rest was in living.

I returned to my room by the shortest route. The word would go around soon enough; at dinner everyone would express outrage at José, or they would sympathize, or want to know the details. There weren't any details. I was moving on and this was one more step.

Opening the Smith Corona, I wrote the first of five nearly identical letters to business contacts in D.C., addressed and stamped them, ready for the morning mail. I didn't know why I was writing them as I was going to Georgia, but who knew . . . maybe magic would happen.

Sharon and I sat together at dinner. These past weeks we had been set adrift by the breakup of the inner group and found some solace in each other even if we talked of nothing more important than the curve of night holding us. I asked her if we could work together once more. "There's a carapace of grief binding my chest. I want to remove it." Sharon nodded.

Together we lit the candles; we offered a prayer. I lay down and sank into relaxation.

I saw barriers, sharp rocks, and heard Sharon's voice guide me around them. I climbed a red granite boulder, flat on top. I could see grass ahead. Echoing circles of light filled my body. A hand grew out of the grass and beckoned. I climbed down and followed a cleared pathway.

I heard Sharon ask what I needed to understand about my grief.

"Here," a voice said. And I felt myself a wall, a stone wall, fixed, holding my consciousness at its center.

"I'm inside a wall," I told Sharon.

"Ask the wall if it will speak to us," Sharon said.

I opened my mouth to speak for the wall, and a deep gurgling sound rose, searching for shape to form a word. My throat contracted and loosened, contracted and loosened; word fragments coughed themselves into being: "foun . . . da . . . tion."

"You are her foundation?" Sharon said.

I felt the struggle in my neck, sensed the wall, silent for eons, find thought, find sound. It broke through my throat in a gush of gritty words.

I am the temple piece she carried with her, the wall said. I heard the voice loud, rasping, felt my back arch as the force of black-gravel words erupted from my throat.

Her work was dark to the dark. Her work was secret. I AM THE WALL. I divide the halves. I stand between light and dark. The voice stopped.

My back relaxed.

"Can you see the wall?" Sharon asked.

I nodded.

"Choose one stone in front of you. Thank it for its protection. Now, can you slide it out?"

"It's in my hand." My voice a whisper but it was my voice. "I'm to keep it for a new foundation. Stones are my totem. I'm told that grief washes; it's not to be feared." I waited, eyes closed, tears sliding into my ears, hair.

"The wall has dissolved. I'm to remember the day I grieved beside the sweat lodge. I'm to take my joy and heal whatever in the world I can heal."

Sharon waited.

I felt weightless, untethered. "I'm afraid to walk without the wall," I said. "All I see is open space." Sharon lightly touched my arm.

"Walk like you always walk with one foot in front of the other," she said.

"How can I keep this open space?" I asked, and I heard in reply: *remember it.*

The voice said, *What she's done now is the preparation. She understands wanting, and yearning closes her off. The wall is gone; the rock is in her pocket. She has chosen to use it for a new foundation. She must stay in her body, walk in the now, and welcome the pain of grief as a sword to cut through dark and cleanse. The sword separates the old from the new.*

Memory can return like a picture book, bringing fear, rebuilding the wall. Love is the new wall. When she centers herself in love, as a toad revels in a pool, that which emanates from her and surrounds her will be a bubble of love, permeable. She will be provided for in the right time. She must allow newness.

The rock symbolizes all of the pasts for her to stand on. She may choose to believe in the sorrow for her father, but it is an old sorrow, and her task is to send sorrow to the light. If she does not, she will make men her protector, her father. When she sends sorrow to the light, she sends past negative karmas with men. She will no longer need her connection to pain.

This is the lifetime when the sorrow must go. When sorrow is released, her life opens to others, a chain reaction that continues like the ripples in a pool. Every healing radiates out and touches another life. Her work is to heal herself. She is a rock woman.

The voice fell silent. I heard faint scratchings, pen on paper.

I sank deeper, saw nothing.

"It's time to return."

Sharon's voice came from the end of a deep passageway, a life line of love to guide me. My body shuddered as it drew breath. My breath attached itself to Sharon's voice and followed as if Sharon reeled me in from the depths of a dark, crystalline pool.

"Take another breath," Sharon's voice said. I breathed. My spirit lifted into my body, my legs, my arms, resting alongside my body. I rolled my head from side to side.

"Whenever you are ready, you may open your eyes," Sharon said. I didn't want to open my eyes. For a bit, I could linger.

But I didn't. My eyes opened as my head rolled, and I saw a candle flame beside Sharon's knee. My gaze traveled up to Sharon's face, to a gentle smile as if she were the Madonna, birthing promise.

"Hi," I said. Sharon briefly nodded. "Thank you." Sharon nodded again.

We worked together a last time during the weekend's Vipassana meditation, although separately, and in silence, as we followed each other in walking meditation. We sat near each other in sitting meditation, touched from time to time as if to make physical the link we'd forged.

I was learning to release the death of my father linked to the death of my time at Kalani. I saw how I held on to friends, attachments, my room at Kalani. How the tightness in my shoulders came from holding on. I practiced meditation with my hands open, shoulders relaxed.

All letting go was painful. And difficult. And possible.

Early morning meditation was the best, clear and light, followed by walking meditation in the dew-wet grass. A bird pecked at seeds near my foot. I moved so slow, it didn't notice. In a meditation, I saw the man, my partner, practicing shamanic techniques, a therapist, and a healer. I looked at my anger and how anger took me to my father's death and holding on. I examined my boredom and saw the Arkansas little-girl-me running down the road, tripping in her enthusiasm. I wanted to go faster and farther than I was able all the time and tripped, fell over, spilled things.

On Monday morning, one last Tai Chi class. My body shifted into each new position as Ken named it, and I listened to the soft sandy slide of feet on the wooden floor. At the end of class, Ken and I bowed to one another and held each other's gaze a moment. He knew I was leaving; everyone knew. Our friendship had formed itself in movement; we trusted one another. I bobbed my head slightly; Ken mirrored. I turned to my room.

I'd said my farewells the night before at dinner and so avoided the gathering around breakfast. Instead, camera in hand, I walked to the sweat lodge where the altar stone and antlers lay, a bowl of cornmeal beside them. I sat and remembered the final sweat with Ben three days earlier: no visions, a quiet waiting, grieving, salty tears and sweat mingling in the dust between my crossed legs. Something of me left behind would always remain part of the earth in this sacred place.

From the sweat lodge, I walked the path beyond the A-frames and beyond the hales' sight lines until I could see nothing but jungle, absorbing this breath of wildness. I listened. No words, rather the sound of birds, crackling twigs, rustling vines. I hadn't learned the names of the birds here, didn't know which sounds belonged to which animal as I had in Kansas. I closed my eyes and listened, breathing the sounds deep.

I returned on the gravel road to the garden. No one there: not José, not Tootsie, battling the washing machines, no Michael Koob, no Miles. I had the gift of solitude to say my farewell to the land. Rain had scattered overhead in the night and the garden gleamed. Weeds sprouted through the lettuce and the basil needed harvesting. I resisted the urge.

Beyond the garden, I passed the massage room, hot tub, swimming pool. Remembering the day Marian left, I touched the jade beads at my throat. I felt invisible, already gone, no longer a part of the community. I passed the office, heard the light chatter of people. Someone laughed. No one noticed my passing.

At the end of the lane, I crossed the Red Road to the point overlooking the sea. No flowers on the stone tower today, no lei transformed the pile into altar. I found one small stone and wedged it into a space between other stones. Below, a large wave crashed its good-bye. Briny spray sprinkled my arm. I licked a splotch, tasting sea, and lifted my head, remembered the day I'd come here, wrapped in a hooded raincoat.

The sea . . . the sea . . . how it calls, rocks . . . remembers . . . lets go.

Retracing my steps to the kitchen, for a moment I was not alone as I snapped photos: Bari, holding a can of lemon cakes in front of her, grinning; Oona, hoisting a community-sized box of cereal onto her shoulder; Kathy, hoe in hand, raking beneath the bushes around the lanai.

Sharon and I had said goodbye the night before at dinner: me, wearing the green ti-leaf print muumuu to look festive; she, wearing a white gauzy shirt and color-beaded necklace. When she rose from our table, she'd leaned in, rested the curve of her neck on my head. Her shirt's nubby woven fabric, almost like gauze, brushed my cheek. Sadness lay between us, sadness and blessing. Behind us, others laughed and chattered in their own moments. We were dust motes woven into time's dense layers to blow along some other road, some other journey, a mysterious chain linking one thing to another.

Jeanne arrived before lunch, and we sat with the community—laughter and jokes, lighthearted banter. Sharon was not at lunch, avoiding my leaving as I had avoided Marian's.

And then the rush: stowing the last things in the car, waving goodbye goodbye goodbye as we drove down the lane and onto the Red Road. The chord between me and Kalani would not let go, its silken claw gripping between my shoulder blades. My eyes burned in unshed tears. I turned my head to watch the sea slip between trees.

NINETEEN

EATEN BY MYTH

I returned to North Kohala five days before the program officially ended, just as I'd moved to Kalani five days before the program began. In the course of sixteen weeks, my fears and expectations had turned themselves inside out to reach depths I hadn't known existed in me; the new task was to reshape myself into a container to hold all I'd learned. What would it look like? A bowl of light? A crystal vase? A pot of earth to nurture growing sprouts? The answer remained elusive. Turning to tasks seemed doable. I cleaned the fountain, caught up on laundry, cleared out the refrigerator, and vacuumed the pool. Returning early meant two weeks with my sister before leaving and taking up life with my children. Moving out of my D.C. apartment and putting stuff in storage felt overwhelming—how would I move; where would I find storage? My mind chattered. I'd tell it to trust and the chatter settled, but I was keenly aware how worry over my apartment grew deeper than details. If I gave up my apartment, where would I go after . . . well, after what?

Leon phoned. He'd seen an advertisement for a Birth of Hula Festival on Moloka'i with Uncle John. I wanted to go, wanted to be eaten alive by myth and grieve goodbye, grieve an ending to begin a beginning, to feel a land that could not be mine, yet thundered with an ancient force so familiar I was stuck in its power. I did not want to leave Hawaii, and I knew I must. But first I'd go to Moloka'i. Jeanne wanted to go as well as Leon's friend Loo. We made our plans.

Krysta phoned. She'd returned to Kalani from her travels around the island. "Janet! I was so sad to find you gone," she said. Her voice held the same melancholy it had the night she'd burned her finger.

"I'm sorry. I didn't know you were coming back." My own melancholy resurfaced. "Can you come up for a visit?" Krysta said yes.

Everything was moving too quickly and I operated out of a scattered sensibility, sorting and packing and carrying boxes to the post office, some for D.C. and storage, and others to my son's in Georgia. After a post office trip, I sat on the patio and looked out at sea. I'd be on the road for several weeks. If I didn't get myself together, I'd get cranky and irritable. But if I sat here staring at the sea, I'd start crying. Leaning into the deck chair, I closed my eyes and sank into the warm sunlight. Mynah birds chattered in the kiawe tree. The palm fronds danced their rattling waltz. Rain had passed through in the night and the grass smelled green. Water lapped at the pool's edge. Do not fear. Be like water. Do nothing before its time.

Russ, Sharon, and Krysta traveled up from Kalani in the old and battered Russ Truck, the truck that had carried us to adventures. Now we wandered on one last quest, up through the pastures where Sonny Solomon had driven me, to walk the trail to the falls.

I took photos of this last journey: Russ, his hair slicked wet after diving into a waterfall pool; Krysta, sunlight setting a crown on her Swedish hair; Sharon and Jeanne, sitting on rocks. And one photo from behind the falls where the trail curved against the mountain face and water fell like a curtain, shielding me from the world.

THE NEXT WEEK, LEON AND LOO, JEANNE AND I BOARDED A BOAT through the air to cross the sea. From the plane window, we watched Lanai rise on the horizon. At last we crossed Moloka'i, coming downwind and low over the Makanalua Peninsula where the white clapboard village of Father Damien's leper colony butted up against a cliff in isolation. Seen from the airplane, the setting's simplicity invited, a place where no one would find me. We circled the mountain spine, and Jeanne leaned against me to look out the window. "The legends say Laka's remains are hidden beneath that spine."

Moloka'i Ka Hula Piko (Moloka'i, the heart of hula).

Jeanne rented a car at the airport, and we drove to the little house that Loo, who knew someone who knew someone, found on Moloka'i. A small house but sufficient for our needs. Loo's face shone in a perpetual smile; we all smiled on Moloka'i.

After unloading the car, we drove to Ke Nani Kai Hotel at one end of the island, overlooking the sea, to listen to Uncle John's stories. He filled a chair in a big room with windows and gestured with his huge arm as he repeated the ancient story of giant lizards and the warriors who hunted them. His other great arm encircled the neck of a drum as if it were his lover. Sacred lizards—what a dichotomy—the sacred that terrorizes. Hawaii's push-pull of destruction and beauty, myth and legend, swept in and shook us.

After Uncle John's lecture, our quartet wandered the island toward the far end, driving the one highway that gradually diminished from a two-lane blacktop to a narrow not-quite-two-lane to a one-lane gravel road between boulders, to Halawa Valley. Ancient Hawaiians had once settled there where the mountains' freshwater streams flowed into the sea and the waves rolled gently ashore.

We gazed up into misty valleys. Clouds hung low, obscuring the backs of sleeping lizards, and we considered climbing the path to a waterfall. Jeanne and I, having climbed to a waterfall two days previously, decided we wouldn't. Loo agreed. We wore sandals and skirts, hardly mountain trekking gear. Instead, the three of us walked barefoot along the freshwater stream flowing into the sea and bathed our feet in the lapping waves at ocean's edge. We didn't talk. I searched for the stone that wanted to return mainland-side with me and found a heavy, hard-packed, red and black striated rock that fit in my palm, ridged on the top like a sleeping lizard's back.

Two fishermen were talking story with Leon as he gazed into their bags. "Come look," he called, and we left the gentle surf to gaze into the depths of gunny sacks filled with shellfish and seaweed. And then we drove the island's road, redoing the way we'd come—the winding trail through boulders, along the narrow two-lane highway past fishing ponds, stone walls grown from land's edge into a barrier reef—and stopped at Father Damien's tiny, whitewashed clapboard church with its white-painted steeple.

Inside, a scrubbed wooden plank floor lined with narrow pews, four on each side; the altar a simple table covered with a white cloth. Jeanne and I sat quietly, our hands lightly touching on the pew seat. We had spent many years together in our home church, sitting in wooden pews. At last, we rose and walked outside. Well-tended grave plots lay side by side along a gravel path. None bore the name of Father Damien although his statue stood guard. Fresh flower leis hung around his neck and circled the brim of his bronze hat. Food offerings lay in the crook between his body and hands. Loo ran to fetch a guava from the car and placed it as an offering.

A tragic hero, Father Damien. His actions also his downfall as he worked at a reckless speed, careless of wounds and cleanliness, and developed the Hanson's disease of his charges. Brother Dutton, a Trappist monk who arrived on Kalaupapa in 1886, never contracted the disease and stayed until 1931, but he'd served in the Civil War, had dealt with gangrene and the deaths a lack of cleanliness could bring. Was Father Damien's faith his strength or his downfall?

Obsession feeds itself, and a belief in a higher power, whether the power is named God or Great Spirit or Sarah, can impel risky behavior. Others had often said how brave I was to risk all in my moves and changes, but I'd never knowingly risked my life for what I believed myself called to do. I studied the face on Father Damien's statue and wondered if he knew the dangers he faced, or did he move so fast, was he so driven, that he ignored them? Did he consider the costs worth the journey? I couldn't ask. No one to ask about change, grief, and moving on, about trust and fear, no one except a channeled voice with no face other than my own.

From the church, we drove to Pala'au and walked through the old Ironwoods to the trail at cliff's edge leading down to the leper's colony. Clouds hung low in the trees, the wispy shards clinging to droopy branches covered in hundreds of pearl-shaped water droplets. A slight brush with an elbow, a passing breath of air baptized us into a reality out of all time and place. We stood in an indecipherable place belonging only to the shadows of myth.

Legend, and there are many about Moloka'i, says the island was home to sorcerers and priests, a sanctuary for those who had broken tabu, and a place of magic. Moloka'i was never attacked because of the power in its sorcerers and, some say, balls of fire called *akualele*—tapa cloth filled with wood chips from poisonous trees, set afire, and flung over the night sea to ward off marauders. Whatever the truth of those legends, the grove at Pala'au rumbled in potent silence. The four of us wandered through trees to the Phallic Stone—to see it because everyone did—none of us needing more fertility than what we had. We returned to the little house and retired as evening snuffed at the windows.

At 2 a.m. we woke and dressed in darkness for a blind quest to Pu'u Nana's spine and a rumored celebration of the day's birth in fire and water and dance. No one knew how the rumor started or who to ask if it were true. Leon had talked to someone who said someone said . . . but Uncle John had said nothing, other than the ancient *kumus*, those dancers with the fluidity of water and the spark of fire trained in the spiritual essence of fire and water. None of us questioned which way to go—just one way, toward Pu'u Nana. Leon had learned there was a gate opening onto a pasture and a foot-climb to the hill, but not where the gate might be. Jeanne drove with Leon beside her. He pointed and murmured as we drove through a black night sliced by the narrow band of headlights. No other cars followed; none ahead. Loo and I sat silent in the back. Leon leaned forward, his eyes searching. With unexpected force, a bump on the road flicked the headlight's beam and reflected two red dots, gleaming ahead. A giant lizard? Slowly, Jeanne inched the car forward; Leon's arm shot forward to point. "Look!" he said. "Cars!" There were cars, silent, dark, parked along the side of the road, taillights reflecting in our headlights. Jeanne cut them off and parked.

"This must be the place," Leon said. "I guess we wait."

We waited as minutes and darkness stretched into a muffled, lagging delay. A car pulled up behind us and cut its lights as it drifted to a stop. We heard the quiet *grrrrrrt* of a pulled emergency brake. We waited.

Far ahead, shadows wavered, and then closer, car doors opened and bodies emerged. Some unknown-to-us-time had arrived.

The air cut cold as we got out of the car. Jeanne handed me a windbreaker. We followed the silently moving crowd through an opened gate and up the side of the mountain. Leon carried a flashlight so we avoided rocks and holes. At the top of the mountain, the wind blew harder and colder. Jeanne and I huddled against a small boulder, not big enough for shelter, but enough to deflect some wind. Leon and Loo sat against another. We looked out to sea, at stars clustered above. Rustles and murmurs. We couldn't tell how many people had gathered in the scattered clumps.

Shadows moved against the starlight. Muffled drums thudded into the night. Dancers danced and my skin shivered, not from wind, but from the drum's call and the echoing thud of feet. I didn't know how many . . . the shapes twisted, bent low, turned. Supplicating arms lifted toward a dawn yet to come. The drums spoke louder; the dancers danced faster.

A gold thread etched the horizon . . . wave tips blushed pink . . . the dancers swayed. Rays of pink and gold grew above the sea.

The sun's rim seared the horizon.

As suddenly begun, the drum stopped, the dancers melted behind us down the ridge. People stretched, bundled up blankets and quilts, left to walk down the hill. Loo, Leon, and Jeanne followed.

I stood for a moment to watch the sun's birth into day. Too much of leaving lay heavy in my heart, but that other world, far beyond this horizon, waited. Who would I be? When the sun separated from the sea, I turned and followed my sister. That evening Jeanne and I flew home.

Home. There was no home now. Only the journey.

TWENTY

THE RETURN

In my whirling fashion, I packed the last boxes and sent them to my son, said goodbye to friends. I would carry the Smith Corona. Jeanne drove me to the airport.

I'd chosen. I didn't want to cry anymore. But I did. When I left my sister and walked to security, I felt Jeanne's eyes, felt the bond between us stretching. I turned, we both lifted a hand in unison, turned in unison, and walked on. Grief welled through me. Even gritting my teeth, I couldn't stop the tears, and kept my head down, following the shuffling feet ahead.

As the plane lifted along Kohala's coast, I saw the black lava fields, a last glimpse of the Puakea house roof, the point of land, and Hawaii slid behind me. Fear twisted my belly: the hero on her return journey, carrying steel wool, pretending Golden Fleece. No ruby slippers in my bag. No comrades, no companions, no one to bolster or convince me the journey worthwhile, that the world needed what I had to give. No map to guide me. *Carry your bowl of light. You are thrust from the womb into a new life. Alone you must go as all go alone. There are no companions in birthing.* At least my trusty voice was coming.

The plane wasn't full, so I could put up the seat arms and rest. Okay. Notice the gifts. The thought of D.C. as home/not home stretched my body as tight as Uncle John's drum skin. I squirmed, there on the less-than-bed seats. Your fear and sadness is your addiction. Leave it! I breathed deep. The plane leveled. Pay attention; pay attention. I slept.

Arriving in Seattle, loud flight announcements and loud news from monitors marched with the overwhelming streams of people. I'd left a land where myth fashioned reality; now I scrabbled between worlds, no name for the new growing in me, nothing concrete to call into shape, no surface on which to stand except an ice-hard floor, gleaming in freshly buffed shine. Judy saw me, waved to get my attention. I wound through people to reach her.

"I was just thinking I should have worn a red shirt like Mom so my big sister could rescue me," I said. "I'm glad you saw me. Thanks."

Judy laughed and with practiced navigation led me down and around corridors to luggage and into her little canary-yellow CRZ. My sister, in her wisdom, drove us to Bellingham on the coast road rather than the freeway. Outside my window, forest and hill, and outside hers, the Puget Sound.

A week in the country with my big sister anchored me in my body. Judy's home overlooked the bay at the edge of the Lumi Reservation's green space. I told her stories of Hawaii; she told me stories of Bellingham. We each donned bib overalls—Dad's, brought back after his funeral—and drove to her friend's farm where Judy's horse, Val, lived. We cleaned his stall. Her friend snapped our picture: the two of us clad in striped overalls, holding pitchforks. Another day, we dressed presentable and walked through downtown Bellingham. Mostly, we hung out and cooked and laughed.

I'd phoned Cynthia from Jeanne's house to fill her in on my plans, or what I could fathom of them: putting stuff in storage, going to Georgia. Now she tracked me down at Judy's.

"Janet, Hans is moving to D.C. for a year. He wants to rent your apartment." Hans, her German lover from some fifteen years back. Shocked, holding the phone to my ear, I said nothing. "Sit down, darlin'," Cynthia said. So I did. "He'll get there around the middle of July."

"Tell him yes! And thanks." I wouldn't have to give up the apartment; it was like having stuff in storage without moving.

Too soon, Judy drove down the same coastal road, and I boarded my last plane to Washington, D.C.

Willy met me. Driving the city in evening rush hour was not like riding angel wings. Cars and trucks pinned us to the road and sent violent fumes into the car. My head ached, my stomach nauseous. Horns sounded on all sides. Welcome home, Dorothy, I whispered, rubbing the space between my eyebrows, the skin chafing beneath my fingers.

Willy's words swam in and out of conscious understanding as the city materialized... "art gallery... meeting..." Who? Who was he meeting? "Not tonight," I said and wondered if I replied to an invitation or forestalled one.

Willy unloaded the two bags and carried them to the elevator.

"Thanks, that's okay," I said to his offer to take them upstairs. "You go ahead. I'll see you tomorrow." He said something, I could see him talking, but the noise of the elevator gears, someone talking at the front desk, a phone ringing distracted me. Was it always this noisy? Had I forgotten?

As I got off the elevator, a woman I knew casually, a long-time resident, came down the hall. "Are you coming or going?" she said. "Coming." I said. "I've been in Hawaii for the past year or so." Her eyes widened. "I thought I hadn't seen you in a while." She asked how it was, and I said it was wonderful and asked how she was. "Oh, I'm fine. My life never changes." Yiiiikes! How was that possible? But I didn't say anything. I smiled and nodded, propped the Smith Corona on one of the bags and tugged my life down the hall to the apartment door. I'd never met the student renter; he'd arrived after I left and left before my return. I had no idea what faced me on the other side. Pulling out the keys I'd retrieved from the front desk, I opened the door.

Evening filled the windows along the south wall. By the reflected light, the apartment appeared as clean as I'd left it. Shutting the door with one heel, as was my custom, and walking to the sliding windows, I lay my forehead against the cooling glass. A plane tracked its landing down the Potomac and dropped from view. The boxes sent from Hawaii were all carefully stacked in the wide coat closet beside boxes stored before leaving. Setting the Smith Corona on the desk and plugging it in felt somewhat normal. Not normal normal, but the desk didn't wobble.

As dusk gathered, my body on West Coast time and restless, I walked to DuPont Circle. Saturday nights on P Street were hangout nights, couples waiting to enter restaurants, guys hanging out to hang out on stoop steps, at sidewalk tables, homeless guys panhandling. How was it possible nothing had changed? The wadded up papers under the benches looked like the same wadded up newspapers from the year before. The placid statues stared back at me as I stood at the fountain to feel spray on my face, a poor substitute for ocean spray. When I left Kalani, a cacophony of goodbyes followed: Victoria, banging a spoon on a kitchen pot; Bari shouting and whistling; everyone waving and waving.

P Street was a cacophony of hellos.

I skated the city's surface, looking for work, revisiting haunts, moving through time that sped so much faster than time at Kalani. Michael phoned, "Grandma, aren't you coming yet?" My kids wanted to see me, friends wanted to see me—pieces of me snipped and eaten away, my bowl of light filling with stones, the Golden Fleece shredded, faded to iron dust. I rarely wrote in my journal—random notes, random dreams. Instead, I wrote to Kalani friends to ease the knot in my chest. At the secondhand bookstore, I found Dan Millman's *Sacred Journeys*, set on Moloka'i. Catherine and I met for lunch and she gave me *The Fruitful Darkness* by Joan Halifax. "Here," she said. "I thought this might be the right book for the right time."

Willy took me to southern Maryland.

His father had died the previous fall, so we did chores for his mom, Jane, at his childhood home on the Potomac's wide slide into the Chesapeake. Willy roared the lawnmower to life while I handled the weed eater. Shutting it down to reposition myself, I heard Willy talking to someone down by the dock, the lawnmower silent.

"C'mere!" Willy yelled over puttering boat motor.

"This here is my cousin Bull," he said, pointing to a big man, standing in the middle of the motor boat. Bull nodded, the gold chain around his neck anchored by a gold and onyx bull pendant shimmered on his open-shirted masculine chest. "We're going for a ride," Willy said and climbed aboard. He reached out a hand to steady me as I climbed in.

Bull took over at the wheel and off we putted down the river to pick up more friends and a cooler of beer. I settled on the padded back seat and watched the cormorants—huge birds, wide wings—as they skimmed the water, claws open for fish. Willy pointed out their nests, twig and branch-built on poles in the middle of the river. The men slid into a southern Maryland dialect as story followed story. "Now I never heard him talk about that directly, I only heard the story sideways," Willy said as an opener to a neighbor's story. When we returned, Jane, who was on the outs with Bull, said, "They're a good family. Some of them let out to weeds but the rest all right." I laughed out loud. We went to a crab festival at a little stone church where, Jane said, Willy had once been an altar boy.

On our last evening, Willy used concrete to repair the sea wall, and I sat with my little sketchbook and played on the pages with colored felt tip pens, stuck on a tiny flower and bits of paper and filled up facing pages.

"I have two pages but I can't pull them together," I said, staring at the painting.

Trowel in one hand, Willy picked up a fine tip purple pen, "Here," and squiggled in some lines: a thin line from a triangular piece of paper built a kite, faint lines connected the pages, broken lines outlined paint swatches along the bottom. One bold vertical sketch anchored the right hand page. Perfect. I returned home with a wonderful painting and a wonderful case of poison ivy. A gift in itself, it kept me home to soak in Epsom salts and dose the blisters with calamine lotion.

Finally healed of blisters, I rode my bike to the mall past the Lincoln Memorial and the Reflecting Pool, past the Washington Monument and over to the Jefferson Memorial. Tourists walked everywhere. Oh. Yeah. This was Washington. Off the mall, I crossed K Street and stopped at the bar where I'd been fired. One of my old regulars sat in his usual place, an intelligent man, editor of a publication, a man with whom I'd had more or less spiritual and wondering conversations. "Hey! Where you been?" he said. I briefly recounted Hawaii stories, the sweat lodges, Shamanism, and calling in spirits. His eyes gathered into thought, "Shamanism. Now that's not something you hear talked about every day around here."

That had to be a sure enough fact. When I asked him what he'd been doing, he said, "Oh . . . everything's the same . . . work, relationships, you know." He was still drinking and still smoking at the same bar with the same people at the same time. How could anyone keep living a life where everything was the same? Peddling home, I pondered. True, I'd only been away a little less than a year, but how could so much of everything not change? A red light stopped me and cars passed: Mercedes, a Chrysler, two BMWs, a Lexus amid a gaggle of smaller Fords. I pedaled home to sit at the wide open windows, looking out at sky, but it wasn't real sky. Even with the windows open, I couldn't smell it or touch it or feel it.

Bicycling the city to some of my favorite spots—the Hirschhorn to see a Dubuffet show because he was a favorite, the East Wing of the National Gallery, the Peacock Room at the Sackler—anchored me in a city I had loved even more than New York or Los Angeles.

In my apartment, alone, I wore the green print muumuu. I found no work. Money dribbled away. I kept reminding myself not to worry about money just because rent was coming due, but that was as much a challenge as training my mind to stop chattering. And then the mail brought a Hans letter from Germany with rent money.

Voltaire wrote, "God is a comic playing to an audience who's afraid to laugh." I still laughed from time to time, but the strain of city and no job heaped noise upon weary.

One afternoon, alone and silent, I put the headset over my ears and dropped into drumming and meditation. I walk to the crossroad, my power animal, porcupine, with me. I greet the Keeper of the Crossroad, the Death figure, and ask if I owed him a boon. He said, "Remember your death every day and remember to live in the now. Be careful with wishes. The rules are basic. Keep it simple and specific. Trust this journey."

Surfacing from the meditation, I realized I no longer fit in D.C. But I also didn't know what was coming, other than a grandson. All I had was trust.

A dream woke me as dawn inched over Washington, D.C. I'm struggling to pack and move out of a hotel. Someone else moving in when I thought I had more time. Jeanne had come, gentle but a little annoyed. "You aren't paying attention to the signs," she said. That message easy to decipher. I got out of bed, pulled out my credit card, and found the number for Amtrak. The agent offered a miracle. "Would you like to add a sleeper to this ticket? It's on special for ten dollars more."

I would.

Reservation made and paid, I opened the Smith Corona and sat, waiting, listening.

This is a year of adjustment to anchor the changes you put in place. You were right in listening to Spirit and leaving earlier than you'd planned.

Your presence is needed. There are many paths to the light; this path will have its share of pain, but it is not your primary path. Be with spirit; be with your family; serve their needs. The center is within. This lesson is for the traveler and the teacher. Walk the line between listening and hearing. Be there for the words said and unsaid. Listening is absorbing into the depths of your spirit; hearing is the surface knowing.

I closed the Smith Corona, pulled a sheet of paper out of the desk drawer, and wrote "Trip List" at the top.

Four days later, Willy drove me to the train station. A porter escorted me to my one-person sleeper. He showed me how to open the sink, where to hang clothes, how to lower the bed, and said he'd come help me with it later. "Put your shoes here when you go to bed," he said and pointed to a cubbyhole near the door. "I'll polish them and get them to you in the morning." He lifted my travel bag, placed it in the overhead rack, and left.

I watched Washington, D.C. recede from my window, grateful for the tiny sleeper, grateful to be alone. A sign on a building near the metro stop at King Street read: Association of Old Crows. Amusement relaxed my jaw. The towns slid past, and I dozed, woke in dusk, swayed my way to the dining car, swayed my way back, and found the conductor had come by and made up my bed. I sat for a time as the night deepened, switched on the overhead lamp, dislodged my pen from the journal's spirals where it always lived for safety and found two last empty pages.

What have I sacrificed for this journey into spirit? My independence. Death is a transformation of matter into spirit; i.e. to sacrifice is to make sacred. Making sacred is about a spiritual calling, and for me, that's human relationships. I suppose sacrificing my independence is necessary if I'm to be in relationship. The end of June, end of the D.C./Hawaii/D.C. phase. The end of this journal. Funny how those things go together. I'll be in Georgia tomorrow.

I switched off the lamp and gazed aimlessly through the window into the passing woods—the deepness, the flicker of light. Placing my shoes in the cubbyhole, I undressed in the dark and crawled into the bed. The train wheels clacking lulled me to sleep.

TWENTY-ONE

BEING MOM

I left my sleeper room sanctuary and stepped into a pile of life. Nathan and Michael met me at the train station, my grandson wrapping his arms around my middle. Nathan put his arm around my shoulder for a one-arm hug. "Thanks, Mom." He picked up my carry-on bag and led me inside the station to collect baggage.

"Is this all?" Nathan said as he collected my large suitcase from the cart.

"My bicycle's against the wall. Did the boxes come from Hawaii?"

"Stacked in your room already." Nathan grinned, looking pleased at his emphasis on the words your room. My room. There was a kind of finality in that. I smiled. He led us to the car, me pushing the bicycle, Michael's hand over mine on the handlebar. "I have something in the boxes for you," I said to Michael. "Some Hawaiian toys." I could see I'd chosen toys too young for him, a bobbling bear in a hula skirt and a flute carved from reed. He wore a baseball T-shirt. He'd soon be six, too old, I guessed, for silly toys. I didn't bring a baseball or a bat. Hadn't even thought of it. "How's the new store coming along," I said, wanting to break my silent walk.

"Oh. Well, I didn't tell you because I didn't want you to worry. It burned down two days before we opened," as he loaded the bike onto a rack.

"Burned down?" It was next door to their restaurant. "Did the restaurant burn?" The restaurant hadn't burned, he said, smoke damage, lost the contents . . . contents of what, I wondered . . . we bought a bar . . . a bar? Too much too fast, my head crammed with information. " . . . thought since you've managed bars, you'd be good at managing this." This? I would manage a bar?

I stared through the windshield, seeing nothing of the town as we passed, as Nathan talked, as I nodded, not understanding anything. A bar? "How's Kyong?" I said. She was at the restaurant, but she was thinking of selling it. He didn't sound pleased.

The Fouth of July weekend came. Things seemed tense in the house, so Michael and I attended a ballgame and watched fireworks. I unpacked. A desk faced one wall of my room. It had two shelves for books. Two windows, one high above the bed and the other high in the wall facing the carport. When Michael had lived with me in D.C., my break came each morning when he sat in the high chair, ate Cheerios off the tray, and watched Sesame Street. Now he preferred Power Rangers. It was louder.

Anger, which I thought I'd dealt with and passed through, came to rear its head and make me deal again. My spiritual life consisted in not losing my temper. Grandma . . . and Grandma! . . . but if I said, "Michael, I'm at the edge of cranky and need to be alone for a while," he heard me. Smart kid and amazingly hard-headed. I couldn't imagine where he got it. A nap-time dream of traveling to Russia woke me . . . Russia? The next night another dream of Russia, carrying a lot of baggage in an underground train struggling for the surface. Siberia? Exile?

Nathan knocked. "Mom, let's go do some errands." Michael rode in the backseat, pointing out his favorite stores. Jeanne phoned. A family reunion in Oregon. She'd get tickets for me and Michael with frequent flyer miles. I'd stopped meditating, stopped writing, one task led to another, details to settle with the jukebox operator and the pool table deliverer. Yes. I could be there to let them in. One afternoon home, I lay down, centered in meditation. My throat tightened with unshed tears and fear. I'd never be the wise woman or healer I wanted to be. And then I remembered to breathe. I rested. And bolted upright . . . take the joy of your solitude to heal whatever sadness in the world you can heal.

I had to quit feeling sorry for myself and be with whatever was.

The new moon on a day of white-hot glare beat us into sodden lumps. I slept until noon. The house was silent. Michael had spent the night with a friend. I'd seen a library four blocks from the house, so I dressed and walked through the glare to cool, quiet, books: a refuge. I found the section with spiritual writing and pulled down *Bringers of the Dawn*, channeled writing by Barbara Marciniak. I didn't recognize her name but I thumbed through the book. It was interesting. I checked it out along with a Carlos Castaneda book I'd already read, but it would help me remember Mexico, a talisman to keep me balanced. Taking them home, I found the *I Ching* and my Tarot deck in a box, waiting to be unpacked. One way or another, I had to start listening to myself again.

The pattern of days began to take on a regularity. I had a couple of hours each morning before Michael woke, needing breakfast. We played games or watched movies; we went to swimming lessons. There was nothing quite so requiring service as my particular five-year-old highly intuitive, individualistic, focused, and basically fearless grandson. He dove into deep water, eyes open, blowing bubbles. On Mondays, I worked at the bar from four to ten so Nathan and Michael could play. I had the nights. Dreams came with regularity: traveling in a car that runs by fits and starts; a man casts a fishing line and hooks me in the front of my shirt. One night, I woke touching my head at the crown. My other arm reaching up like in Hawaii. I recognized the movement but couldn't remember what I'd said or heard.

Leon Khalil phoned. The sound of sea in his voice wrapped me in comfort, and with the receiver pressed into my ear, we remembered Moloka'i and Uncle John, laughed at retelling the story of the red lizard eyes startling us and becoming tail lights. When we said goodbye and hung up, my heart felt like I'd said goodbye to Hawaii all over again.

The airline tickets arrived. Michael and I would fly to Denver to meet son Stephen and drive to the family reunion at Crater Lake in Oregon. It would cost me in energy, but I wanted to see my family and longed to be with Jeanne. Jeanne, as much as Kalani, brought Hawaii to me. In an afternoon meditation, I remembered a moment, she, a young baby, crying in her bassinet, me three-plus years old. I'd guided her thumb into her mouth, me, her big sister and a master of thumb-sucking. She took to it right away. I ran into the kitchen. "Mommy, I teached the baby to suck her thumb." I lay looking at the ceiling, smiling. Somehow that memory unlocked a storage folder in my brain and the memories tumbled: a rocking horse at the top of the attic stairs; riding the heaped-high cotton wagon behind my father; a neighborhood boy; and suddenly, the memory of a temper tantrum, lying on the floor kicking my heels, furious, and a dipper of cold water dashing my chest. That was a story I'd heard many times. Once, when Grandpa and Grandma Sunderland were visiting, and I was in the midst of a tantrum, Mother distraught, Grandpa told Mother to toss a cup of cold water on me. "That'll stop it," is the story's tagline. I guessed it would. How long would I keep doing anger before I was done, as if it were a birthmark I couldn't erase? Above me, a mottled ceiling, sparkles left over from someone else's sky, someone else's story.

Michael and I flew to Denver to meet Stephen, and he drove us across the sage lands of Wyoming. A relief to enter Utah's green fields and trees. Michael played in the back seat, fell asleep, and woke hungry. I fed him sandwiches we'd packed, passed one to Stephen. We drove. We were all meeting in Bend and together, we'd caravan to Crater Lake.

Those few days became the family reunion everyone wanted: Uncle Kenny taught Michael how to handle a fishing pole and he caught his first fish, a whole four inches long; we drove up to the crater and played in the snow, Lia holding Michael by the tail of his shirt so he wouldn't slide down the steep incline; we cooked meal after meal, laughing and telling stories. And then it was over, and we were on the road to Denver and to the airport to fly back to Atlanta where Nathan and Kyong were happy to see us and happy with each other. We resumed our routines of restaurant, bar, and care-taking Michael.

BILL PHONED FROM COSTA RICA. HOW HAD HE FOUND ME? HE'D called Cynthia, he said. After the hellos and the how-are-yous, he said he was calling for an ulterior motive. I laughed. "What can I do for you?" It was Weezer, the silver-gray tabby who'd adopted us as a kitten when she lived under our steps in New Orleans. He'd had custody, found sub-letters who would care for her when he traveled. Now the girls had moved out of the apartment and left the cat. "Are you going to D.C. anytime soon?" I wasn't. He didn't press. It was easy to laugh at his stories. After we hung up, I missed him. At the bar, I let down my guard and entered into a long and involved conversation with a tall, lanky man named Jim who tipped well. A threatening dream followed: I'm afraid and closing all the windows and doors in the house, and when I go outside, I'm lost.

Okay, no more flirting with Jim.

But I had lost myself. Too often becoming impatient; too often skipping meditation for tasks. My life felt cramped and small. I longed for the Hawaii garden, the time to ponder, the screened window opening to sky and jungle. I even missed José and laughed, a short and sharp guffaw. No chanting, although sometimes I sang with Michael: "This little light of mine, I'm gonna let it shine." He liked that one. Sometimes we'd dance. But my center drifted as I did laundry, read him stories, sat to watch videos, drove to swimming lessons, noise, constant noise. I was in a car, driving somewhere, daily. Being of service was exhausting and dangerous, one day bruising my leg cleaning at the bar and on another, scratching a wound down one arm carrying a bag of potatoes into the restaurant.

I wrote about anger and wrote about anger and wrote about anger. It didn't help, so I pulled out my Hawaii journal and reread the messages: "Discipline is the key. Discipline in the way you work, in the way you breathe, in the way you love, in the way you walk; forgiving self leads to self-responsibility leads to healing. You have much to learn." I sighed.

Nathan and Michael were in the living room, watching a movie, so I drove out past the edge of town to the river road, followed it to water, sat on a log, stared at the river, allowed my mind to empty, focused on breathing. My body relaxed. You're feeling trapped. And when you feel trapped, you fight. A big breath whooshed out of me. I shook myself. So, okay. I felt trapped. Well. At least I understood.

That evening, as I lay on my bed reading, Michael came in, rocked for a minute in the desk chair, and then closed his eyes. He became the stillness you'd hardly believe possible in a boy. I waited until his eyes opened.

"What were you doing?" I said.

"Talking to my angels."

"Ah. And what did you say to them?"

"That I wanted to go to Chuck E. Cheese."

"Hmmmmm." I suppressed a grin. "And what did your angels say?"

"They said I could go."

I laughed, whooped actually, and got up from the bed. "Then I guess we should go."

Finally, the day came for Michael, his birth certificate, and his grandma to visit school and register for kindergarten. We stood at the office counter, his head reaching high enough for his eyes to peer over. Three check boxes remained for race: White, Black, Asian.

"He isn't any of these," I said to the woman behind the counter. She blinked when she looked at Michael, his dark, straight hair, almond eyes. "I guess Asian?" she said.

"He's Asian and Caucasian. You need another box."

"We don't have another box. You have to choose." Her lips tried to stretch into a smile but her voice had an edge.

"How am I supposed to choose between Asian and White?"

"Use the father's race. That's what's usual." She wasn't even trying to smile anymore, her face as tight as her blond curls. The warrior in me rose. Michael looked from my face to hers. There was no point. I checked White, held Michael's hand, and we walked out, heads high.

"Someday it will be different." I said. "There'll be more kids like you. But right now, the most important thing to remember is you're both. You're not White and you're not Asian. You're AmerAsian. Be proud of both." Michael nodded. He half-trotted to keep up with my stride, but he glanced up, grinning.

In that night's dream, I opened a box of dreams. I hoped it wouldn't be Pandora's.

TWENTY-TWO

GOING TO SCHOOL

Michael began school the last week of August. I woke him, fed him, and walked the two blocks with him. He'd have a full day in kindergarten, so I checked again to see if he had lunch money. Michael stuck his hand in his pocket, felt around, and nodded. "You're okay then? About school and all?"

He nodded. "Maybe I'll know some kids," he said. He spoke slowly, a tip to his head.

"If you don't now, you will soon. You're a good kid, Michael. Look at how many friends you have at the restaurant."

Korean families brought children with them, the kids free to play between tables.

"They don't go to this school."

"I know." His steps were lagging so I stopped and squatted in front of him. "Look. All you have to do is be you. It takes time to make friends; like it takes time to grow up. Usually making friends is a lot faster." Michael, head down, listened.

"Hey. Do you need a hug?" He looked up and gave a brief head shake no, his eyes on the school over my shoulder. I stood up, offered my hand, which he took, and we went to school.

The rhythm of days shifted. After walking Michael to school, my day quieted until I picked him up and listened to his stories on our walk home. I continued to work happy hour at the bar. Nathan and Kyong both worked late into the night so they slept late into the days. I biked, exercised, read, ran a few errands, meditated. In one, I moved forward through a wall, textured like stone, but with no solidity. I saw a crack of light and stepped toward to it. The light allowed me to stand near it but not enter the next room. Another day, Kyong woke with shoulder pain. I called Jeanne. She said Kyong had a rib out of place and told me how to put it back in. I did, and Kyong felt better. I carried books to the library and checked out more. Joan Borysenko's book suggested thanksgiving.

My head jerked up and I stared, unseeing. When was the last time I'd said thank you. To anyone. For anything. I repeated the words learned and forgotten: hope, trust, avoid judgment, and most of all, avoid desperation. And say thank you.

A week after Michael began school, I cut off all my hair. It hadn't been cut in months but I didn't expect such a drastic decision. The thing was, I'd colored my hair for years to lighten its dishwater blond into a more interesting blond, but I hadn't colored lately. Staring into the mirror, I parted various sections. Nearly an inch of roots were white. Might as well let it grow out and see what it looked like. Driving to a beauty shop a few blocks from the house, I walked in. A woman, sitting in a chair reading, got up and said hello. "Do you like to cut hair?" I said. It was one of her favorite things to do she assured me. "Then cut it all off down to where the white starts."

"All of it? That won't leave much."

"I know. But I'm tired of coloring it and I want to see what I have."

"Let's do it!"

I walked out with a fringe of white on my head. I'd said thank you several times and gave her a generous tip. Running my fingers through it felt like I'd left some of my past behind.

Michael was a happy boy. He liked school. Friends came in the afternoons to play, and laughter tumbled from the backyard. They raced back and forth, Michael's dog bounding beside him, and I remembered standing at another window, watching Michael's father run with our dog Shane some twenty years before in Belton, Texas, both of them leaping through tall grass. I'd written a haiku poem about the tow-headed boy and dog and published it in the literary magazine at the community college where I took classes.

One afternoon, I dressed business casual and crossed the river into Alabama to the Chattahoochee Valley Community College. My task was to put up fliers for a city-wide darts tournament that the bar was co-sponsoring. Lawns rolled between big pine trees. The campus on a hill so I could see into distance. My shoulders softened in the same release I'd felt during my first visit to Kalani, and I heard myself say, out loud, "I want to work here." Passing students looked at me, curious.

The building in front of me had a sign that read Arts.

"Hi," I said to a woman at a desk inside. "I'm Janet." The woman clasped my outstretched hand and smiled. "Kathy. Kathy Ledbetter. How can I help you?"

"Well, I wondered if there might be any openings here. I've taught English grammar and pronunciation for several years, and I really like the campus. I thought I'd ask."

"Let me take you to the Dean's office. I need to get outside for a bit anyway." We walked across campus, visiting. Since it was obvious I didn't have a southern accent, she asked where I was from. Trying to relate that story was more than I wanted to do so I said I'd come to Columbus to help with my grandson. "How nice!" she said. After a moment's reflection, I agreed. "That's the Dean's office, in that building." She pointed ahead. "I'll introduce you to his secretary."

Kathy introduced me to Mrs. Brannon, older, more formal, dressed in a slim gray suit, stiffly polite. "Come by and say hello again," Kathy said as she left. Mrs. Brannon leafed through a weekly planner. "He has Monday afternoon open. What time would be good?" We settled on 1:30 and I left for home and the Smith Corona and pulled up my resume.

Kyong explored the idea of visiting her mother in Korea. They hadn't seen each other since Kyong married Nathan—against her mother's wishes. She worried about seeing her now.

"You're a great mother. You must have learned it somewhere," I said. "It'll be okay. She'd probably like seeing you." Kyong nodded.

Monday afternoon, fresh resume in hand, I met Dean Williams. Mrs. Brannon held my resume as I waited in front of her desk, feeling like a kid in fourth grade. She glanced at it, marked a check beside my name in her weekly planner, rose in one smooth movement, and led me into Dean William's office. She indicated a chair with a tip of her head, handed him the resume, and left. The Dean studied the resume for a moment and looked up. The blueness of his eyes, a blue I hadn't seen since coming south, startled me.

"You've taught English grammar," he said. "Tell me about it."

I told him about teaching English in Mexico and my work in Washington, D.C.

"How about spelling? Are you a good speller?" he said.

"Yes. My mother was a writer and insisted we learn to speak correctly and spell. I attended a one-room schoolhouse, and each week we had a long list of words to memorize and practice for a spelling test." I saw myself bending over a list of words at the farm's kitchen table, but stopped myself from saying more. I had to quit trying to please people by entertaining them.

"Well, a funny thing just happened. The writing lab teacher quit last week. Think you could run a writing lab? Do tutoring with students?"

"I think so."

"Good." He wrote something on a pad and studied the schedule at his elbow. "There's a class beginning in October for pronunciation. We have a lot of students from Vietnam. Think you could do that one, too?"

I nodded. If I said anything I might say too much.

"Give Mrs. Brannon your information. She'll send you to personnel.

You'll start tomorrow. Here. Take this with you." He handed me the resume.

"Thank you," I said in my best professional voice. I had to get out of there fast before I burst into whoops.

Mrs. Brannon wrote down my contact information, wrote down the building number for the office of personnel, and handed it to me. She actually smiled. "Welcome to CVCC," she said. My trip to the personnel office was brief and efficient.

I released my whoops in the car. I was faculty at a college! Well, tutor, but it was a start.

When I parked behind Nathan's car, I noticed a blue mountain bike, but dashed inside to give him the news. "Nate, I was hired! I'll start teaching tomorrow. I can take Michael to school and be out in time to pick him up." I was so excited my sentences ran together.

"Cool," he said. "You see the bike out there?"

"Whose is it?"

"Yours. I saw it at a yard sale. A lot better than that raggedy bike you came here with."

"Oh, Nathan. Thank you! Can we go look at it?"

"Sure." He unfolded his six feet four inches from the chair. He even let me hug him. We explored the new features and gears. I had a bike with gears!

Two dreams bloomed in quick succession. In the first dream, a dead body was floating away on a barge. My dead body, I guessed, the life gone from my old life. Waking from the second, I wondered if I'd dreamed of my spirit lover. He'd been in my apartment to water the plants, he said. He had allergies, but he thought I'd want him to water the plants. He didn't know where I was until he read some notes on the desk.

I stared at the ceiling. Darkness lightened as dawn inched into the skies.

Another shift in schedules. Michael and I dressed for school, left in the car, first to his school and then to mine. The first day I had three students, but by week's end, the word had gone around, and I was busy.

Kyong came home and said it was her last day at the restaurant. She'd found a woman to run the restaurant, and she would go to Korea. She shopped through the following week, gifts to take to Korea, and Nathan drove her to the Atlanta airport. Michael would not be consoled. I cooked rice and gave him sheets of seaweed to tear up and wrap around the rice, his mother's comfort food. His eyes stayed sad, but he ate.

"Want to watch a movie?" I waited until Michael lifted his head. He nodded. I pulled out *The Three Musketeers* and showed it to him. He nodded again, more half-heartedly to please me that in real interest, but I put it on, and he curled onto the couch, his head on my lap. Ten minutes into the movie, he fell asleep. I lifted the remote and studied its buttons. Usually Michael deciphered it for me. Okay. Up and down volume; down. VCR off. I switched to a news channel. We didn't get a paper and I rarely had control of the television so had lost track of the world. Maybe it was just as well. China had set off a nuclear weapon. I found the off button on the remote and trundled Michael down the hall to undress and get into bed.

The next morning, Dean Williams passed me on a campus sidewalk. He stopped. "How're your classes?" They went well, I told him. "That's what I hear. We probably need to talk about next semester soon. Come see me."

I wanted to continue. I did. But the part-time pay was worse than I made in D.C.

I needed a master's degree. So while I agreed to the new semester's schedule, research came next. The state college in town offered a master's in education. I didn't want a master's in education. If I had to put time and money into a degree, I wanted to work on my writing. But to do that, I'd have to drive at least an hour into Alabama and possibly two. Jane wrote and said she had a full-time opening at the ESL school. My apartment in D.C. a ten-minute walk away. Hans, who had sublet my apartment, wrote. He'd left his job with the German station and might be leaving. Once again, I foundered in a pool of unknowing. Just when things had begun to make sense.

An armful of books from the library gave me Rilke and Thomas Moore and Carl Jung. I wrote notes, tried to figure out why and where I might be headed. I drove Michael to school, taught, picked him up, came home, fixed dinner. Nathan was glum with Kyong gone. I couldn't do much for him, but did my best to keep Michael occupied and entertained: Chuck E. Cheese, movies, bike rides, and trips to the museum. One afternoon, with no classes and Michael in school, I drove to Auburn, an hour each way, to visit the campus. It had the degree programs I wanted but it was too big. Not mine. I drove home no more settled. I remembered what Saki said, what Monique said . . . faith is the gift of spirit unfolding. How could I keep my soul attached to unfolding when everything felt knotted up?

At my desk, I stared at the photos on the shelf. I didn't know who I was anymore. Not the woman from the Bill years. I was her for a long time, twelve years, more or less, but now I didn't know who I was—except scared. Even the Hawaii woman in the garden seemed alien, a persona passed through and gone. The one I felt was the little girl sitting slumped, half-grinning, legs crossed at the ankle, on a piano bench between her sisters, Judy and Jeanne. I picked up the picture to get a closer look at that little girl. Michael's face looked back at me. He looked like me at that age! Imagine that. If I was no longer a beautiful woman, what was I? Beauty had bound my life and stripping away that illusion left me vulnerable. Now I looked like any other slightly dumpy, youngish grandmother with short hair. When I studied the Georgia folk and saw them going to work and coming home, taking care of kids and lawn and dog and shopping at Walmart, I'd think maybe I made too much of life . . . maybe I watched too much for tides and omens and wisps across the moon. Maybe it all came down to going to work and coming home and taking care of kids and dogs. Why think it should be different for me?

TWENTY-THREE

WATER AND FIRE

Jeanne phoned and we visited in a long, meandering conversation. Life was as crazy for her as it was for me; we missed each other. The craziness had nothing to do with living in Georgia or even Hawaii where enlightenment reigned. Cynthia phoned with much the same message: Austin was not immune. So there we were, boggling along, things curiouser and curiouser, as Alice said.

The pronunciation class began. Now I was teaching four days a week. I wrote and received a copious number of letters, many with Kalani friends who'd also moved on and mourned the life we'd left. Marion sent photos of her baby boy; I sent her photos of Michael. Bari was in Washington State but thinking of moving to another Pacific island. Bill wrote. He'd frantically flown to D.C. to look for Weezer, had walked the alleys for hours, whistling and calling, until Weezer made her entrance, garbling, fussing, dirty, and complaining.

I expect he sat down in the middle of the road and pulled her onto his lap. He didn't say that but he probably did.

My friend Ralph, who'd been my astrologer since New York days, compiled a cartography map and mailed it to me. My most desirable places to live, it showed, were either west of Brisbane, Australia; the center of Mongolia; or the high desert south from Denver. A stern Saturn line ran through Columbus, Georgia, a least desirable place for me, filled with family challenges, illnesses, responsibilities, and "other inhibitions." Do tell. The challenge was not to feel like a martyr, obviously something I needed to work on.

Michael and I formed a clear bond as he blossomed. His vocabulary increased, he brought home boy treasurers, mostly rocks and dirt on his pants legs, and walked around singing.

November became chaotic. My ex-mother-in-law, Mary, Nathan's grandmother, whom I'd loved, died, and Nathan and Michael flew to Nebraska for the funeral and a family reunion. I taught during the day and spent nights at the bar, keeping track of things. Nathan returned to customer complaints of my rudeness. I could barely tolerate them when rested and in good form, my temper not much different than when I was three years old except it was too much trouble to get down on the floor and kick my heels. And nobody threw cups of cold water on me, though they may have wanted to. I placated Nathan with home-cooked meals. Hans phoned to say he was returning to Germany and gave a month's notice. I contacted the apartment manager and gave her notice for the end of December. I'd figure out how to get up there once the semester ended. With a week off before Thanksgiving, I drove to Savannah for three days. I had to get away.

Savannah was romantic with Spanish moss hanging from old wide-spreading-oaks, big old houses, trellises, columns, ironwork balconies. It reminded me of New Orleans. I wandered, explored crannies, talked with people. One, the owner of an antiques store, a socialist-phrase-spouting self-taught non-conformist, showed me a newspaper article, complete with photo of him out front of the shop, repairing the sidewalk in his fight against the powers that be. Central City, in particular, was going to hell in a handbasket. This after I'd asked, "Is Savannah a good place to live?"

As I was leaving, he walked me to the door. I smelled a sudden familiar smell. "Does Savannah have chemical plants?" Ah, my yes, six or seven down along the river, paper mills. Oh. A chemical plant southeast of Columbus wafted noxious smells when the winds changed. So I drove on to Tybee Island, east of Savannah on the Atlantic. For a weekend, I had ocean. And sky. An eclipse was coming and the tides high. The winds strong. I walked on the beach, ears wrapped by a thick muffler, sat to watch the surf, and washed away my angst. I returned home in a much more pleasant mood.

Late December, I prepared for Winter Solstice, bought and lit candles, prayed for peace. I wasn't tired or even sad. Melancholy perhaps. The image of me going to D.C. at the end of December bloomed in my head like scenes from *Blade Runner*. Hans phoned. He'd decided to stay through December and two cameramen would then sublet my apartment through May. I contacted the apartment manager and canceled my notice for the end of December. Rent paid for another few months brightened the semester break. I baked. Nathan perked up when he smelled chocolate chip cookies. Michael and I put up a little tree and decorated. We shopped. Wrapped presents. Kyong phoned from Korea. We talked to Stephen. Nathan and Michael went to the movies and gave me a quiet and slow afternoon.

When I wasn't occupied with Michael or bartending or fixing a meal, I read and wrote, dabbling away at a manuscript of my life in Mexico. Car dreams of driving, not knowing where I was going, kept my nights busy. Nathan and Michael slept late. I read and wrote, regurgitating old stuff, old stories.

I was boring, my life was boring. "Michael. You want to go bowling?" Of course he did. When all else fails, play with a kid. We played the rest of the Christmas school break, and life lightened up. Nathan was even happier. I baked banana bread. And runzas from the recipe my ex-mother-in-law had taught me. "I smell runzas!" Nathan said when he walked in. He laughed in the same way he'd laughed as a ten-year-old, coming in the door and smelling Mom-food.

The books traveled back to the library. We checked out funny movies. We became bear and cubs, tucked in whenever possible. I had mornings; I had space; I had quiet. Sometimes I slept and sometimes tea and a book propelled me to write conversations with myself. On New Year's Eve afternoon, I cooked split pea soup, my concession to the New Year's tradition of black-eyed peas for luck.

Michael and Nathan resumed their lives, and I had a down week before classes.

Reworking my personal mythology, which I had first worked before Hawaii, helped me look at this transition, as did rereading Joseph Campbell and Carl Jung. Was Jung's individuation about peeling away layers evolving? A professional peeler—sounded like kitchen help. Or a stripper. Well. Perhaps my sense of humor was reviving.

I was trying to figure out something. I just didn't know what.

Now I kept two daily notebooks with different-colored covers, one for exploring my own mythology and what it meant, and one for dreams, passages from books, astrology. The mythology exercises squirmed me in recognition and amused me with discovery. Right brain/left brain or maybe the same brain on different channels. Except the channels fed each other. What I learned in one, I saw in the other. The pen scratched, wasn't right, switch pens, the paper slid, my arm burned, shoulder ached, keep writing, fingers cramped, do your practice. Writing is your practice, pray in it every day. And like a greased lock, my mind opened soundlessly.

Time after time you've tried to see where something would lead and it's to the same spot, or a spot like all the other spots, a crossroad, a turning, a new life. Is that what the traveling and doing has been about—to know myself? Old woman, have I frittered away time or have I used it for the highest good?

The good is served by being true to your nature.

My nature seemed to be a seeker, but I wasn't sure anymore what I sought. Love? A home? My family loved me. I had more "homes" than I could keep track of if you counted Hawaii.

In personal mythology, I wrote about rage. I had to see and I had to understand in order to release it. "Rage is the result of ghosts not laid properly to rest," wrote Clarissa Pinkola Estés. Maybe the rage ghosts grew from my father's death, but hadn't I released them? And what about lying on the floor and kicking my heels as a toddler?

My nights filled with dreams of struggling with a car that wouldn't go as fast as I wanted. Or wouldn't go at all.

Mystery lived inside my struggle, and I did not have its name. I kept thinking that finding its name would give me power over it. All the old stories promised when you had someone or something's name, you had its power. How could I name something I didn't understand?

Quiet mornings allowed me time to peel at layers.

The new semester began, so I closed the books, left to teach, picked up Michael from school, laughed at his stories on the good days, helped with homework on the less good days, and worked at the bar while Nathan had time with his son. Many of the men who frequented Kings Club for after-work beers and a game of darts wore long ponytails, tied at the neckline, the epitome of long hair not covering red necks. Country music the only music on the jukebox.

One morning I wrote, "Is moving the only way to progress? Can one progress standing still?"

That brought me to a full stop. I stared at the wall as memory catapulted me to Willy's studio. Willy moved all the time, dancing, talking, thinking, telling stories, but in front of a canvas he stopped. I'd asked him how he did that, stand and look at the canvas, and he said, "I give myself a break. I'm looking at what I'm looking at and everything else goes away." In the Kalani garden, I'd looked at a tiny emerald grasshopper and everything else faded away. If I could stand still, would whatever needed to find me come?

The phone rang. "Mom," Nathan said, "are you teaching today?" I was. "Can you take care of Michael this evening? Beth said she'd come so you don't have to do the bar. Just do Michael. I have to go up to Atlanta. Some fool sat on the pool table and broke off a corner leg and the company that installed it said they'd have to ship the leg down and it'll take three days. What a bunch of crap. I'll get it myself. It's Friday. Go to a movie or something."

"Okay."

"Thanks, Mom. I'll see you about eleven."

So much for standing still. Maybe eye of the storm was more appropriate.

That afternoon when I picked up Michael, I said, "Dad had to drive to Atlanta. What do you want to do?"

"Chuck E. Cheese!" he said, with the sparkle of left-over Christmas in his eyes. "And watch *Nightmare before Christmas!*"

"But we saw it last night."

"Yeah," he said. "But I want to see it again."

So off to the dinging bells of Chuck E. Cheese where we played games and ate pizza and came home and put in the movie and ate popcorn. A good balanced meal if ever there was one. I hated scary movies but Tim Burton was okay. We laughed. We were both in bed by the time Nathan came home, although I was awake and reading, book propped on my knees. Since my light was on, he knocked at the door and stuck his head in. "Michael okay?"

"Yeah. We did Chuck E. Cheese and watched *Nightmare before Christmas*. Again."

Nathan grinned. "He asleep?" I nodded. Nathan's eyes looked tired. "I got the leg on. Beth's closing. I'm headed for bed."

"Rest well. I'm proud of you, you know," I said. He grunted and closed the door.

TWENTY-FOUR

OH ... THAT ...

February arrived sullen and gray, the light washed out. My feet were cold. When I picked up Michael, his cheeks were flushed.

"My throat hurts," he said.

With those three words, Flu King reigned. Nathan and I took turns nursing Michael. My throat constricted in soreness. I continued teaching. Michael got well and went to school. I remained sick but functioning. Michael became sick again, really sick, his eyes swollen, his cough deep. Nathan wrapped him in a blanket and drove to emergency care. I got well for a couple of days and then sick again. Really sick. I canceled classes. Nathan got sick. Coughing echoed through the house. I dragged myself to the kitchen, fixed Jell-O, dragged myself to Michael's room, spoon-fed him, returned to bed. Nathan dragged himself to the kitchen, fixed soup, fed Michael, set a bowl on my bedside table. In the middle of fever, I decided to leave Columbus and stop looking for miracles. I'd return to D.C.

A day dawned soft and fuzzy. My throat didn't hurt. No coughing rang through the house. A clinging fog bound close around the windows. I could smell it—raw cold like vacant rooms. I dressed warmly and walked outside. Gray fog curled around my legs, shifting. Monsters could hide in such a fog, fanged monsters with three-pronged staring eyes, and I wouldn't know. It slid over the roof, restless, seeking a toe-hold. I found Nathan in the kitchen, heating a skillet. "It's foggy. How you feeling?" He grunted. "Michael okay?" He grunted. I heard the sound of water in the bathroom shower. It seemed we'd survived. Even with monsters in the bushes. The sun peered through to lift forgotten fog-shreds. We ate scrambled eggs and toast and watched a movie.

The two weeks of sickness left me feeling raw and vulnerable. Vulnerability like a fog, no shape, amorphous. No edges, no boundaries. Nothing to see. I remembered Ben lifting the shell off my back. That kind of vulnerable. A childhood memory unrolled: sitting in my father's car on the afternoon of his funeral, my hands gripping the steering wheel, pulling myself higher to see out the windshield. Grief like ice in my heart. How could I possibly live from my heart? How could I let someone inside my fears and longings? Did I allow Bill inside? Why didn't I see rescuing the boy in his novel, rescuing himself, was his necessary task? How could he possibly rescue me? Did I really need to pull away these layers...to find what? God? God at the center of me? Was there a center of me? I was so tired of thinking and plotting and figuring things out. There was no perfect me. Sort of like there's no place like home. Or you can't go home again.

If home was where I was, then I had to make peace. I put away the work on personal mythology and returned Jung and Newman and Mercea Eliade to the library. Even the tape recorder I used when half-asleep to record dreams was weary and went to the factory for renewal. Outside, with the March sun warm on my skin, I wondered if I'd ever be the writer I wanted to be. Sidetracked by fantasies, I daydreamed of being on the farm. Maybe for summers. In an old trailer. It couldn't be that expensive.

Mother phoned. She was home from Hawaii. She said she had a weeping eye and had to have it checked. "But Mother, we weep all the time!" I said. "It's what we do." We laughed. "But this is different," she said, "It's...oh, what is it called? What was it Mary had in having Jesus?"

"An immaculate conception?"

"Yeah. That's it. I have to remember that, when I can remember that, before I can say macular degeneration."

I absolutely howled.

When we got off the phone, I sat in a kitchen chair and stared at the phone. I could hear my mother's wit and felt a grin, tugging like a lost reminder, at the corners of my mouth. My sense of humor had derailed. Oh, I'd laughed at Michael's stories and laughed at Nathan's tease, but laughter and a sense of humor were different. With a sense of humor, you could get through anything. I'd allowed this time to shape and weave layers of frustration so invisibly dense that somehow, in all this finding my way, I'd misplaced myself.

Something had broken free and instead of ruminating, I began seeing: redbuds bloomed, azaleas, white pear trees, yellow forsythia. Michael came home to tell me a boy teased a girl and he told the boy to be nice and a girl needed help adding and he helped. We dug out his baseball glove and I pitched in the backyard. He'd outgrown the pee-wee league and joined the junior somethings, a six- and seven-year-olds league, and wore his blue shirt and blue cap with the M. "M's for Michael," I said as we walked to the schoolyard for team practice. "No, Grams. It's my team," he explained in little boy seriousness.

A review for an author I followed, Natalie Goldberg, showed up in the Atlanta paper, so I walked to the library for an interlibrary loan. The librarian and I had talked books for weeks. He'd come from Atlanta, and we'd commiserated on our current living environment.

"Just finished reading it," he said. "It's in my desk drawer. You can borrow it."

I took it home, and reached a section on how she'd traveled across the country to St. John's College in Santa Fe. My heart woke in a tickle, and I heard *bing* ever so soft as if a tiny angel sat on my shoulder. I kept reading. St. John's program was an education in the classics. Even with an undergraduate degree, I was largely self-taught, although somewhat erratically. But the foundation of western civilization might tie all my reading and searching into some semblance of... well, something. Stability?

Well, get up and call. If you don't call now you'll forget! So commanded the voice.

"Okay! Okay!" I stuck a pencil between pages to keep my place and looked up the number.

"Graduate Department. This is Susan," a lighthearted voice said.

"Uh. Hi. I'm Janet Sunderland. I was reading a book by Natalie Goldberg. She wrote about attending St. John's College."

"Oh, yes," Susan said.

"I've been looking for a graduate program. Could you tell me about St. John's?" That sounded pretty lame, but Susan explained the program, the history of the school, it's beginning in Annapolis in the 1700s, the sister campus now in Santa Fe, the graduate degree four semesters long. She said, "Do you happen to teach college?"

"I teach remedial writing."

"Well, a funny thing just happened. We received a huge grant for college teachers to come here for the summer. Why don't you apply? Maybe God's telling you to come."

There it was again: "a funny thing just happened."

"I teach in a community college. Does that count?"

"Yes, I think so. Give me your address. I'll send an application."

We visited. She'd always wanted to visit Hawaii. We both had sons. I said I'd been looking at maps and wondering what could take me to the mountains south of Denver. We laughed.

By the time I was off the phone, I felt high on possibility. I loved being with my family and loved being Michael's grandma, but I couldn't see a future in Georgia.

Reality crashed: leaving D.C., leaving friends, leaving my apartment, starting over.

The application arrived and I filled it out, put it in the mail, and sent a check to K-State requesting they send transcripts to St. John's. I said nothing to Nathan or Michael. There would be time if accepted, and if a grant came through. Fear crawled over my shoulders at the thought of driving a U-Haul truck by myself out of D.C. and across the country.

That night, startled awake by the feel of a body pressed against mine, I patted the bed to see if Michael had crawled in. I stared at the still-dark ceiling, rewinding a convoluted dream: traveling in a big elevator car sideways. I'd shifted to the back, didn't want to be the first out, didn't know where to go. Others surged ahead and onto a bus. I walked. Multicolored baskets in Native American designs hung from trees. My path led along the edge of a hill banking sharply. I struggled for balance and a strong hand grabbed me, balanced me, and held me safe.

Dreams drew me into a future I longed for, wanted to believe, and mistrusted. But all of me longed for this desert I'd never seen. With or without St. John's.

I PHONED MY BROTHER, JACK. "DO YOU HAVE DAD'S OLD PONTIAC?"

"Yeah. Got a for sale sign on it."

"Well, take it off. I need a car. I'm moving to Santa Fe."

That single step, having a car, solidified my decision. At the library, I researched St. John's and Santa Fe and found other colleges: College of Santa Fe and Santa Fe Community College. Maybe I could work at one of them. I was so done with bartending and the excesses I fell into: swearing, drinking, smoking. I'd gotten better at avoiding flat-out anger, at least outwardly, other than drinking and smoking and cursing.

Songbirds migrated northward, and one morning I heard a robin, a Kansas robin, heading home. I needed to tell Cynthia I was moving to Santa Fe. When? Soon. Why? I told her the story of the Natalie Goldberg book and the dream, the phone call, the application. "I haven't heard whether I'm accepted, but I'm going."

She was quiet on the other end of the line.

"The message was right," she said into our silence. She laughed. "And you would have forgotten if you hadn't called. Santa Fe feels like a yes."

Cracks, like light shifting through tangles, appeared in several of my students' papers. One student said he wasn't afraid of writing anymore. An older man told me he'd taken the course twice before but finally learned how to make a sentence. He began to write beautiful and philosophical papers. He had a voice. That's why I had problems with the Mexico book I was writing, had been writing, for years! I had no idea what it wanted to say. I could teach "topic" but I hadn't done a topic. I'd written living in Mexico.

Reading and writing and acting grew from roots on the prairie, but the only real study I'd been consistent with seemed to be pinning myself on a wall and examining the carcass. Perhaps if my life had led me to being a scientist, I'd have found a road with enough twists, bends, hills, switchbacks, and rocks to keep me interested. As it was, my subject was me.

Kyong came home from Korea. The acceptance arrived from St. John's with a grant for the summer semester. I told Nathan I would leave the third week of May. Michael was so happy to have Mommy home, my leaving drew no tears. Same with Nate. I packed, graded papers, turned in grades. My brother was meeting me in D.C. with his truck. We'd drive to Kansas and pick up Dad's Pontiac. I phoned Mom to tell her I was moving to Santa Fe and asked if she wanted to come along. Ever ready for an adventure, she said yes.

Nathan and Michael drove me to the Atlanta train with my boxes and bicycle and suitcases. Willy picked me up in D.C. This time, I allowed him to help me get everything upstairs. The Germans, who'd taken over the apartment from Hans, had left.

Everything except kitchen stuff was already in boxes stacked in the closet. The grocery store next door to the apartment building made procuring boxes for the kitchen easy. Jack arrived. We cleared out the apartment, cleaned, and loaded the truck.

One last time, I stood alone at the wide windows and said goodbye to Washington, D.C. Closing the door and locking it, I patted the outside of the door once, took the elevator back down, and handed my set of keys to the desk clerk.

Moving with my brother was a wonderful thing. Packed boxes filled every nook and cranny in the U-Haul trailer, and in late afternoon, we drove west. As dusk slid into evening, about a hundred miles out, we discovered the headlights were hitting mid-treetop level. Too much weight at the trailer's front had tilted the truck up to run on its back legs, so to speak. We pulled off at a handy truck stop and parked. "Well," Jack drawled, "there's food here and bathrooms. I guess this is where we stop." We'd packed a couple of pillows and light blankets in the back seat, so after our truck-stop dinner, we curled into separate corners and slept.

The first rays of sun stabbed me awake. I stretched carefully and shook Jack's shoulder. "That was remarkably uncomfortable," Jack said, and pried himself out from under the steering wheel to open his side door. "Yup," I said, tossing his pillow and blanket into the back seat. "Let's get coffee and breakfast."

One of the best things about truck stops, besides great biscuits and gravy, is the accommodating bathrooms. We cleaned up and ate. Jack brought the thermos in. After refilling it, we went out to survey our work. "I guess we'll need to pull out about half the boxes," Jack said. I nodded. We began pulling out and stacking boxes behind us, reloaded and rebalanced, and with each few boxes, reexamined the hitch to make sure it wasn't complaining.

Jack drove. The landscape was beautiful, trees green, but I was weary. Pulling a pillow from the backseat, I dozed and woke to signs for Pittsburgh. "Jack! Where are we?" He'd missed the fork where I70 and I76 divide while his navigator, me, slept, and we were on an unexpected detour.

We discussed alternatives. There weren't any good ones, so we turned around to find I70. I stayed awake, but east of St. Louis, the truck coughed. Coasting toward an exit, we stopped. "We're out of gas," Jack said. We stared at each other and burst out laughing. Jack pulled out the gas can, completely empty, and took off walking. At the top of the exit, a car picked him up. Fifteen minutes later, clouds rolled in, lightning and thunder combined in a sudden crash, and a Midwestern downpour began. I figured he'd wait it out at the gas station and opened my book, but when I glanced up, there he was, striding down the exit through the rain, his Stetson as umbrella.

"I thought you'd wait it out," I said as he crawled into the truck's cab. "Well," he drawled, "I was already on the overpass when the rain started so I thought I'd come on. What worried me was that I was the tallest thing up there and I had a gas can in my hand. I'll wait till the storm passes to fill the tank."

Finally reaching Topeka, we picked up Old Blue, as I came to call Dad's car. It had to have a name beyond "Dad's car," although names rarely change easily. Early the next morning, Jack drove on toward Santa Fe, and I drove up for Mom. "Hi, there," she said and patted the hood of the car as I got out. She looked up, a smile lighting her face. "It's good to see Dad's car. You too, Janet."

And then it was Mom and me in the Pontiac and Jack in the truck. Mom told stories and fell asleep, her head propped on a pillow against the window. We caught up with Jack in Elkton, Kansas, and drove west. Nothing quite as beautiful to this Kansas girl's eyes as acres and acres of rippling wheat fields, not quite gold but turning.

I'd reserved rooms at the Super 8 in Santa Fe. It was a long drive. We arrived sometime near midnight and parked side by side in the rear parking lot. The next day we began the apartment search over two fruitless days. "I've gotta get back soon," Jack said a couple of times. Where to leave the boxes and if I stored them how would I move them? "Can you give me one more day?" I said to Jack at dinner on the second evening. He nodded. Somewhat reluctantly, but he agreed. The next morning as I read the newspaper over breakfast, I found a small ad for a small adobe in the country. $500 a month.

"Jack! Look at this." Jack took the paper, read the ad, and grinned. "Think you might've been saved again," he said.

Leaving the loaded truck in the parking lot, we drove out to look at the adobe. Fate or Angels or the Kindness of the Universe once more intervened with a six-hundred-square-foot old adobe, a kiva fireplace in one corner, a paving stone patio bigger than the house, surrounded by a low adobe wall. Perfect. Seton Village. I noticed an old and rambling adobe on the hill above. We dashed into town, signed papers, drove out with the truck, unloaded, set up the futon couch/bed and placed my drop leaf table from New York days under the east casement window, my bookcase against the wall, and piled boxes in the middle of the room. We slept one last night at the motel, and Mom and Jack left the next morning.

TWENTY-FIVE

UNPACKING HISTORY

Old Blue drove me out to Seton Village to park on the gravel drive in front of 3 Seton Castle Trail. My shoulders relaxed as I stared at my new home. A woman walked to my car window. "Hi. I'm Susan from across the road." She tipped her chin toward the house behind us, half-hidden by piñon trees. "Welcome to Seton Village. Want to stop and have a cup of coffee?"

Tempting, but I shook my head. "Let me unpack some, and I'll see where I am," I said. "As soon as I can stop, I'll come over." No time for stopping, hardly even slowing down. Shuffling boxes to find bedding, I made up the futon. I had a bed, a table, a bookcase Stephen had built in D.C. with space for my even older television. I set up the Smith Corona on the drop leaf table and plugged it in. The table wobbled on the uneven wooden floor. Well practiced with wobbly tables, I cut squares of cardboard and shoved them under the legs. The box of dishes went to the kitchen, down three steps.

The house had two entrances: one windowed door led into the upper living space, and the other, also windowed and catty-corner on its left, led down steps into the kitchen: a two-room adobe split level on a down-sloping hill with white-washed interior walls. As I set the box of dishes on the counter, I realized all the kitchen stuff could have come in that kitchen door. Ah, well. Moving in. The kitchen, thankfully, came equipped with a Formica-topped table below a north-facing window, and a double sink with cabinets beneath a long window with a view of the western range of mountains. An apartment-sized gas range sat at one end of the sink, a water heater at the other. A closet and a bathroom with a shower completed the downstairs room. I unpacked towels and hung two in the bathroom. No idea where to store the rest of them as yet.

The next morning, a trip to St. John's registered me firmly into graduate school. Classes would begin Monday. I bought books and scanned syllabi. No time for a trip down to the fabled Santa Fe Plaza;

from the schedule, it looked like I'd have little time for anything. Over eight weeks, I'd attend two evening seminars, four morning tutorials, and two afternoon preceptorials. Weekly. And do a lot of reading. The fall and spring semesters were each sixteen weeks.

I'd learned the classes were small, but I was surprised at how small. Ten of us gathered at a long and oval wooden table with Tom Simpson, my first tutor. I'd signed up for the history semester, thinking history might be a useful foundation, the tutorial a history of thought: St. Augustine, Vico, Hegel; the seminar, ancient historians: Herodotus, Thucydides; the preceptorial: Shakespeare. At least I had familiarity with Shakespeare, although how the Socratic method might work with something written for the stage lay beyond my understanding.

Mr. Simpson asked the opening question and a conversation began. I'd read the assignment. Read it three times, the syllabus said. Three times? Like, when? I could talk about books. But my presumption frayed as I realized not only were we talking, we were pointing out specific passages to support our ideas. That week, I read, made many notations on page margins, and continued unpacking. Other than at class, I didn't talk. Even in class, I didn't say much. Once, I made it to neighbor Susan's for coffee, my one casual conversation in a week.

Opening boxes unearthed memories since before New York when boxes from Austin moved to my folk's. I'd picked up one or two boxes each time I visited and carted them to New York. Those went into storage during the Mexico years. After Mexico, Bill and I rescued them, along with his, when we rented the apartment off DuPont Circle. Some were opened, some stayed closed and stacked in a closet. When we separated, we separated boxes, mine stacked in the long coat closet in my studio apartment-in-the-sky. Still taped shut. Now with me. Who was this woman, unpacked from boxes, contents spilling out on the floor, piling up in corners, whispering?

An entire box contained books on the Great Mother/Divine Feminine, some from the early 70s, some from D.C. bookstores: Joseph Campbell, and Robert Graves, C. G. Jung, and some less well known: *The Hebrew Goddess; The Great Cosmic Mother; Gods, Goddesses, and Images of God in Ancient Israel;* a copy of *Prolegomena to the Study of Greek Religion.* When or where in the world did I buy that? It might come in handy as I studied at St. John's.

Years of journals and unfinished manuscripts erupted from another box. Sheaves of poems collected under a paper clip so long the clip had marred all the pages. Stacks of headshots all the way back to when I lived in Germany. Germany! How that face loved a camera. How could I possibly understand the history of western civilization when I couldn't understand my own span of years?

I arranged books on the Stephen-built bookshelf/television stand, repacked boxes of photos, mementos, pieces from Mexico. The papier-mâché Mexican dragon that had guarded my D.C. apartment was liberated to guard my adobe. The soft gauze skirts from Mexico and the muumuus from Hawaii hung in the closet to add to what might become my Santa Fe style. One small box, a sturdy, white plastic box, held the fragile Magic Forest, each piece carefully wrapped in tissues, white low-fire clay from my college pottery class and hand spun into a tree, a dancing queen, a king, and a dragon. I repacked them, settled the white box in a bigger box, and stored the refilled boxes, along with a roll of paintings with no space to hang, including one by Willy and one by the Spanish artist, Gonzalo Torné, who'd once stayed with us in New York as he'd made the rounds of galleries, above the small closet where a deep cubbyhole held my past. I kept one out: a framed lithograph of Raphael Soyer's *Mother and Child*, propped against the wall on top of the bookcase.

My birthday inched close. I'd spent most of the last year dreading its coming, jockeying with what aging meant or didn't and what I was doing with my life anyway.

A graduate program tour for Tsankawi, Anasazi ruins in Bandolier, was scheduled for Saturday, my birthday. I signed up. As we drove north out of Santa Fe, the van driver kept up a stream of information. Tsankawi was built by ancient Pueblo Indians in the early 1400s, although archaeologists said Pueblo Indians settled in the area around 1100. In Tewa, the Pueblo language, *tsankawi* meant "village between two canyons at the clump of sharp, round cacti." Kansas farmer to the core, notwithstanding my years elsewhere, landmarks made sense. We'd been encouraged to bring hats. The driver passed around sunscreen. "There aren't any buildings, there's caves, so as you're walking, watch out for snakes." The sunscreen bottle passed to me. "If you get all the way up, you'll have a great view. The trail's about a mile and a half. Be careful. There's places where it's worn right down into the rock." And what should we do if we come upon a snake in a deep down worn track? Likely back up slow. Snakes aren't a problem unless you scare them. Sort of like people. I'd once wandered onto a den of rattlesnakes in a farm pasture where limestone cliffs made a perfect den, but it was in early spring, the snakes yet groggy, and I wandered slow. And backed out slow.

"Most of the people went barefoot, but I wouldn't recommend it," the driver said.

We hiked in hot, crystalline air, glad to have the water bottles the driver handed out. At the top of the mesa, I walked to cliff's edge, stared at the sheer, facing cliff wall. Tears, unchecked, rivered down my face. and I breathed a prayer of thanks.

This barren landscape had called me in a voice I didn't know, hadn't expected, and couldn't name. My soft chant followed the tears... *hello, I've come... thank you for calling me.* Behind me, a row of cave openings faced the valley. I sat in the shade of a cave mouth on a natural sitting-place stone ledge and gazed over the valley. Tears streaked my face.

Without warning, the first laugh I'd had since moving to Santa Fe burst out.

Centuries past, someone had carved a sitting place that now served me. And I worried about reaching fifty?

A pair of swallows darted and swooped in an updraft. One peeled away, dashed past my head into the cave, darted to a crack. I had disturbed nothing. Satisfied, it swooped out again, its wings fanning the scent of cold... dark... age.

That evening, in my little adobe, laughter and fiddle playing in the big house floated down the red, gravely hill. Cactus dotted the landscape between us. The neighbors had a party, celebrating my birthday unknowingly, and the sky blushed a deep red-orange like a thousand candles along the horizon.

The mail brought a hand-drawn birthday card from Michael, and a birthday card and package from my big sister Judy. Inside the card, a check with a handwritten order to use it exclusively for fun; inside the package, a pen to click and change the ink from red to green to blue and black, which I picked up several times to make a note and then became so engrossed in choosing colors, I forgot what I meant to write.

I read the Peloponnesian wars between Sparta and Athens.

Monday through Friday, I read, wrote, exercised, attended classes, read, wrote, and slept. I inserted eating into the schedule, but sporadic and hardly timely. The grant gave me enough money for tuition, living expenses, and supplies.

Weekends, part of the time I studied and read and sometimes I played. At the Taos Powwow, a three-year-old boy danced instinctively beside his powerful warrior father, oblivious to the crowd or whether others saw or approved or even if his father approved. He danced. A young Lakota woman from Denver floated like cottonseed over rough and dusty earth, her face glowing. I wanted to be like her. Confident enough it wouldn't faze me what people thought or said.

Susan and Jeff, the couple across the road, invited me to a party, and I acquainted myself with neighbors who filled me in on Seton Village, built by Ernest Thompson Seton. He'd built the house above me on the hill for himself, a rambling many-roomed abode. His daughter and her husband now lived there. The neighbors called it the Castle. Maybe that's what Seaton named it. He built houses around an open grass space on the other side of the main road as workers' quarters, hence, the Village, added to and expanded over the years into roomy homes. Maybe he'd built my little adobe, too, and everyone just left it alone.

My open casement window filled with the sounds of chirping bugs, bird calls—no sirens, no traffic. The days hot and we waited for rain. Clouds formed in the late afternoon, thundered, but rain played in the mountains, not the desert. I had class on Monday, July 4, so missed the annual Seton Village fireworks, but driving home, the sky sparkled in all directions. The people I met kind and generous: a stranger stopped to help change a tire; at no charge, a mechanic welded the new exhaust pipe that had come apart. Waiters at the Old Santa Fe Trail Coffeehouse served unending coffee when I tucked away reading. One afternoon, a conversation of tumbleweeds gathered to welcome me home at the kitchen door.

Most evenings, when I wasn't in class, I was at the new desk I'd built from two file cabinets, one stuffed with writing and old letters, the other empty for school files, topped by a 4x8 sheet of half-inch plywood I'd carted home in Old Blue's trunk, varnished, and set up in front of the west-facing window in the upper room. It didn't wobble. I read and wrote, watched the range of mountains across the valley, watched as clouds filled the horizon or a sunset bloomed. Finally, the heat reaching sultry point, an evening wall of rain walked from the mountains into the valley, crossed the road, ambled over the top of my adobe, dust strong in its breath as it thundered up the hill.

A news story said comets struck Jupiter in mega-ton blasts, rippling through the cosmos. That evening, most around the table had the same dark circles around their eyes as I did. Late that night, Cynthia and I talked. "How's it with you?" she said. I replied, "Jupiter!" and we whooped.

In class, we gelled as a group, discussions more orderly and considered, more comfortable with saying Mr. and Ms. followed by a person's last name as we addressed each other, formally. Early on, one of the tutors had said, "Our task as scholars is to be aware of various ways of thinking." I wrote it down.

Could anyone really understand how another thought? We could probe at what someone wrote, but could we really know thoughts? Communication such an iffy skill. Words had various flavors, the word "love," for example, could taste sweet or it could taste bitter.

I had no idea how I thought. Thoughts came to me. I'd blurt something in class, but no, no, that's wasn't it; it was this, the group agreed, and discussed, while I listened, unwinding sentences into some kind of sense until they came to the same idea I'd blurted too early.

Do nothing before its time.

I practiced learning to think.

The tutorial tutor asked me to come and talk to him. He thought me too abrupt, too threatening in my voice, and I seemed to be against organized religion. I listened, didn't explain my years of fighting with Sunday school teachers when they said things like "God took your father." God didn't "take" my father; a heart attack had. Didn't tell the tutor about the preacher who had pulled me to him in the summer camp swimming pool and cupped my budding breasts in his hands. I didn't say St. Augustine had whored his way through early adulthood, but blamed women for his downfall. Redemption was a word without meaning when you blamed those whom you'd abused. Thus was Christianity led male-centric. I didn't say that female leadership in organized religion was stupendously lacking. It wasn't Christianity I was against, but the seemingly nearly universal need to keep women subjugated. But I talked less in that class, and when I did, asked a question. There was one Augustine line I had underlined in the book and written in my journal: *The past is all we know of the present.*

Mr. Simons, in history, encouraged me. "Take the theories presented and add to them," he said. "You can do that." I absorbed Hegel: his theory of human history as a spiral of spiritual evolution resonated in the deepest parts of me. While my own evolution did tend to spiral out of control from time to time, a deeper, surer part also resonated, even if I didn't have its name.

Every couple of weeks, I'd call home—home being where Kyong, Nathan, and Michael lived. Nate had left for a restaurant management school in Carolina. Kyong didn't know whether North or South, but she was alone with Michael. I talked to Michael, reminded him to be home before dark. "Dad's gone, so you have to be responsible."

Suddenly it was August. Classes ended with a final picnic for graduate students and oral finals and final papers, and time was mine again for three weeks. For a week, I drifted, head weary, dug in the sandy dirt, and walked the desert gathering stones to border my makeshift garden. My bicycle sat in its crate against the adobe wall, so I unearthed it, oiled the chain, but did not go for a ride. My nights filled with dreams and my days with empty-headed puttering, visits to art galleries, drives to explore New Mexico. The second week, I looked for work.

A fall grant would pay tuition, but not living expenses. I visited state agencies and applied, found the penitentiary and applied to teach, read want ads in the newspaper, and applied at the community college with my resume of teaching experience.

TWENTY-SIX

TEACHING AND LEARNING

A bruptly, life shifted. Santa Fe Community College offered a teaching position in remedial English. I said yes, drove over to sign a contract and attend orientation. Emboldened, I stopped at the College of Santa Fe, found the Dean of Theatre, and talked to him in the off chance there might be something. He took my proffered resume. "You're a professional actor?" I nodded. "You could teach speech, couldn't you?" I was game for anything. And suddenly, I had a morning speech class at College of Santa Fe followed by a twelve noon English class at Santa Fe Community College. Most fall classes at St. John's were in the evenings. I wouldn't have to teach at the penitentiary.

That kind of news had to be shared, so I drove up to St. John's to tell Andrea, manager of the bookstore, and the closest thing I had to a friend. She was pleased for me.

"Andrea, I need to find some kind of a regular spiritual community," I said. "I need a steady anchor."

"I've attended this odd Catholic but not Roman Catholic service at Loretto Chapel. It's called the Church of Antioch. Why don't we go together?"

Sunday morning, Andrea and I sat to one side in the chapel. Meditation music began. I twitched. My history with religion was complicated. My mother born Quaker, but once the family left Jewell County, following her father's railroad job, there were no Quaker communities. She'd raised us in small Christian churches. My father had never gone with us, and from the research I'd done into the Sunderland name, I figured he'd been more Celtic warrior than well-churched. Dad went after he and Mom married. Those were the years of arguing with preachers and Sunday school teachers. Over the years, when life turned chaotic, I'd god

BODY, MIND & SPIRIT / Generalgod

a Roman Catholic Church in which to sit and meditate, but

my politics, especially around women's rights, had kept me from conversion.

As the opening song at Loretto Chapel propelled us to stand, the procession, the robes, the incense looked Catholic. The priests with servers looked Catholic. But when the presiding bishop, tall, dark hair, graceful hands, began the opening blessing and intoned, "In the name of God, Father and Mother, Son and Spirit," my mouth fell open. Literally. My last membership in any church had been St. Ignatius in New York, High Anglican with "smells and bells," as they say, and while a statue of Mary was prominent, we sure hadn't had Mother God. In Mexico City, I'd once visited an Episcopal Church, but the parishioners were all diplomats and the service felt stilted. St. Matthew's, just off DuPont Circle in D.C., was a favorite spot to sit in meditation. And Hawaii was . . . well . . . Hawaii. Loretto Chapel felt welcoming and beautiful: white walls, an arched ceiling, sunlight streamed through windows. A statue of Mother Mary flanked one side of the altar; a statue of St. Joseph on the other. Maybe this Church of Antioch would fit all of me.

September began with a rush. Monday, I subbed for a teacher at the community college, and in the evening, entered the philosophy and theology semester at St. John's: a 5 p.m. tutorial and an 8 p.m. seminar. Tuesday, I taught my first speech class at College of Santa Fe and my first writing class at Santa Fe Community College. Wednesday, I subbed at SFCC again, and on Thursday, I taught classes and attended classes, and after the St. John's seminar, we had a party. I drank too much red wine and woke up the next morning with a hangover.

A very long semester lay ahead, especially if I kept going to parties. And drinking.

In the midst of being freaked about time and work and reading and classes, I attended Mass the following Sunday. I didn't have to do anything. I could simply be. Standing with others around the altar, we raised our hands as the priest raised his to bless the bread and wine. We gathered as equals in peace. When I left, the bishop, Father Richard, stuck out his hand. "You've been here before." I nodded. "Welcome back. We're having coffee in the room around the corner." He pointed down the hall linking Loretto Chapel to the hotel. "Why don't you join us?"

Following others who seemed acquainted, I walked to the room, picked up a cup of coffee, and positioned myself near a wall. The priest who'd presided that morning walked over. "Hi, I'm Cliff." We shook hands. "Janet." He asked why I was in Santa Fe and smiled when I said to study at St. John's. I'd noticed his shining white hair as he presided; now I noticed a wedding band. A married priest? Another woman came up and claimed Father Cliff's attention. I slid away and walked to the end of the table and put down my cup.

"What's your name?" Father Richard said behind me, and I turned. "Janet. Janet Sunderland."

"Here, I brought you some information about the church. Thought you might be interested." He handed me several pamphlets.

"Thanks. I'll get them read, but right now I need to go home and prepare for tomorrow's classes. I'm studying at St. John's."

"Ah, St. John's. You must be pretty smart."

I didn't know how smart I was, and I'd be less smart if I didn't get the reading done. I smiled and said goodbye.

"See you next week," he said.

I wrote to Mom. I felt ambivalent about church and didn't know how to think about God.

Her letter came in return, and after a wandering sentence on why she didn't like narrow writing paper because she didn't have room enough to complete a thought, she wrote, "I empathize with your dilemma. Make no mistake. God is not a theory. All of this earth, sun, moon, stars, planets, tides haven't just happened. They all had to be made by a mind that loved colors, as in a rainbow, yet variety as in flowers and trees, growth and shape as in pines and evergreens as opposed to deciduous trees, sunflowers as opposed to roses and lilies, violets, and dandelions. Nothing stable just happens. Love, Mother."

She might have fit in well at St. John's. Nothing stable just happens. In trees or in life.

The fall semester proceeded in philosophy and theology. Philosophy, one of my reading passions in years past, sometime after Dostoevsky and the Russian phase. Rereading Plato, I remembered how he resonated with my spirit and my mind. From Plato to Aristotle. Pages and pages that I read and reread. Prime Mover who moved. I imagined God, sitting on a big, black motorcycle in the sky, kick-starting the universe. I could say that to my mother—she'd laugh—but I couldn't say that in class. Someone would say, *No, no that's not it!* And it wasn't "it" but I had to believe something larger, deeper lived in us now and not just at the beginning of time. Whatever time was. Or was not.

My schedule had, once again, become routinized, as it had in Hawaii, in Georgia, even before. People always wondered how I did so much. "I keep busy," I said. Like a giant cane spider, I build my webs as far as they can go to see what gets caught.

A hummingbird pair hovered beside the cactus outside the casement window and feasted on cactus blossoms as I read Aristotle, searching for a point between confusion and clarity, the fulcrum point of one toe touching perplexity, the other a crack of light.

The hummingbirds hung mid-air.

Andrea said I had to attend the Burning of Zozobra, a Santa Fe fall tradition to burn away the gloom and worries of the past year. She did not say there'd be hundreds of other people singing and talking and drinking beer. When the fire leapt Zozobra's gauzy and papery white pants and forty-foot-tall wooden frame, a frenzy of howling and screaming and drum beating ricocheted across the throng. Streams of acrid smoke, swirled by sparks, flew heavenward. I could not imagine any God thinking this a propitious offering. But Andrea had driven and was enjoying herself, so when she shouted something that sounded like "isn't this great," I smiled and nodded. I'd smiled and nodded at incomprehensible words in Mexico too. From the spectacle of Zozobra, we drove to a party with several St. John's people. Faculty and staff. The conversation lofty. I smiled and nodded. Yet in the following weeks, the intuitive hits sluicing through my head calmed, and I found my brain thinking logically. Even Aristotle was making sense. In bits and pieces.

On a rare morning when Dame Time gently stretched an open portal, I walked into the desert and followed an arroyo. I'd chambered myself like a medieval scholar hunched at her desk for so long, the desert looked as alien as a moonscape. How many years would it take to dig these deep furrows in the rocky sand? Indian summer skies struck my eyes in enameled blue, the chamisa golden, the asters purple. I walked in a painting.

My life as a solitary pleased me. I wasn't battling anger anymore; I didn't feel like a failure. A Jean-Paul Sartre quote, taped to the wall in front of my desk, read: "Freedom is what you do with what's been done to you."

Several inches of snow fell in the mountains. Beautiful, but a warning: cold weather. I'd have to invest in boots. I sighed, thinking Hawaii. My muumuus would move to the back of the closet. Neighbor Jeff carried a pile of firewood from their place, and I built a fire, lay in front of it, propped on floor pillows, reading.

Pascal: "What completes our incapability of knowing things is the fact that they are simple, and that we are composed of opposite natures, different in kind, soul and body." "Man is to himself the most wonderful object in nature; for he cannot conceive what the body is, still less what the mind is, and least of all how a body should be united to a mind."

Pascal understood mystery. I wondered if he'd written this as an argument to Aristotle's logic, but if I wondered aloud in class, wandered, I guessed one could say, it was hard for others to hear me. And so, I remained a silent admirer.

Father Richard's weekly Wednesday evening healing service went onto my schedule. One evening, as he lay hands on me, I saw a flash of a strong wooden cross, and the following Sunday at Mass, it occurred to me I might study for the priesthood since the Church of Antioch ordained women. That brought me up short. I wasn't exactly priestly material.

Maybe study healing with Richard? Along with all my other reading for classes and reading for teaching, I bought Elaine Pagel's *The Gnostics*. *Gnosis:* to know. I'd spent enough time excavating self-knowledge to claim that tribe! Genesis and Plato and Elaine Pagel. What a combination.

Why this Abraham and Jacob and Noah and Sarah? They all had their flaws, and yet it was these people with whom God made a covenant. Was it because they listened? There was choice, and the choice could have gone either way, or could it? That was the part I didn't understand. Did I have a choice, or was I somehow compelled to do what I did? I had dreams. Were they compulsions? And then I remembered Mother's line: *nothing stable just happens.*

You had to choose to do the work.

I applied for a spring semester student loan and worried about the debt piling up for something as esoteric and possibly unmarketable as a St. John's education. I would earn a degree in thinkology like the Scarecrow. Well, it kept him in Oz. Maybe it would get me there too.

A week before Thanksgiving, Mom arrived. She was as adaptable in my little adobe as in my small Kalani room. While I was teaching, she visited with Susan, sometimes they shopped. Through Susan, Mom became acquainted with others in the Village. Susan and Jeff invited us to Thanksgiving dinner. I gave finals and graded papers, wrote St. John's papers. Sometimes Mom rested or read while I worked and sometimes she visited Susan. Sometimes we sat and watched television in the evenings after cooking dinner, and laughed and criticized story lines or the writing. Those were the best times. She went to church with me and liked Father Richard's sermon.

Two weeks later, I drove her to Albuquerque for her flight to my sister Judy's. Driving home from the airport, alone, shadows stretched long, and silence lay across the desert

Old Blue felt empty.

One more week of precept and tutorial. And grades to post and a dinner dance at St. John's and a holiday, end-of-semester potluck at SFCC. And then, four silent days before my sister Julia, brother-in-law John, and niece Raven arrived for Christmas. We drove to San Juan Pueblo to see the dances. My son Stephen drove down from Denver, and we all trooped out to Tent Rocks, white, windswept towers in the desert, to hike. Then there was Christmas Eve and *farolitos* on the plaza and along my little gravel driveway, the tiny candles inside brown paper bags flickering in the promise of light returning, and eating and laughing and shopping. We attended church. We cooked meals and wandered into the desert. Stephen left for Denver, and finally, there was New Year's Eve and packing and driving my sister and family to the Albuquerque airport on the first day of the New Year.

Leaving the airport, I turned south. Mexico pulled at deep currents in me, currents I did not understand, and I needed to smell ocean. Parking the car in an El Paso grocery store lot and checking to make sure all doors were locked, I walked to the bridge into Ciudad Juarez. Finding a place to get a visa on New Year's Day proved troublesome. I'd lived in Mexico and sent a courier to the border to stamp my papers; how could a visa be a problem? The Mexican generosity and kindness I remembered—and so missed when I left—appeared in a Mexican couple who joined me mid-bridge and translated while my fractured Spanish explained I needed a visa. The official took my passport, made some notations, and handed me a visa. Once across the bridge, I found the bus station and bought a bus ticket to Los Mochis, where I spent the next night after the bus broke down in the middle of the first night and I missed my connection. I found an ATM machine, figured out how to charge money on my Visa, and caught the next bus south. I couldn't get to the Pacific on the time I had, so I headed for Topolobampo, Sinaloa, on the bank of the Gulf of Cortez. Years ago I'd fallen in love with Mexico, an all-consuming love as with a new lover, exciting, unknown, mysterious, and with a complicated history.

I may have discovered the least desirable place in Mexico to spend a week. However, the hostel clean, the bed adequate, and a table sat next to a casement window that opened onto the sea. The table wobbled at one corner. Unused to people staying for more than one night, the kindly young desk clerk, when I asked if there was an electric pot and a cup, brought them along with a candle and set them on the table. I had a window, the sea, one book, my journal, my tea bags, my pen, and a folded up matchbook under one table leg to keep it steady. I unpacked.

Late afternoon, walking along the beach, I watched the waves soft in their nudge, and watched two fishermen clean and repair nets. One of the men worked in slow determination, but the other man's hands danced through the ropes. They didn't talk, they worked at the end of a good day or a bad day fishing; regardless, the nets needed care.

On the way back to my room, I passed a *tienda* and bought a notebook with a beautiful ballerina on the cover, stretching to reach her lifted toe. It would be my Topolobampo notebook, larger than my usual size but fewer pages, bought fruit, cheese, crackers, and a can of Carnation milk for my tea. I'd packed my Swiss Army knife. The Mexican cats and I slid the streets, wary, them in hidden pathways behind buildings, me on the wider path in front.

I slept early and soundly and woke before dawn, lit the candle. Tatters of fog slid across the opened casement window sill. I wrapped in my wool shawl, plugged in the teakettle and brewed tea, sat to meditate, my fingers circling the warm cup.

With my back to the window, I did not see the lights coming across the bay, did not know my picked hostel a ferry landing.

A slithering chain rattled, an engine coughed, and a shuddering gangplank clanked to the ground outside my window.

The ferry from La Paz, I would learn, arrived every morning.

The town woke, cries rang through the curved streets, roosters crowed, passengers clambered down the gangplank, trucks growled up an incline from the behemoth's belly and grumbled onto the road. Disgorging its last remaining crumbs, the ferry yawned, open mouthed, as the sun mounted the ridge over Topolobampo.

The trip to the Visa machine in Los Mochis had not resulted in cash, rather a message to my bank to wire funds to Topolobampo. Determined to reach freedom, I had been careless. I hadn't thought through details, and my impetuous desire drove me to the impossible. The ferry reloaded trucks, passengers, mysterious bundles bound for somewhere, and off they went across the water. I asked directions to the telegraph office. I found the telegraph office; the money had arrived.

I was safe: tea and hot water, papaya and melon and crackers, a notebook, a warm bed, a less-wobbly table, and money.

Dreams slid in and out of my nights. I'd wake briefly but by morning they'd drifted with the tide to another set of dreams, another storehouse of memories. Now that the tension of money was over, I settled into the routine of pre-dawn writing in the Topolobampo notebook with the stretching-dancer cover. The darkness erased all sound until first light shifted black into dark gray, lighter gray, and the ferry arrived. Some mornings, fog, ghostlike, rose from the sea. It hugged the wharf, the beach, the embankment. The ferry, out of sight, waited.

The pages I wrote and wrote, scrawls against time and memory, layered like refuse and broken pottery shards, a flow of words, and anything at all—no space, no time, as if either was more than nothing—and on these foundations, everything was built. If the foundation was a nothing, could that which was built be anything? Philosophers had mulled for centuries to tie down those ephemeral, invisible concepts. Perhaps the ancient Chinese, who saw everything as illusion, had merit. Everything upon which I built my life was invisible: time, space, intellect, emotion. Players and observers, we cemented foundations to wonderings as if that could hold invisible time bound by invisible mind. Illusion built on illusion.

Where in the storehouse of memories did I need to look for the depths of my yearning, ever searching, not knowing what I searched for, or what to find. I was my own dragon, guarding rusty treasures.

Watch and listen, the voice said.

A dream fragment surfaced: a house beyond a field set up against a cliff. I wanted to see if I could live there.

I closed the dancing ballerina notebook and went for a walk.

Each day I wandered the beach, stared over the water, left the beach at random streets, and climbed into town. When I found a reasonable café, I stopped for lunch, sat outside, watched the street or people or the sea. I didn't talk to anyone. On the third day, I found the restaurant Grecia and sat on the sunny patio, away from beach and children and radios, to watch sky and space and rocky hilltops poking up from the sea. I didn't think; I watched. A halo circled the sun and haze slid over the mountains. My skin smelled salty. Mexico brought memories of Bill—the house in Cuernavaca, scarlet bougainvillea along a wall—and it surprised me to realize we'd parted more than five years ago. What thorn did Bill Joyce hold that anchored him to my side?

Before dawn, I woke rested, fixed tea, sat with my morning journal to record a dream of traveling, and remembered an exhibit in Washington, D.C. of the Scythians. They wandered. I'd bought a pin in the gift shop, a black square with a golden coiled beast. I was a coiled beast, a beast who crackled and crunched on pieces of time left in old books, old journals. Nietzsche wrote, "The attraction of knowledge would be small if one did not have to overcome so much shame on the way." Was shame a thing of society? Was part of the task of individuation to walk past those shames? Shame and power circling, in the same way beasts circle a fire. Life carried power and death carried shame.

The television came on loud against the wall of my room. Steps thudded in the hallway. The ferry's horn tooted long and hard as it shuffled toward the wharf. I sighed. My quiet time was over. Was death the reason for the noise in Mexico—radios, music, shooting rockets—to chase away shame for one more day, or was it to frighten the beasts, push them back to the space of dreams?

The ferry docked, unloaded, reloaded, the rhythm of its ritual familiar. After it left, I dressed and walked into the streets. Perhaps memory lay in front of me rather than behind, the path unwinding as it would.

Too soon it was time to pack. One last early morning at the open window, one more ferry arrival. I closed my bag, unplugged the teapot, returned it to the front desk, and said goodbye. I caught a bus to Los Mochis, the next to Cuidad Juarez, walked over the bridge, found Old Blue where I'd left it, and drove to Santa Fe.

TWENTY-SEVEN

WINTER ANGLES INTO SPRING

S alt smell faded from my skin as Old Blue began the last rugged climb
to Santa Fe, stretches of dry mountains on one side, desert and dried
scrub on the other. I did not know how long I could live in the desert,
even with an annual rebirth in the sea.

But I had quiet days. Unpacked, the humidifier plugged in, I shifted
my morning writing to the drop-leaf table facing east. I built a fire. A gas
heater, beside a wall in the kitchen, hardly warmed the place. I'd bought
plastic sheeting for the windows weeks earlier but time had conspired in
such a fashion as to have none of it. Pulling out the sheeting and tape, I
covered the windows from the inside. Instead of watching the sea, I sat
at the east window as light inched into morning and watched the flames
in my kiva fireplace. Money worries scrawled across the last pages of
the Mexico notebook. I'd left the feeling world, the sensing world of
Mexico, to reenter the thinking-thinking world. Each morning, after
setting the teakettle to heating, I put on a coat and stepped outside to
stand transfixed in layers of stars beyond stars until my nose felt each
breath freeze.

Sometimes the day dawned crystalline blue and white and some days
a high fierce wind heading for the prairies flew too close to the ground
and buffeted. My fingers were cold; my feet were cold; I bought silk liners
for my gloves and boot socks. I wore wool scarves around my neck and
hats on my head: my black Mexican fedora for the good days; a tightly
woven round wool with rolled sides on the bad days. Rolled up it looked
like a Thomas Aquinas hat; rolled down, my eyebrows covered, slits for
my eyes, a wool scarf pulled over my mouth, I resembled a rebel from
Afghanistan. I was cold all the time. Maybe I complained to Mother and
she told Judy, or I complained to Judy. At any rate, the middle of January,
a down comforter from my big sister and my mom arrived in the mail. I
took to reading in bed, comforter to my chin, switching from one hand
to another when the hand holding the book grew cold.

Teaching and learning and church became my out-of-house routine. Teaching classes, recycled from the semester before, was fine. At St. John's, I began the mathematics and natural sciences semester: Lucretius, Aristotle's Physics, Books II, III, IV, and VIII, followed by Ptolemy, Darwin, and James. I could probably understand James. The tutorial was Euclid, eight weeks of Euclid. I studied. I drew lines. I worked with a study group and a student tutor. It didn't help. The lines boxed me in.

The preceptorial, atomic theory, began with Newton. The lab experiments were the closest I'd come to pure magic. The Periodic Table fascinated me; keeping it in my head proved fruitless. The tutor, Mr. Sacks, suggested I might like *The Periodic Table* by Primo Levi to see again the earth, air, and water from which I was separated by a gulf that grew larger every day. Reading Primo Levi so much kinder than studying geometry. He opened my mind while Euclid tangled it.

Readings on Lucretius enchanted: "A half can always be in halves divided/No limit to all this. So how would they differ/The universe from the littlest thing?"

I dreamed I was attending another graduate school after St. John's, followed by dreams of traveling fast, but the roads I wanted to take were under construction. I slowed down.

Time once more my daemon.

The church was warm at Mass on Sundays, as was the healing service at Richard's chapel on Wednesdays. In the middle of February, the phone rang. Father Richard said, "I'm on retreat this week and want you to lead the healing service."

In the midst of writing a paper, my eyes went blank. I slumped in my chair. "Me?" I'd practiced laying on hands beside Richard, but lead? I shivered. The fire had died.

"You said you wanted to be a healer. Now's the time to start."

"What do I do?"

His chuckled. "Do the same as I do. Open with a reading, do the prayers, walk around and lay hands on people." We said goodbye. Father Cliff agreed to lead the prayers. I led the healing service, open to the energy that rose from my chest, down my arms, and through my hands. I gently placed my hands on shoulders, felt them relax, almost melt. Cupping my hands at jawline, I lifted a head, felt the neck release. A pulse flowed from me.

That night, my dream put me in a car, moving forward.

I could not like Euclidean geometry, but it trained me in logical steps. Actually, Matt Stewart taught me how to think in steps during our tutoring sessions. He was patient and kind and big and sandy-haired and handsome. I was smitten. But he was too young and too much like my father and I hadn't gone through all these years of studying myself to turn stupid. Smiling and laughing at his jokes were the most I permitted myself.

Euclid: "A boundary can only be definite because it's imaginary."

With a borrowed shovel from Jeff, I shoveled snow from the driveway. The wind blew down the chimney and scattered stale smoke and ash smells. The tips of my fingers turned white. The fire rebuilt, I pulled a chair and rug nearby and wrote to my mother by hand. She'd traveled to the Northwest Territories after leaving me in November, to Judy's, to my sisters' Julia and Jolene, back to Judy's. My own solitary life taught me pages about my mother. She wrote "It must be time for the weather report" when she ran out of things to say and had space left on the page. She was at Judy's and Judy worked nights, slept days, so Mom's days stretched long. "Nothing much to do this morning except sit here and watch bananas ripen. And that's difficult for them since it's partly sunny as opposed to partly cloudy." She'd visited her brother Kenny in Oregon. They'd had a lot of rich food and her system was out of whack. Judy cooked some rice. It helped. "And then I remembered Grandma Moore telling my mother to boil rice and save the water and give it to a sick baby. Can't remember which baby. Look it up—might come in handy sometime."

My mother's letters brightened my life and mind.

Aristotle not so much, but I made headway with learning to think.

One night, in front of the fire, I laughed aloud at reading Lavoisier: "it was necessary to guard against the extravagancy of our imagination." All told, that was unlikely to happen with me.

Time slid by in a blur: school, school, school. Church my only refuge where I didn't have to think, I could be.

During spring break, I flew to my sister's in Bellingham for Mother's eightieth birthday. Masses of purple, yellow, and pink blooms sprawled luxuriously out of the hanging baskets lining Judy's deck. A misty rain washed leaves.

"Look at these!" I said, cupping a purple flower with pink wings. Judy cultivated masses of flowers around her little place. My strawberries, planted the previous summer against the wooden pole fence at the end of the drive, prospered fitfully. We laughed. We cooked. Ate cake. Retold stories. One afternoon as Mother napped, we siblings sat around Judy's round oak table for the "talk." "She's forgetting a lot," Judy said and named times Mother repeated the same things or asked the same question. She'd always been absent-minded and woolly, a condition in part from the head surgery after the car accident with Little Joe. But this was different, we agreed. Mother could no longer keep living alone. Judy proposed she come live with her. So big sister took on the role of Big Sister and became the head of the clan. Jack said he'd get Mom ready to move in the summer. I flew to New Mexico, feeling sad, feeling relieved.

We ended Euclid and began Lobachevski—curved lines—I could imagine space as curved. Lobachevski invited me to suppose, to enter the uncertainty, the world beyond the looking glass where things became "curiouser and curiouser." After jumping down my own list of rabbit holes, my affinity with Alice had no bounds.

After the spring semester, one would remain, the summer term and graduation. Then what? Snatches of dreams said my spiritual home and material home were one. Classes at SFC and the community college went well. Both schools had scheduled me to work in the fall. Did I need to stay in Santa Fe? Where else would I go? Long, chaotic dreams, multiple images overlaid in a mosaic: an actress, a healer, a mad scientist, and lines of Asian men beating sticks.

Pat Golden, the casting director whom I'd worked with in New York, phoned. "Are you paid up with SAG?" I was. "I think I have a role for you." She was coming to Santa Fe as casting director for a Japanese director, *East Meets West*, shooting in New Mexico at the end of May during my break from all the schools. Not exactly Asian men beating sticks but close. Nathan phoned. He and Kyong needed some time together and could Michael come for the summer? A chorus line refrain ran through my head: "Yeah . . . I can do that . . . I can do that." And not for the first time. Old Blue, after its El Paso run, needed work. I could drain and flush the radiator, I'd worked on my car when I was at K-State, so I could do it again, but the oil leak was bigger. For now, I could keep checking oil and adding oil. With pay from a film job, I could get it fixed. My spirits lifted. The winds lessened and sunny days grew.

Easter Mass at Loretto bloomed in stunning white and gold. With a full house, it felt like a cathedral from some exotic locale, a miniaturized version of the immense Gothic cathedrals I'd visited in Europe. Three priests and three servers processed the center aisle in a blaze of light and music. Bishop Richard lit the Pascal candle and held it for servers to light their small candles. They walked the aisle, pausing to pass new fire to the first person in each row for them to pass on.

Driving home, I wondered at the many holy places where I'd felt, well, comfortable, but a big gap lay between being comfortable in God's houses and uncomfortable with God. Was it the rules, or was there a spirit in me that responded to the spirit in others that responded to . . . well . . . there it was again—God.

Cynthia and I talked late that night, a timeless conversation of losses and loves, as we relived twenty years of confessions. We'd often wandered in the land of our histories, what made us who we are. Talk wandered to lovers, hers with Dean had ended as badly as mine with Bill, and we'd both stayed wary. "I've been having dreams of a man for a couple of years but nobody's shown up," I said. "A couple nights ago, I dreamed of walking hand in hand with him, and we came to the edge of a cliff and fell over. Maybe I need to learn to fly." I laughed, our conversation sliding on to siblings and family and my sons whom she loved with a fierce protectiveness. Because that's how our stories wandered, the years between us not needing details to understand. I told her about the acupuncture student I'd met, Christie, who worked on my bad hip. She told me she was dancing again.

An April eclipse fell heavy, my students tired and grumpy, the St. John's classes more contentious than usual, and a lab experiment-gone-wrong burned my hand. I was not perky. On the first Sunday in May, we held the Graduate Institute May Day picnic, a catastrophe in the making amid a lack of cohesion in settling on a site for the Maypole. Matt Stewart carried it across his shoulder as we wandered back and forth on the hillside. I left and walked up the canyon to sit on a rock under trees. I'd grown up in a large family and the best way to dodge most anything was to walk to the pasture and sit on a rock under trees. When I rejoined the group, the pole was up. Kelsey Stansbury handed me a blood red carnation. "I wish you a love that burns the flesh," she said. The Maypole secured, we danced. I carried the red carnation home.

Two weeks left in the semester—papers to grade and finals to give, a preceptorial paper to write, a seminar paper to finish, a trip to the airport to pick up Michael, and . . . make a movie. A late storm blew in, gusty, cold, and inches of snow. I stayed home, built fires, graded papers, and read and wrote. The moisture was good. I'd trailed a stick through the dirt in March and planted peas, the hard dry nubs like winter in my hand. But Dad always said to get them in by St. Patrick's Day, so I had. Now they'd get a good soaking. I'd get the rest of the garden in soon. I'd bought seed corn to plant in a spiral to the west of the adobe wall, beyond the survival-mode strawberries and north of the pea plot but close enough to water them all at the same time.

By a stroke of fortune, I'd discovered the acupuncture school lab with graduate students in residency and met Christi Nichols. I wanted healing for my perennial bad hip, but our work soon soared into the sacred. I'd pretty much lived in terror of needles from the time I was six years old when they tied me down for penicillin shots after yanking out my tonsils. Hers felt like silk: needles high on my buttocks, needles near the hip joint, needles in lower thighs, the outside of calves, at wrist points. I saw a huge spiral of energy, felt her place a needle in my crown. The spiral settled into colors, purple to violet, sea green to green. After removing them, she helped me turn face up. Christi placed one needle above my pubic bone and one in each inner knee. I felt her hands on my ankles ground me, and an old, deep sadness rose.

"It's like something's deep asleep in me," I said and felt her remove the needles, felt her hand at my pubic and one at heart level. A long deep sob shuddered up my body, and I burst out in tears. Christi released her breath in a flood of words, "I only asked the energy between your heart and pubis to be connected!" she said. I laughed my customary startled laugh. "I guess it worked."

In class that evening, I could see energy waves around people, not colors, but energy. By the time of preceptorial and lab, I felt more grounded in my body. Nothing jumped to bite me.

I turned in grades.

I finished writing the precept paper and the seminar paper.

Pat Golden arrived. She had a free weekend before movie work became work, so we drove up to Abiquiu to see Georgia O'Keeffe's house. Pat had introduced me to Ralph Weston, the astrologer, so Pat and I talked a common astrological language as we traveled, stopped, bought food, and drove to Christ in the Desert Monastery on several miles of rutted dirt road. The chapel quiet, so quiet I could hear a fly buzz fitfully against a window near the altar.

Pat left, and I had four days of rest and filing papers and organizing folders for my final summer at St. John's. And studying a script. And costume fittings, and a quick read through before three days of filming. I arrived at nine each morning and signed out each evening, high on the energy that both sucks and gives, wanting more and more, rerunning scenes in my mind, the surprise of the Japanese crew and director when I swung the rifle up in one swoop and pointed it at the window. I was a frontier woman, wasn't I? The Japanese director, Kihachi Okamoto, famous in Japan, smiled and nodded. "Good." Maybe I incarnated my great-great-grandmother Lucinda, a Quaker who migrated to the Kansas frontier in the 1800s and, no doubt, had learned to handle a rifle.

On Saturday, I slept, and on Sunday morning, Father Richard initiated me as a server along with Casey.

We walked to the front with candles, Father Richard blessed our hands with holy water and laid his hands on our heads. What was this I did?

And then another full week of working on the film. I finished. They paid me. The IRS, for reasons unknown and totally unexpected, sent a refund check. SFCC sent a final paycheck I didn't remember was coming. Old Blue revived with a tune up, a repaired oil leak, a wash, and an inside clean out. The Smith Corona, after years of sacred duty, was on its last legs, so I shopped for my first-ever grown-up computer, drove home, and unpacked a Hewlett Packard with Windows and Internet and email. I lovingly wrapped my beloved Smith Corona in protective paper and put it in a box over the bathroom along with a carefully wrapped box of small disks that stored my history in letters, three screenplays, and several stories. After hooking up the Internet, I signed up for an email address. And in between other tasks, filled up the refrigerator and cupboards and watered the garden. New spinach was ready to harvest, so I harvested, brought it in, fried up a piece of bacon, tossed the spinach in the hot fat like Dad might have done.

So much of me started with someone else.

TWENTY-EIGHT

TURNING ANOTHER CORNER

Time, that most generous gift, was mine before the summer semester started and grandmotherhood began. Pat would return when the film wrapped. I sat at the computer, an email begun: "Dear . . . " appeared on the screen at which I stared, hands curved in my lap, but I could not remember who I meant to write to. I slept long and hard. The second week, I staggered into resurrection, found my summer reading lists folder and the bag of books I'd bought and hadn't opened. Sitting on the rug between the open front door and the futon bed filling the rear wall, I spread the books around me.

The best I'd saved for last: literature. To savor. Homer's *Iliad* and *Odyssey*; Greek theater—*Agamemnon, Antigone, Oedipus, Media*—Shakespeare's *A Midsummer's Night's Dream, The Tempest,* and *King Lear;* Aristotle's *Poetics;* and Goethe—*Botanical Writings, Faust, The Theory of Colors.*

I began with Goethe's *Botanical Writings:* "Clothed in wonder I am here" and lifted my head once light grew too dim and evening crept through the open door.

When Michael walked off the plane, I almost didn't recognize the chubby-cheeked boy with a basketball under one arm, a foot taller than I remembered, and pulling a suitcase with Going to Grandma's written in bold white letters. His face lit up when he saw me. "Grams!" he shouted. We stepped into familiar territory. Susan's son Chris, a year older than Michael, met us when we parked at home. They became instant friends. I carried Michael's suitcase inside and unpacked. Susan said Michael could stay with them when I had class, and Chris decided that meant Michael was his. That first evening, Michael came home covered in red dust.

"We went to see his fort and then we climbed on a big rock and jumped off and then . . . well, I don't remember what we did then but it was fun!" he said as he stripped and walked to the shower. In the morning, he disappeared with Chris while I sat on the floor and read.

On Saturday night, invited to a party with the film folks and the Japanese press, my AmerAsian grandson was a hit. On Sunday, we showed up for church, and after, picked up Pat Golden who'd returned for the press party and drove into the Jemez mountains for a feast day dance and came back to grill hot dogs and hamburgers on my tiny hibachi on the stone patio. On Tuesday, I took Michael and Chris to the set so they could see a movie filming and have lunch. Wednesday evening, Michael and I attended the healing service.

"I saw you looking around as I was working with Father Richard," I said on our drive home. "What'd you see?"

"Dragons!" he said.

Dragons?

"They followed you."

"You can see dragons?"

Michael nodded. "I can make the lights change too."

He pointed through the windshield to a traffic signal, its red warning clear. "Watch." He lifted both hands. "Change." He kept them raised until the light changed as we reached it. Michael looked at me and grinned.

Oh my, I wondered. *What have I here?*

An old woman came to my dreams that night. She lay hands on me and energy coursed through my body. Michael lay tangled in the sheets beside me. She rolled me over, placed her hands on my back, and as she merged into me, layers of ancient shamans, holy men and women, passed through me. And through me to Michael.

Michael thrashed, muttered, settled.

But day-to-day life remained. My bank account shrank and no teaching jobs until fall. A random ad in the newspaper jumped out: Professional Psychics Wanted. I'd read the cards for years, mostly for myself, and Ralph had taught me enough astrology to be dangerous. Maybe I could qualify. I called, read for the office manager, and was certified a professional psychic, a job I could do from home between reading for classes and grandmothering. A job that traveled wherever I had a phone. So between meals and feedings and boy-stuff and classes, I counseled on a psychic line.

July entered hot. We waited for the monsoons, tumbling at the horizon and threatening to start any day, which would make us all happy, the garden included. Tomatoes, squash, and peppers liked the heat, the beans not so much. I wrote Mom that crickets were eating the new growth and she suggested baby powder. It worked; the crickets hopped elsewhere, but the advice came a little late and only a few beans recovered. If it stayed warm long enough, I'd have tomatoes, but summer could end the first of September and leave me with a mound of green. I'd have to ask Mom for her green tomato pickle recipe or fix a lot of fried green tomatoes. My birthday slid by. Age didn't seem to make much difference any more.

Too many sparking irons in the fire to worry about age. Michael was fine, having a boy summer in the country. He was tall enough to ride my bicycle and roamed with Chris over hills and down along arroyos. At the Village Fourth of July picnic, Chris's dad oversaw both boys as they helped with fireworks and returned home streaked with soot and sweat and smiles.

Michael was so much like his father. He slammed through the door, gave me a hug, and stood at the open refrigerator door. "What do you want?" I said.

"Something."

One afternoon, he sat at the table, waiting for lunch as I stood on a step stool and gingerly screwed a bulb into a shaky ceiling fixture. As I twisted a final turn with the bulb, I heard a loud POP and jumped. Michael, chewing bubble gum, laughed and laughed as he peeled gum off his face. "Michael! No popping gum when I'm doing something dangerous!" He nodded and peeled.

He liked church and liked being admitted into the sacristy while priests and servers donned vestments. He asked Richard if he could climb the spiral staircase and Richard allowed it. "Once," Richard said. Michael stood at the choir loft railing and looked over the empty sanctuary much the way I looked over the sea, an absorbed expression on his face. When I asked him if he saw dragons, he shook his head. "Dancing dots of light."

Of all the beauty and wars and heroes in the *Iliad*, I was most imprinted with Hephaestus, the blacksmith, forging Achilles's glistening shield. I understood the blacksmith's misshapen form and his love of fire. In my final two semesters at K-State, I'd blacksmithed and shaped iron from fire, had loved the feel of a heavy hammer in my hand, the plasticity of iron pulled from the fire at just the right moment, so much more satisfying than the silver wire, thin copper sheets, and tiny blow torches of my metalsmithing major. My major professor was not impressed and had written I was not graduate school material on my final form, less, I'd thought, from my work and more from my refusing his romantic outreach.

The *Odyssey* brought no such memories. Instead, the long journey home was my story, as forever, it felt, I was tossed between Charybdis and Scylla, sucked into whirlpools of reflection only to be flung out into a battle of one sort or another as long years passed and I searched for home. My constant need to understand the power in words from the root meaning of words pushed me to sign up for a non-credit course in Greek with Mr. Stickney. We managed to progress through ten chapters of *The Freshman Greek Manual*, which all undergraduates began with, and I regretted having only four semesters instead of four years at St. John's.

The mix of present, past, and future swirled, and the eclectic pieces of my life began to shape a whole. Although never sure of where or what led,

I wondered if seminary was the next step. I talked to Richard and wrote to Matriarch Meri Spruit, asking advice. They encouraged me to apply.

My paper on Goethe and Gnosticism in a dialectical argument required enormous concentration. When Michael flew through the house, he flew quietly. After Goethe, I'd have two papers: one on *King Lear*, the other on poetry—that paper required writing a poem.

When I read the myth of Medusa, I found my topic: Medusa's face.

I am civilized now: the menses stopped.
No sacred blood stains my passage,
no Pegasus born from my pain.
Promises made for tomorrow have arrived
not yet filled, but neither broken
and my eyes that see your future cannot see mine.
Yesterdays rustle at the edges of my mind:
a white mist/the sea—
days purple as plums
that once grew in my family's orchard.
How many days are left to me?
In the darkness of dying
a soul's touchstone uncovered;
in the darkness of birth burns the fire.
I am what I was: wild-haired snake woman
shattering mirrors I once held before me,
pushing the boundaries of knowing past knowledge,
wrapping the red coral beads round my wrist.
Who will listen to my stories?
How many words are left to me?
I press the touchstone to my palm face down, feeding nerve ends.
You will not see the hissing snakes,
their teeth bared to devour.
But do not come to me backward,
your brazen shield held by illusion.

I was surprised by its fierceness.

On the fifth of August, I drove Michael to the airport. When the steward called his name, he wrapped his arms around me, burrowing his head into my center. "Soon," I promised to his downturned head. The steward took his hand and walked him to the plane. At the bridge door, Michael stopped, looked at me, and raised one hand. I raised mine in return. I already felt empty. For all the added responsibility, he was my shining and laughter-filled child and brightened my life.

Graduation was upon me, a year to be tallied like abacus beads in memory's setting: Marilyn and John and Duffy and Tom Simpson and Mr. Bart and Shakespeare and Homer in a blaze of phenomena, portending tomorrow. Like Achilles, I'd carry my master's degree as a brilliant shield and discover if it provided protection. I'd miss Mr. Cornell and Goethe and re-looking at the German romantic in me; I'd miss poetry with Basia Miller and Mr. Rawn. I'd miss Euclid and geometry and the struggle to make sense, the synapses firing in my head, a physical snap, when understanding grounded. Where would my flower of knowledge bloom in this blue desert of mountains? I would not be the same, and yet, what was the me of me if not the soul who knows and needs uncovering to know that it knows? That pondered with some sense of amusement. What was written on the touchstone of my soul? Which line belonged to Mr. Stickney, leading me in a waltz, and which to Mr. Bart, expounding on Shakespeare?

Mr. Stickney took his place after undergraduates received their diplomas, and as Graduate Institute graduates, we walked forward, one by one, and he handed us our master's diploma. We celebrated and laughed and toasted each other and said we'd keep in touch, but when I returned to my empty adobe, deep loss, deep tiredness, and deep relief filled me. My rubber band had snapped and left me with whiplash. I had a master's degree. My face looked tired, more tired than in the last weeks of school when Michael was here and I was pumping out papers. My emptiness did not know how to fill itself.

In the time before fall teaching, I rarely left the house, culled books, and cleared space for the many I'd bought and read in the last year; tossed papers, filed others; stared at mindless television. I slept long and deep, and I completed the application for seminary with a personal inventory: what are your five (five??) favorite books; what is your philosophy of life (sharp laugh); what do you think needs most changing in the world (me). I answered the questions rightfully and put it in the mail. The last chaotic corner was my long sheet-of-plywood desk and the top of the cold space heater that served as an extra shelf during summer. The house inched into order. Indian Market was slated for the coming weekend, and a Native American medicine man would dance at a special church service. I pulled out the white gauze ruffled skirt and blouse from Mexico and hand washed them. They were showing age but would do for wandering around the plaza.

I hated giving up dearly loved clothes and saved them, thinking I'd do something . . . use as a pattern for a new one . . . the sewing machine I'd bought when my kids were young more or less functioned . . . or keep them in my closet until packing for another move. Maybe if I stayed put, I could make a rug. So much of my stuff carried stories.

Each morning, beyond the drop leaf table, a hummingbird dashed to the opened window to see if I were awake.

In the afternoons, monsoons swept the dusty desert clean.

I dreamed and I meditated.

The dreams chewed on failure—a paper not handed in, rewriting a second paper—and all the time, in the dreams, aware I had my diploma.

A notice for a College of Santa Fe faculty meeting arrived via email. The greeter seemed surprised when I said I was an adjunct. But polite. She ushered me to a seat, and I learned the meeting was for full-time faculty. I did not belong. But then, where did I belong? What would it mean to belong to or with something? I had no idea, having lived a life of not belonging. I belonged to the divine and to my family, but place was never one of the things I'd been given to belong to.

But it was a wonder how inevitably right church felt. There was a good amount of resistance to calling Jesus my master, but then I had trouble calling anyone my master. I practiced praying. I'd have to inch into it.

What I believed was that everything—masters and teachers, visions and dreams, stars and planets and physics—played in the universe. How we played determined the outcome. I vowed to play well. In a meditation, I heard, *you make the choices . . . destiny is blind.*

On the psychic line, my readings grew deeper and resonant. Often I woke in the night with my hands reaching up, as in Hawaii, but couldn't remember the message. The new moon arrived, a quiet night, no traffic noise, no insects, no lights except for blistering stars throbbing against a sky so black it had no color. A yard sale garnered a round, glass-topped garden table with chairs, and I carried them home in Old Blue. On a deep night, alone, I sat on the patio, head tipped back to layers and layers of stars beyond stars, the immensity growing, expanding. Feeling very small and very frightened at my insignificance, I scurried into my little house and shut the door behind me.

The tomatoes ripened.

The time had come to begin reading for seminary, not because I had to—I could take as much time as I needed, Richard said—but because it was in front of me and I didn't know what else to do on this journey of evolution.

I began with *The Rule of Antioch* by Herman Adrian Spruit.

As an Independent Catholic Bishop, Herman Spruit began The Church of Antioch, or, formally, The Catholic Apostolic Church of Antioch Malabar Rite because he thought it time to ordain women. He'd been ordained a Methodist minister, but his Old Dutch Catholic heritage sent him on a quest for a deeper sense of spirit. A pragmatist and a mystic made sense to me.

The inside cover page had a simple drawing of an open palm with the words "Love, like Quicksilver, must be held in an open hand."

"Jesus made it abundantly clear in words as well as in attitudes and actions that LOVE is both the center and circumferences of his philosophy."

My body sighed deep and all of me relaxed.

Bishop Spruit must have been a good teacher. Richard had trained with him, loved him, and carried on his words. Richard also a pragmatic mystic. Bishop Spruit died about the time I'd first begun attending church, so I hadn't met him. The Matriarch, Meri Spruit, had visited once, and I liked her. And I'd heard some of the hoo-ha around a woman elevated to head of the church over other male bishops.

There was one rule in the Church of Antioch and one rule only: love one another.

"We would rather do anything than love," Bishop Spruit wrote.

Love and peace. Those two words resonated most deeply in my body. My mother said I'd laughed when she fed me, my older sister picky with food, and I, she said, loved to eat. Do tell. Love and peace. I'd had my own battles across continents searching for whatever love or peace felt like.

I lifted my head. Sunset on the way. I left the books and the computer and walked into the desert's evening light.

Along with Bishop Spruit's book, I read Thomas Hickey's *Independent Catholicism for the Third Millennium* and *The Pilgrim's Way*, translated from Russian. A wanderer, the pilgrim wanted to understand "pray without ceasing." He walked across Russia to ask wise people what it meant, all of whom gave him different or incomplete answers until he decided to make the prayer his own: "Lord Jesus Christ, have mercy on me, a sinner." This was the prayer I needed, not a petition in the exact sense, and not a save me, rather mercy, mercy for wherever this journey took me, was taking me, demanding I go—where, I didn't know. I walked with the words, keeping time with my steps.

I dropped a sinner from the prayer as I walked and practiced. It was enough to ask for mercy. Goodness knows I could use it. When I asked Father Cliff how I should think about the word sinner, he told me the word sin evolved from ancient Greek, an archery term meaning to miss the mark. All you needed was practice. If there was one thing I knew how to do, it was how to practice. My legs grew tired walking the arroyos and "have mercy" gained a new perspective, but I'd stopped arguing with myself and learned the silence of the desert.

TWENTY-NINE

TRANSITIONS

Fall teaching began: three English courses at the community college and two speech classes at College of Santa Fe, the classrooms stifling, sweaty-smelling, and the students stupid in end-of-summer heat. The School of Court Reporting hired me to read for the speed class on Tuesday and Thursday evenings. Other nights, I worked the psychic line and read for seminary. An odd combination, I noted from time to time. With all that, money would be at a breathing easy stage, although somewhat short a breeze.

On the last day of summer, the casement window stood open through the night, and I woke to a cold wind. I shut the window, but unready to light the gas heater pilot light, plugged in a space heater. By afternoon, the air was pure and golden. But it was fall. I stopped on my way home from school and loaded Old Blue's trunk with firewood, put on my gloves and work clothes, stacked wood against the adobe wall, carried pieces inside. I shuffled through the closet and brought warm clothes to the front, summer to the back, and pulled out a shawl. When the sun set, the chill grew. I built a fire and sat in front of it reading. I'd need to buy plastic and reseal windows.

Too fast, the world turned too fast, and yet the desert was glorious in its purples and golds and soft light. The nights silent, the crickets somewhere else. The air clean-smelling with aspen and pine and the early scent of burning wood.

I decided to write a paper on fate and free will in response to reading *Catholicism for the Third Millennium*. Which had I chosen? Which was foist upon me? Which was concept and which reality? The aspect of consciousness that enables us to discover structure is the sacred... consciousness becoming more and more aware of itself as holistic. Yes, this is what I believed, this is what I'd said, in one way or another, this a place I wanted to find.

St. John's College drew me back for a performance of the *Iliad* with the actors holding masks as in the ancient Greek productions. I heard Hector say, "but as for fate, I think that no man yet has escaped it once it has taken its first form, neither brave man or coward." What the first form might be, Hector didn't say. Birth? The first fateful choice that set a particular path?

After the performance, former classmate Meena said, "Let's get a drink," and we settled in to wonder on fate and free will, which allowed me to forget I meant to put gas in the car, and therefore, cause and effect being what they are, ran out of gas past midnight on a dark road with no reasonable option but to settle in for a cold night, propped on Mom's car pillow. I dozed. Headlights signaled a car. It stopped. A Good Samaritan knocked on my window. Did I need help? I did. He figured out where to buy a gas can, I didn't have one and neither did he, and left. "I'll be back in twenty minutes," he said. And was. And put the emptied gas can in my trunk. "Now you have a gas can. I bought one for me too." He grinned at my thanks and we shook hands. My car took me home after 2 a.m., grateful to crawl into a bed I'd not expected to see that night.

With a full roster of classes and a new course of study, it was another one-foot-in-front-of-the-other time. I had to look down each morning to make sure I had shoes on.

A letter arrived from my sister Julia in Oregon. She'd worked through years of print shop jobs to Master Printer. Now she owned the shop. She'd been working seventy hours a week but had to put a stop to it at seeing herself on the verge or crying or screaming or both. All the time. Now she limited herself to eight hours daily at the shop and two hours at home learning the new computer system. What was it about this family that we could not stop working . . . oh, yeah . . . Kansas pioneer stock.

I liked teaching, but my students were in chaos—families falling apart, cars burning or in other ways failing, coughing—the students, maybe the cars too. I talked to Katy in Montana, she whom I'd met in Mexico and climbed Popocatepetl with and who'd taught at university for years. "Sounds like a normal fall to me," she said. "If you lighten up, they'll catch up." Reasonable. Classes evolved into freewriting for the last fifteen minutes, which gave my voice a rest and from which the students' writing bloomed. In speech class I taught outlining, and in English I taught outlining. The simple kind: no A/B/C or numbers, just stars and circles to rearrange. And rewriting. A lot of rewriting.

A Sunday afternoon seminar at the Episcopal Church on pastoral care focused on listening without judging. It was what I believed confession, forgiveness, and reconciliation were, in a church sense, and what I'd learned from trees and grasses in Hawaii. After talking through the process, we paired to discuss how we each needed forgiveness. I surprised myself by saying, "I need forgiveness for being a mother, for being the young woman who simply wasn't conscious." My sons and I were close, but not being a better mother when they were small dug at me. They'd both grown into good men. It was time to let that go. In the late afternoon, in another dyad to talk about a grief we'd experienced, my father's death rose, once more, and I recognized my resistance to letting it go: I'd built my life around it; what would be left if I let it go? It was there, always, like a too-picked scab that wouldn't heal.

Nearly every week, I served at church. Father Richard became Richard and Father Cliff, Cliff. Wednesday evening meditations began after a late summer break, and Richard asked Cliff and me to alternate leading the service. I prepared a short talk on energy and how we identify our source, appropriate for the fall leaning upon us.

Hickey's *Independent Catholicism* continued to wrap me in comfort: "Faith involves placing one's trust in the Spirit as an all-powerful evolutionary force guiding each of us to perfection, as well as the Creation as a whole."

That sounded like Hegel. And Mother. I believed in evolution. If life evolved, step by step by step, would not spirit, the breath of life, the energy of consciousness evolve too? And in evolving, would we not also be responsible for our choices? Was physical evolution fate and spiritual evolution free will, using an evolved consciousness to make the choice to use challenges as gifts and go where one was led? I wanted to use both in clarity, rather than deny the one at the expense of the other.

I learned liturgy from Cliff, and learned, as I sat beside him, to recognize when his body shifted from stillness to movement: usually, when the toe of his shoe twitched we rose in tandem, like a dance. I held my hands like Richard, but I moved like Cliff.

A full moon eclipse announced itself days ahead of arrival. I had cramps and hot flashes and my face broke out in pimples. Three nights of frost followed the eclipse and the garden kaput, but I'd managed to pick two full bags of green tomatoes before it hit, thanks to a Kansas habit of watching weather reports every night. "My word," I said aloud, looking at the tomatoes. I sounded like my mother. Maybe next year I'd stick with cherry tomatoes.

The Pilgrim's Prayer—a background litany while walking, driving, washing dishes, sweeping the patio—replaced the usual chatter in my head. I asked for a dream to show me what more I needed to let go of and death chased me: death in a wolf mask, death in a human skull; I ran and death followed. Startled awake, I stared at the vigas overhead, got out of bed, and found Hegel: passions, private aims, and the satisfaction of selfish desires, are effective springs of action. My passions had often sprung me into action. Now I had to stand still and allow death to show me what I needed to know.

The management company to whom I paid my monthly rent, finally, after much badgering, sent workers to stuff insulation through a crawl space and under my wooden plank floor. They weather-stripped the windows and screen doors. I taped plastic on the inside of windows, and bought a white, heavy-cotton nubbed blanket to use as a rug. I had wood and a full propane tank. Old Blue needed an oil change and high-desert winterization, and new tie-rods, as it turned out. As tomatoes in the house ripened, I sliced and dried them in the oven and packed them in mason jars. As usual, I had too many irons in the fire, which often felt like a blast furnace. One of my young speech students, Eric, angry at the program, angry at wasted time, wanted to do his persuasive speech on Amnesty International and focus on apathy because nobody wanted to get involved. "This doesn't serve you or your audience," I said. "Help us see what you see and what drives you to speak on apathy." The next class, he did a most remarkable speech: "You get up, all your clothes are dirty, no underwear. Your hair won't comb. It's going to be a terrible day. In the meantime, Carlos, who is fifteen, is waking up in a Guatemala jail with a lump on his jaw and bruises on his arms." He held the class spellbound, and I remembered years and years past, vowing to no longer stand at the barricades but change the world one person at a time.

One evening, coming out of the bathroom from a shower, body damp, an opening lay between me and the kitchen door. I could see the door, yet I stood on the edge of time and glimpsed the world in itself, luminous. At my feet, the edge of dark emptiness. In that moment, I saw myself grounded and free from the abyss.

Mom phoned to tell me Uncle Kenny, her brother, had died suddenly. He'd spent many years in the Navy, and one year on leave, came home with small, carved cedar boxes from Lebanon for Judy and me, a box I'd carried since childhood. It stored important papers: passport, my sons' birth certificates, a letter from Jeanne when she'd traveled in Nepal. Mother was the oldest of six, the one who had watched over others as they grew, and now only she and her youngest sibling were alive.

"I don't know, Janet. No one's left except Doris, and I haven't seen her since Dad's funeral. Was that at Dad's funeral?" I assured her she remembered correctly. "I visited Kenny a month or so ago. I think he was building birdhouses or maybe showing me old ones. I don't remember." She wasn't crying, but her voice sounded scratchy, as if gravel clogged her throat. The family planned to gather for Thanksgiving at Kenny's house before it was sold.

I phoned Katy. "I'm flying to Oregon for Thanksgiving. Can you drive over?"

She could, she said.

I phoned Matriarch Mary Spruit. "My coursework for cleric is nearly finished. I'm coming to Oregon for Thanksgiving and I wondered if I could visit you."

"I'd be so happy to see you. You write well. I like your papers. Perhaps I could elevate you to doorkeeper while you're here?"

"Yes, thank you!"

I talked to Richard, explained my trip to Oregon. "I plan to visit the Matriarch while I'm there."

"Ask her if she'll elevate you to doorkeeper," he said as if reading her mind.

The Tuesday night before Thanksgiving, I flew to Oregon and met my brother, Jack, at the airport. Julia, her husband John and daughter Raven, picked us up. When we were children, before death took our father as well as John's father and we all played at their farm outside Barnes, Julia and John would run away to the Kansas hill pasture and "get married," they said. This before Uncle Kenny married John's mother, adopted John and his twin brother Jim, and they moved to Oregon. It took another thirty years for Julia and John to find each other. We drove to Uncle Kenny's house across the mountains.

Mother and Judy arrived, my sisters Jeanne and Jolene and Jo's husband Mike. Judy slid into responsibility; Jeanne slid into universal it-will-all-work-out; Julia organized among several cell phones; Jack sat on the back porch reading; and Jolene showed up when she showed up.

We only got older, not different. Except we laughed more.

Katy arrived with her bedroll, and we laid our sleeping pallets next to each other on the living room floor. John's twin brother, Jim, arrived with his family the next day, and we had seventeen for Thanksgiving dinner. I retreated to the kitchen to wash dishes as others laughed and visited in the living room. The kitchen both warm and quiet.

On Friday, the semi-adults loaded up cars and drove to the ocean to play on the beach as rain drizzled. I snapped pictures of Katy, laughing, my brother and sisters, laughing.

We separated on Saturday, Mother returning to Hawaii with Jeanne, Katy loading up her car and driving back to Montana. I was leaving with Julia so I could visit the Matriarch.

When our family circled for prayer before we separated, a family that grew up praying, men, women, and children, Mother, as eldest, asked me to pray. I prayed for Uncle Kenny and for all of us, for family, and then I hugged and laughed, said goodbye and wiped at tears.

On Saturday evening, I went to meet the Matriarch. She ran the school, read my papers, and wrote letters back. I loved her immediately. Her square face shone and her eyes laughed. She loved to laugh. It was infectious. We fixed supper together and talked story, church history, seminary, but mostly story. The walls were covered in bookcases and books, decades of church, church history, lineage, theology. The same turmoil occurred down the ages of the Independent Catholic movement as had occurred down the ages of other churches. Bishop Spruit, when he became ill, appointed her Matriarch. The panoply of male bishops quivered and balked and several left the church. We talked books and resources and the Kabbalah course I would study. She said the Tree of Life was also the Tree of Light. On Sunday, she elevated me to the Order of Doorkeeper. When she lay hands on my head, the same surge of energy as from Richard's hands—strong, quiet, and loving—ran through my body.

On Monday, I got up at four to leave at five to fly to Denver to meet Stephen for lunch, then fly to Albuquerque to drive to Santa Fe to teach at four to go grocery shopping to return home and balance the checkbook. Change was a rotation of phenomena, each succeeding the other, until the starting point came round again.

By Winter Solstice, finals over and grades in, I sat in the early dawn's glimmer of Sun Return and remembered my years-ago journey to Mexico. I taped a Mexican wool serape to the cold adobe wall in front of my desk below the window. The plastic-covered windows looked like I'd shrink-wrapped the place, but the house stayed warm.

THIRTY

TRANSFORMATIONS

Alex and Olga, Russian friends I'd met in Hawaii and who had moved to Albuquerque with their nine-year-old daughter, Stacey, came on Christmas Eve. We walked Canyon Road, lined on both sides with candle-lit *farolitos*—lunch-sized paper bags filled about a quarter of the way up with sand to add ballast for the small, lighted candles stuck in each. More *farolitos* lined the rooftops of houses. The streets were ablaze in beauty. Small bonfires, spaced along the road, gathered wanderers to sing carols and warm up with hot cider. Stephen drove down from Denver and arrived by the time we returned from Christmas Day Mass, so there were five of us in my little house as we rustled each other through the kitchen, preparing food. In celebratory fashion, we feasted. And then everyone left, and there was only Stephen and me. We laughed at the same dumb things, went to see a movie, and wandered the Christmassy mall.

And then he left, the house quiet, and I returned to reading and dreaming and meditating.

And writing.

From some perverse impulse, I decided to work on the Mexico book and turn it into a novel. So, in a large and thick spiral notebook, red cover, I began writing in the early morning, by hand, page after page, and couldn't seem to get past the opening, although I'd introduced Jenny and Jake, as I renamed Janet and Bill, and memories and farm and light and movie making. Why did I keep writing when I couldn't find what it wanted to be? And why was I writing about Bill as if he were a residue I couldn't clean out of my blood? But if I didn't write, I would forget, and I didn't want to forget, neither Mexico nor what I'd learned. Giving myself permission, I wrote page after page. I built fires, switched on both electric space heaters, and turned up the flame in the gas heater. The radio related temperatures of seventeen, nineteen, twenty-two. The mountains wore white capes.

Two weeks of freedom lay ahead before classes began. In the

afternoons, I studied for seminary, wrapping my head around more than a thousand years of Talmudic history out of which had grown the Kabbalah and its two lineages: Practical and Speculative. I drew the lineage on page after page, studying connections. Both Zoroaster and the Old Testament described the early human journey from spiritual to creative to physical/intellectual. Were we now, in this age of computers and connections, beginning an ascent through new levels, physical/intellectual to spiritual? Would we evolve into understanding how spirit works through everything? Wasn't it time to expand our limited vision of God to God-of-many-names?

Temperatures returned to a more or less moderate level and snow melted on the patio. New Year's Eve I spent at home as one year dissolved into statistics and the new one strode in as if it knew what it was doing.

A cat named Chama became my companion. She belonged to Francis, Richard's mother, but Francis entered a nursing home, and her beloved cat couldn't go. She came to me. At night, she curled beside me under the comforter, and in the morning, she'd go for a walk while I looked at stars. Cat food went on the grocery shopping list.

Old Blue broke down and I replaced the alternator. Along with my college teaching, Court Reporting hired me to teach a grammar class one night a week and two nights with speed building. I pushed my reading and their writing to go faster and faster in order to prepare them for witnesses who might speak fast from nervousness on the witness stand. I better understood Bill's craziness at teaching so many courses to make a living. On the evenings when nothing else demanded, I worked the psychic line, building my client list.

I held tight to my seminary self, but the writer took over at dawn—although the novel itself galloped at a snail's pace—and the teacher took over on work days. Every Wednesday night I reconnected to the healer, and every Sunday morning to the ritual as if it were a dance I'd performed all my life. A friend of a friend told her husband about me; he'd had surgery and asked me to do some healing work. When my hands became a conduit for spirit, a part of me stepped aside in awe of the love that flowed through me, in awe of the shifts I could feel. He soon left the hospital, encouraged by his body's ability to heal. I felt humbled. Instead of a goal to legitimize the Crone/Healer, this study for the priesthood had become its own journey. Why was I, with my less than holy background, called to a destination so outside the way I'd lived?

Phoning Cynthia, hoping she could help me see, proved futile. A new lover, who came and went, had left her feeling angry and betrayed, as had life and work. Had I been so long out of a relationship I couldn't relate? I listened and said the appropriate words, but I couldn't help her any more than she could help me, a hurt deeper than my unanswered questions.

I read and reread Paul's Letter to the Philippians. To some, he said, "I write to you as children" and thundered rules, but to the Philippians, he said, "I write to you as mature followers to find the God within." In my childhood, Paul's words were thundered from preachers who chose the Paul of thunder, especially the women—"keep your heads covered and your mouths shut." But now I heard a voice I used with my own students. "Look inside," I said. "Find your own voice." Odd to find a voice in Paul that echoed my own rather than the preachers of long ago. Odd to find myself defending Paul to a woman friend, as angry at his words as I once was. Odd to be able to listen to the rain instead of the thunder.

A letter arrived from my niece, my brother's oldest daughter, Jessica. She was getting married and had talked to the minister about me participating as they made their vows, and he said it was okay so please could I come. I reserved a ticket. Last summer's movie had garnered me an agent in Albuquerque. She wanted new headshots. I had new headshots taken.

Four years ago, I'd danced the New Year in at the Hawi Bamboo Café with no idea where I was headed. Some things hadn't changed, but now I had a general outline. Mostly SFCC and CSF and church and seminary. And home to read and write papers.

My seminary studies focused on liturgy, scriptural interpretation, Kabbalah, and the course, "What is a priest?"

What is a priest?

I knew Richard as priest, Cliff as priest; Richard a healer and detailed administrator, Cliff a counselor and thinker. I asked Cliff what being a priest meant. He told me a story: "One night, shortly after our ordination . . . we were all about twenty-five years old . . . we new priests were invited to Monsignor Clare O'Dwyer's for dinner with some of the older clergy. I knew Clare. He was a friend of Tony's and he'd been to our house a lot."

Cliff had previously told me various stories about Holy Rosary, the Polish church catty-corner to his family's home in Baltimore where he'd started serving as an eight-year-old altar boy, and he'd told me stories of the priests and bishops coming to their house after Mass on Sundays. This was a new story.

"We were sitting in Clare's apartment before dinner, having drinks, talking priesthood. One of my classmates asked Clare, 'What's the secret to being a good priest?' We waited, expecting a profound theological or ecclesiastical statement. Clare just looked up and said, 'Be kind.' That was it. Be kind."

Cliff and Richard were both kind. What would I be? I counseled on the phone line, practiced as a healer, but I'd never thought of myself as kind. Driven, yes. But being driven sometimes rolled over people and I could be impatient.

I practiced being kind.

In February, I parked the car in Lamy, an end-of-the-road town scattered with old houses, to catch the train. The station felt familiar: blue and white tiled walls, carved wooden benches, padded leather seats, the kind of station where Grandpa worked when I lived in the Barnes house. In Topeka, I hugged my niece often, and during the wedding, I blessed them. The biggest story came with the rings, tied to the pillow with a knot, requiring a frantic search for a pocket knife to cut them free. A lesson to absorb for later use: ensure no one ties the rings with a knot.

In mid-March, I lifted my head from studies and writing, and behold, spring had arrived. Energy burst out, bluebonnets popped in the front garden, snow tires came off Old Blue. When I drove to Walmart for seeds and returned with spray cleaner and sponges, I figured I was in trouble: spring cleaning—the overhead vigas, the picture frames, the little do-dahs and magic rocks sitting on shelves, the shelves themselves, the floors. A two-tailed comet passed and I sat outside, bundled into a blanket. I did not feel afraid, even when I looked beyond its tail into depths. Why was that? Had something anchored in me? Maybe there was not a one something, rather a progression, from the charge of Barnabas, forgive yourself, to here, this patio and this sky. A pack of coyotes chortled from the arroyo. With a thump, Chama landed in my lap, and I curved my arms around her.

I liked the Kabbalah. It appealed to my scholastic bent and my mystical leanings. Tiphareth, anchored in the center of the Tree and termed a "Mediating Intelligence" by the Yetziratic Text, brought the surrounding essence into balance. For years, I'd felt pulled between the poles of a material life and a spiritual life, but now, work that brought in money, whether teaching or healing, had become a material expression of my spiritual life, no longer separate. The Tree of Life balanced between the poles of masculine and feminine energy.

Jeanne flew in for Easter weekend. On our drive from the airport, we saw people walking beside the highway, and I remembered Mexico and Katy and our pilgrimage to the Basilica of Our Lady of Guadalupe, people on bloody knees, inching forward. Jeanne and I, on foot, walked the last of the Good Friday pilgrimage into Chimayo. A murmur of prayers whispered over us as we slid into a wooden pew beneath the painted icons, the space pulsing with petitions. We followed another line into an adjoining room. A man, sitting beside a hole in the floor, scooped out a dab of holy sand and poured it into our cupped hands. Folded wheelchairs hung on the walls amid crutches and braces. Jeanne had learned the power of spirit in healing. Now I was learning. I curled my fingers around the sand in my palm. The sand remains with me still, cradled in a small bowl among the stones from Hawaii and Molokai.

Jeanne had come to Santa Fe in order to take me on a work visit to the Phoenician Hotel. After church, we drove to the airport and flew to Phoenix, the hotel a good bit more extravagant and polished than my adobe. I sat on our balcony with coffee and looked over the grounds as she met with the spa director. Jeanne worked on the big toe I'd stubbed hard the week before going too fast up the steps from kitchen to desk. We rested and swam. The dark smudges under my eyes faded. "Your feet will heal as you move forward," Jeanne said. All Easter Monday classes were canceled in Santa Fe, so Jeanne and I played through the day and parted that evening at the airport: she to Hawaii, me to Santa Fe.

Designing a worship space was my next assignment. I drew a large oval, windows all around, the altar in the middle, and benches placed on all sides. I'd liked working in theater's Black Box; now I had a white oval for a performance space and gardens in alternating circles and squares, symbolizing the divine masculine and divine feminine, growing separately yet together.

"The Principles of Liturgy" bedeviled me. I began the paper, deleted, made notes on scraps of paper stacked on my desk. I'd heard those words all my life. We broke bread and drank wine—grape juice in my childhood church—to remember Jesus's death. I understood why early Christians did it; they knew how to make wine from vineyards, how to knead bread. The symbols would have resonated on a daily level. Cliff helped me think through it when he said we offered each other service with this meal shared in love. The Gospel of John, written some ninety years after Jesus died and in part a reinterpretation of earlier stories, focused on love. I determined to focus on love.

In early May, with little snow during the winter and no spring rain, the Jemez Mountains burned the western horizon into a glossy, black-outlined blaze. The winds carried a scorched smell and the sky blanketed itself in mourning. The students coughed as they completed finals. I found myself standing outside each sunset, scanning the horizon for either smoke or clouds, like a South African farmer waiting for rain—or locusts. Undoubtedly, I read too much. The flames, day by day, burned out, leaving black scarred sides in my western view.

Another extinguished flame, in the guise of a literary journal, arrived in my mailbox. It carried one of Bill's essays along with an open letter in which he wrote he was living in Cornwall, England, married to "a quiet Wicca witch named Magi," and had a little boy. Finally, he was happy, and we were truly over.

Michael arrived in early June. I quit the job as reader for the Court

Reporter School because whatever extra energy I had needed to be spent with Michael. The psychic line earned enough to pay bills.

Expecting a quiet birthday, me and Michael and ice cream and a movie, did not happen. My niece Laura, husband Angel, and four kids stopped on their summer trip. Stephen called to wish me a happy birthday and say he was late but sending a CD player. Julia called. Susan walked over with her kids, including Michael, and they brought gifts: clothes pins with lady bugs from Alyssa, a flowered candle from Chris, and from Michael, a little bird feeder in the shape of a sunflower. Sweet.

Jeff took Michael and Chris on an overnight camping trip, and Christi arrived to do ritual.

I'd told her about working with a massage therapist who'd found a blockage at my solar plexus. I'd written a paper on Isaiah, and in the process, discovered the *Metaphysical Bible Dictionary* and learned the solar plexus was the altar of the body through which the soul connects to the outer, physical organism. The Kabbalah named it Tiphareth. The center of me blocked integration. I'd told Christi I needed a ritual, a ceremony of sorts. I needed a transformation, a rebirth. Through our months of working together in acupuncture, I'd come to trust her hands and she'd come to trust my guidance.

Flowers from the garden graced the drop leaf table; I bathed and dressed in the white jalabiya, last worn at my Hawaiian Halloween, chose sacred stones, and lit incense. Christi had prepared by talking to her mentor: he told her breath is the fire for burning away the old.

The sun spread late rays through the west window and onto the floor as it dipped into mountains. Night came quickly in the desert. Chama wound around us. Convinced of no play, she curled on the bed pillow.

I lay on the white rug, a crystal in my left hand and a black onyx arrowhead in the right, no idea why they were in those particular hands or why those particular stones, perhaps polarities. Christi inserted needles, and I breathed the fast panting breaths I'd learned in Hawaii. The energy built in my legs, stopped in my upper thighs. Christi said, "Breathe," as she worked the energy up through my groin and into my stomach. The stones slid from my hands as my fingers cramped into claws. I felt my hands go to my solar plexus and claw from side to side, not at flesh, but at energy. Christi chanted, deep, low. The energy grew. I pushed my clawed hands into the air above my chest. They were so cold and so filled. "My hands are holding death," I said. I felt Christi jump up . . . a rush of air. My breathing slowed and fire crawled up my center from pubis to throat. My hands fell to my sides, open.

Light . . . sparkling, iridescent pinpoints . . . blues, greens, yellows, purple reds. Golden threads, one from each thigh, grew past my groin and my belly, chest, throat, face, out the top of my head. I lay stunned.

Christi related what she'd seen, a dark shadow, and being jerked up and sent to open the window... air... I felt air move the darkness. Christi covered my hand with hers and held it. Perhaps I'd completed the work begun in Hawaii.

Two days later, a letter arrived from Mother. Inside the letter's folded birthday wishes, she'd tucked a small golden cross on a golden chain. I've had this a long time, she wrote. I think it belongs to you now. I put it on. The tip of the cross lay between my collarbones. It weighed nothing. I felt tears burn behind my eyes and my heart bloomed, not the sudden thump for my attention, rather, a gentle opening into peace. I wore Mom's necklace on Sunday as Richard elevated me to the Order of Healer.

Rains descended, turning the garden into jungle-like proportions. Morning glories walked the wood pole fence and tumbled over the top. The strawberries sent runners in all directions, more leaf than fruit. The eggplant happy, ready to burst into meals. Michael liked it grilled. He said it tasted like sunshine. We went to movies and ate popcorn. He wandered with Chris. On July 4, the Village gathered on the common grounds across the road and set up tables for a potluck meal while the little boys played with sparklers and the big boys sent up the bigger show after nightfall. It was spectacular.

"I wanted to shoot off the big rockets," Michael said as we walked home. In a couple of years, I assured him, when he was a bigger.

One morning, in the verses of Isaiah, I recognized words from childhood songs and laughed out loud at "declaring the end from the beginning and from ancient times things not yet done." Michael looked up from the kitchen table where he was eating breakfast. "What's funny?" he said. I read him the passage. "What's not done?" he said. Almost everything.

We celebrated Cliff's birthday, July 21, at a Wednesday meditation service. My father died on July 21. I didn't ask Cliff how old he was, but his birthday on such a fated date felt odd. I smiled, wished him a happy birthday.

The days and weeks wound through in simplicity. Michael and Grams and Chama slept through sunrise each morning.

Too soon, it was August. We searched the house and Chris's bedroom for Michael belongings and packed his Going-to-Grandma's suitcase. We were quiet on the drive to the airport. At the gate, he waved one last wave and was gone. I waited until his plane took off and returned to an empty house. I puttered and cleaned out the refrigerator. The sun, sinking toward the mountains, so red, so raw you could almost smell blood.

Billie Holiday's voice trailed me as I walked outside.

In Mexico, floodlights on the Angel of Independence trailed across my balcony. Would I, in twenty years, still be struggling to grasp where that woman had tucked herself away? I could write how Pepe Lobo hired me to work in a travel agency. Joe Wolf his American name. He'd gone to Mexico shortly after the Mexican Revolution and stayed. "When a peso was silver and as big as this!" He'd formed a circle with thumb and forefinger.

Escaping the adobe's silence, I drove Old Blue along country roads and wondered at rusty patches in the piñons. Dad knew about Dutch elms and thistles and milo fields. He left milkweed along the fence line for the monarch migration. Katy and I had traveled to the monarch's wintering-over mountain and walked through a forest of butterflies. One sat on my shoulder. Dad bought the Pontiac new in 1980. Now the valves knocked, but I felt safe. A windmill turned lazy in an empty stretch of pasture. Tires kicked a cloud of dust behind. Dusk gathered. My obsession with time and memory was like digging in rocks and gravel with a dull spade, slow at best. Turning the car at a field lane, I drove home the way I'd come. If I couldn't heal the past, I had to make do with the present, and at present, I drove a country gravel road growing dark.

THIRTY-ONE

WHISPERS

F all slipped away in a blur of reading, writing, cleaning out the garden, and teaching a full load: four speech classes and two English classes. I sped from class to class, and in mid-October, released early for a sudden blizzard, I drove to the tire shop for Blue's change to snow tires, but barely in time, couldn't turn into the driveway, stuck in the middle of the road, so gunned the car backward under the trees outside Susan and Jeff's house. Schools canceled. By noon the next day, Blue had melted free in the sun, and I had finished winterizing the adobe.

A speech class group gave a presentation on the Adopt a Grandparent Program at Pine Ridge led by Grandmother Emily Has No Horse. The speech energized the class; they brought in clothes and shoes and cash and we boxed and enveloped and sent it to Pine Ridge. Grandmother Emily Has No Horse wrote, thanking the students. I read them her letter: "Look what you can do when you are passionate and well-informed, and work together. I am so proud of you," I said. Their faces beamed.

By mid-December, finals over and grades posted, I shuffled papers into files, cleaned house, and packed a suitcase. Or at least started; it lay open on the floor at one end of the bed and created a cumbersome detour. The kids had moved to Atlanta where Nathan managed a restaurant. I'd fly there to spend Christmas, leave my wall of scotch-taped notes, and go be mom for two weeks. I'd shot a photo of sunflowers in a vase over the summer and took it to the photo shop, had it blown up and framed, and sent it to Mother. Chama had to stay home so I bribed Chris to come feed her and empty the litter box.

Christmas brought a full moon in Cancer, and in Cancerian fashion, we celebrated to excess. We had a plethora of presents. Nathan and Kyong had Christmas Eve and Christmas Day off, and enough chocolate filled the house to feed each of us, every day, several times a day. We played computer games and watched movies. Kyong and I cooked. We ate at Nathan's restaurant; we returned home and ate chocolate. Michael and I played more computer games. The sky gray my entire visit. Kyong caught a cold and then Michael got it and I carried it to New Mexico.

The New Year entered as I slept.

An icicle on the north side of the house grew to four feet long and thick as my arm.

Susan waded through drifts from her house to mine and brought warm nasal spray, Nyquil, and Sudafed.

The icicle grew. The cat curled into the comforter. I built fires, which, all in all, didn't help my sinuses but helped me. I recovered.

With an arctic express headed our way, Cliff said he'd pick me up for the meditation service, and after, he took me to eat at Pranzo's as his late Christmas present. He told me stories of his journey to priesthood, his mentor, Tony Dziwulski. I asked him to pronounce Tony's name again and he did. "How do you spell it?" He spelled it, not like it sounded: Javolsky. "It's Polish," he said. I laughed. "I figured that." We talked music. Or rather, he talked, I listened, realizing our influences were different generations, or at least styles, I was a sixties girl, he was seventies. "What year were you born?" I said, confused. He had white hair; I had white hair. "Nineteen fifty-two," he said. And then, "Is something wrong?" My face betrayed me.

"My father died in nineteen fifty-two," I said, "July 21. I just remembered that's your birthday."

"Wow, that's interesting," Cliff said. "And I was born six weeks premature."

I looked down at my lap and curled my fingers. Too much information. I shouldn't have said that. I shouldn't have asked. I'd never met anyone who was born on the day my father died. Not even around that date except my brother five days after. Candlelight flickered off the edge of my plate. Someone laughed at a nearby table. I glued a smile on my face and looked up. I sipped wine. It tasted sour and caught in my throat. Old dreams flickered at the edge of fear. I wanted to get away. The knot in my chest twisted tighter. Cliff wouldn't let me help with the bill. I kept a bright look on my face and asked him something inane about liturgy as he drove me home. When we reached my adobe, he wanted to walk me to the door, but I said, no, no, don't bother, and dashed inside and closed my door. This was crazy! What was I afraid of?

By Sunday, enough snow had fallen for me to stay home. I wasn't ready to face Cliff, and I didn't understand why. So I refused to think about it. Walking out the door to get the paper from the mailbox, a big plop of snow, hanging over the front door, landed on my head.

I was nearly three years in the same house with a cat and a cat box and cat food and a very big tin to hold it. I'd need to get a storage shed if I lived here much longer. I wondered how I could build up . . . like maybe hang shelves from the vigas. No doubt a sound decorative touch. But summer would come soon, and the house would miraculously expand. Well, maybe not soon, but it would come.

Jeanne sent a packet of angel cards, and each morning, I pulled one to measure the day. Most about studying and waiting and watching. At the Wednesday night healing service, a stunning blue light coursed through me and my hands passed on the love flooding me. One rule, and one rule only in the Church of Antioch: love one another.

I chose the path of love. One evening, the moon full, the snow melted, I walked the medicine stone labyrinth I'd built on the north side of the adobe from stones gathered in the desert. In the circle of cosmic change, I lifted my hands, prayed for the sacred marriage, the marriage that joins, that brings light and love. The marriage of equals. I did not know what I should do or where I should look. Standing in the circle, all I could do was be.

I wanted to hear the whispers, not the shouts.

I was not alone in transition. Jeanne, offered a big job in California, didn't know what to do. Jeanne, who always knew what to do. Cynthia was let go from her Austin government job and scared and angry, her retirement safety snatched from her, and after cleaning out her desk, her supervisor said she could stay, in another capacity, with a reduced salary, but she'd been offered a job managing a theater company. What to do. Do what our heart says? Make choices from plenty rather than poverty? I didn't know. My life was simple, if one could call writing a novel—which for all my proffered reasons not to, I continued to poke at—studying for seminary, and teaching college simple. But no decisions to make. I'd become the crazy woman in a Baba Yaga house, minus the magical chicken legs, with a Bible on my lap and a cat. We rolled balls. We took naps.

I listened for whispers.

Classes were fine, students progressed. I graded essays and speeches. My awkwardness with Cliff had passed, and we resumed talking at church like we'd always talked and laughed while vesting or over coffee. On a February morning, sun streamed in the east window when I woke. Pulling on a coat and jiggling the screen door, as had become my habit to check for overhead drifts, I walked to the mailbox. Sun warmth peeled open my coat. I smelled early spring, soft and taunt, green. Paper in hand, I returned to the house and left the door open. The house needed airing, Chama needed to explore the patio, and I needed to finish writing a paper.

On my many personal paths of study and practice—Buddhism, Native American spirituality, Hinduism, Wicca, Huna—I'd learned valuable lessons, but this path was the one I kept wandering back to; now I headed toward ordination. If I was to make a dent in the understanding of how Spirit works—to celebrate what I understood of paired energy—I had to go with what was mine. Christianity was mine. An old memory surfaced: summer church camp, maybe eleven years old, evening vespers, the setting sun sending a stream of gold across a small lake behind the minister. He invited us forward to be baptized or to dedicate our lives to full-time Christian leadership. I'd already been baptized so sat on through succeeding verses until a sudden compulsion pushed me forward to dedicate my life to Christian leadership, beside a wooded lake, outside Fairbury, Nebraska. I paired that memory with one of returning to St. John's with Meena for a performance of *The Illiad*, the actors holding masks to shield their faces. and hearing Hector say, "But as for fate, I think that no one yet has escaped it once it has taken its first form, neither brave man nor coward." What first form might be, Hector didn't say. But now, after all these years, it seemed Christian leadership had grown from my past as my own, personal "First Form" and I was preparing to dedicate my life to Christian leadership.

I read *The Dead Sea Scrolls*. Twin threads ran through the scrolls' discovery: delight and fear. The delight in new information and new findings and fear the documents would undermine Christianity. Why was it so threatening to suppose the Essenes' beliefs influenced Christianity? It seemed possible to view this very recent discovery of the Dead Sea Scrolls as well as the Gnostic Gospels, plus New Age Spirituality, and an acceptance of the mystical as preparation for an evolution of religion in the third millennium in the same way the Essenes proposed an evolution of religion in the first. I knew "fear God" was translated as awe or respect but there had to be more, like a willingness to stand in the transformative energy.

I pulled out my *American Heritage Dictionary*, looked up "fear," and found the Indo-European root, *per*, which developed into many words, mostly movement of some kind. The Sanskrit version means "in front of or around;" Old Germanic, the idea of "danger, retreat, and fear." Movement might be dangerous. So might standing rigid. Could "fear God" mean walk all the way around God and look at it from many angles and then if you get scared, backup and regroup?

Well, it worked with rattlesnakes.

Hopefully, that-which-we-named-God looked on my struggles with benevolent humor.

I'd been cooped up too long. I wanted to strip the plastic off windows and open them. I wanted to sit outside and watch the sky instead of taking quick peeks while carrying in wood or the mail. I wanted to dig in the ground. I wanted to put away wool socks and go barefoot.

A letter arrived from Matriarch Meri. She wrote, "You asked some very good questions about Jesus. It could be he was killed because he felt women were as worthy and equal as men. My feeling about the knowledge taught by Jesus is that when the person was ready, they were told. It was a question of readiness and discernment, of whether they were prepared to handle the energy transmitted. There is no way of learning exactly what happened; in any case, it is always the opinion of the historian, even if a written account was made available." The Matriarch's wisdom comforted me.

The following Sunday, others were scheduled to serve at the altar so I took my place in the pews and began to meditate. My body sank deeper into the quiet, into the peace of no time or place. But while my body meditated, my mind chattered, arguing with the same old arguments— what was I doing? why would I want to be a priest if I didn't believe the whole story? what makes the story true? how can I trust it?

Perhaps, just perhaps, nothing more than perhaps, I could stop questioning and simply be. No one really knew anyway. There was no proof other than Josephus, the historian, who wrote that a man named Jesus had been crucified and he'd had followers. And if he'd died, he'd surely been born. And if he'd had followers, there must have been a reason.

On the Day of World Prayer for Peace, I sat on my white rug in silence, prayed for the earth, for all beings, including rocks. I prayed for peace. For understanding. A freight train of golden light rushed through . . . there goes the prayer . . . a part of my brain registered. A clear column of light washed me down through my chakras to base. Clean. When I surfaced, exhausted and buzz-filled with energy, I went to the drop leaf table and stared out the east widow. No wind, no sound. The world held its breath. Pulling on warm clothes, I walked outside to see what was new. Chama followed.

That night, I woke from a dream of men coming into the house, but this time they came to move out old stuff and debris. I recognized their leader, a man who'd come to me in past dreams. He sat on the couch, put his arm around me, and pulled me close as the men cleaned.

During the Wednesday evening service, Richard elevated me to the Order of Subdeacon. It was the first time I'd lain prostrate; a circle of energy settled over me.

That evening, I gave my first sermon and learned the difference between writing a sermon and speaking a sermon, especially about Lent. But I managed most of it. "Instead of giving something up and then taking it back after Easter, what if we released something we've outgrown, something that's blocking growth?" The idea of sacrifice associated with Lent had such a bloody ring to it, but I didn't say that. A sense of denying the body. I didn't think Jesus denied the body, or he wouldn't have done the healing he did, or the wine with dinner. Mostly, I talked what I thought: love God, let go of fear, be with peace. Celebrate life.

The next morning, Cliff phoned. "I won't keep you," he said. "But this morning I woke up at four-thirty and realized how much you are the mother. You were glowing last night." I didn't know how to respond. We hung up. Did he mean I was mothering everyone?

Maybe he meant Mother like he and Richard were Father.

After Mass on Sunday, Richard and Cliff took me to lunch. Richard was well known in Santa Fe. He knew everyone and everyone knew him. "Coffee!" Richard bellowed as we made our way through the mostly emptied-out restaurant to a table beside wide windows overlooking a pine-blanketed arroyo. We sat, coffee and menus arrived, we ordered.

"We want you to join the staff at Loretto," Richard said. He glanced at Cliff. "We agreed. You'll serve at the altar every week, and when you're a deacon, you'll read the gospel. Once you're ordained, we'll take turns presiding." Cliff nodded. I'd expected new duties, but "staff?" The turmoil up the center of my body blocked any response.

"You'll have some new responsibilities, but you need to be at the altar and not off to one side," Cliff said.

"Anything specific?" My face must have once more betrayed me. My throat felt so tight, it's a wonder I didn't stutter. Cliff laughed. "I'll show you."

Staff. Like I belonged. I stared out the window into pines. Had I found home?

Meri approved my moving through the deaconate orders quickly for an August ordination. My entire family wanted to come but October or November would be difficult for them. We set deacon ordination for March and priesthood ordination for August. I had a lot of work to do. As if that were somehow different than always.

Lunch after church became a staff routine. When Richard couldn't make it, Cliff and I had lunch. Cliff excelled as a liturgist, and before leaving the Roman Catholic priesthood was offered the job of Liturgy Director at the Baltimore Cathedral. I listened and learned as he designed liturgies for the Church of Antioch.

The doubts came at night, alone, staring up at the vigas, unable to sleep. In the liturgy, there were no doubts. I moved with Cliff; I moved with Richard. Was I playing a part or living a part? Was there a difference? Chama leapt from the floor and landed on my belly with a whoomp. I curled around her and we slept.

THIRTY-TWO

A New Identity

B ut regardless, some things didn't change. I rose at five-thirty to write with no idea where the writing was going. I wrote. The whole process might have been easier if I didn't teach writing. Or if I didn't care. Or if I didn't have to. Chama wanted to play. I rolled balls. She chased them. It helped when the balls rolled down the kitchen steps and bounced and pinged into a corner. Or under the table. That took longer, not that she ever learned to fetch, but it took more time before she wound around my feet... *mom mom mom*... telling me to get the ball and roll again.

Spring crept in unwillingly.

A comet rose in the east, its tail easy to see and my reward for getting up early. Everyone seemed to be in the midst of change and most had no idea what that meant or was. Winter was ending in... I don't know... and that perhaps was appropriate after a very long and very cold season. Tulip leaves sprouted through patches of snow. The patio, muddy and moldy smelling, and too wet to rake or sweep.

Katy wrote she was flying into Albuquerque to give a conference paper and after, would come visit. I put aside the Mexico book, cleaned and painted the sooty and dust-smeared white plastered walls white again. Katy wrote the most over my head economic studies and papers, but when she talked, somehow I understood. We'd met in Mexico, each of us sitting in the sun outside the movie theater in Chapultepec Park, me, waiting; she, reading a book, *Open Veins of Latin America*. "What do you think of that?" I'd said. She lifted her head. "The writing's good but the economics don't always follow." After these many years, she was a department head and presenting papers. She'd as soon not be a department head, but she was.

I planted spinach and peas that soon popped up eager for sun. The bluebonnets bloomed with the almost-smell of the violets I'd picked at my knee in Hawaii. I tossed the cat outside. Her pitiful "mom" echoed through the screen door from time to time before distraction seized her.

She preferred roaming at night when I'd sit outside and watch the sky. I'd grab her off the wall to come inside. Too many coyotes to allow the silly child freedom.

Three big papers remained, the most complex on Teilhard de Chardin, which sent me to reread the *Odyssey*. Chardin struggled to find the center between Scylla and Charybdis as much as Odysseus had struggled, and lost, and struggled. Did I really have to know this much? Digging. I was always digging, like a gravedigger tossing shovelfuls of sludge over my shoulder searching for firm ground.

But perhaps I was evolving, inch by inch, elbow to fingers.

And grading papers and teaching. I went to school; I went to church; I came home.

One day, creating a cover page for yet another seminary paper, my head suddenly blanked out when writing the date. I couldn't remember what year it was and scrabbled through the papers on my desk to find a calendar.

When I got tired, I browsed the dictionary: excoriate, to remove, flay. The English language itself a mystery, and other than the root words in the *American Heritage*, I didn't know how English was built.

On Wednesday evening, March 19, I put on a collar for the first time and from the depths of my closet, rescued the pin-striped suit I'd worn as a businesswoman in D.C. My skirts worn shorter in those days, which prompted Richard and Cliff to proclaim surprise in discovering the new deacon had legs. An alb over that, I lay prostrate, energy coursed through me, and I felt something lift, old stuff like a dark shadow. I wobbled when I stood and felt Cliff's hand at my elbow steady me, guide me to face Richard, who vested me in a new deacon stole. When I put on my glasses to read the gospel, they steamed up. I took them off, Cliff handed me a handkerchief, I cleaned my glasses, and read. At the altar for communion, I lifted the cup for the first time, joined in the blessing chant, and realized it was the same chant, different words, as in Hawaii. Richard on one side, Cliff on my other. Energy flowed through my arms and hands.

If I embodied some small part of the whole, would this part complete my whole? If God spoke to Moses, to Abraham as a friend, could I speak to my god-self as a friend? Use it as a mirror? Like any good teacher helping a student struggle through questions in order to uncover answers, maybe finally says . . . just go do it . . . you'll learn as you go.

Still high on energy the next morning, I carefully drove to school. Fragmented by the afternoon, a Hershey, a Snickers, and a bottle of red wine came home with me. On Friday, with no classes, I crashed. Cliff came to take me to dinner.

"This is a lonely process," I said. "Separate and alone." He nodded.

He noticed a Mexico picture of me on the wall. "You look different now," he said. "More open." I stared at the photo. She wore a shield in her eyes.

Impulsively pulling out Bill's poetry book, I read one of his Mexico poems aloud. My voice choked, and I stuck the book back on the shelf.

"Let's go to dinner," Cliff said. So we did. And we laughed. And I was okay.

Saturday morning, the phone rang. Bill.

He was in New York between traveling to Cuba through Mexico. "I thought you were married in Wales," I said. "Married?" he said. When I reminded him of the literary magazine and his open letter, he said no, he wasn't, it was a joke, and slid into stories of Cuba and bars and people.

I'd once been named "wife" in a poem.

"I'm becoming a priest," I said.

"That sounds about right." Odd. He sounded sincere.

He said he'd called to tell me the cat, Wee-wee Joyce, the only child between us, had died. My heart clenched and I felt tears in my eyes.

All the healing and unhooking and letting go I'd done over the years, and with a single phone call, he was back in my head. I had closed that chapter and he was back. All because a silver-gray tabby had died.

Cliff stopped by to talk about deacon duties, and I told him Bill had phoned. "Well, I guess you called that in," he said. I guess I had.

On Good Friday, Cliff picked me up and we sat in the Santa Fe Cathedral, huge wooden beams, clean-plastered walls, before the service at Richard's chapel. Dropping deeply into a meditation, I lost track of where I was until I felt him shift, lightly, at my side. We rose, said no words, and drove to Richard's. As his deacon, I sat beside Cliff, and when he stood to speak, his spirit, full and powerful, stretched above his head. I could see it. Cliff never looked like that. Who was this man, the man under the referential, almost hidden man presented to Richard, to the church, who always laughed and was pleasant to everyone?

Easter Mass was glorious but at the end of March and chilly. I drove home to my adobe and built a fire. Richard and Cliff busy with family. With a week off from classes, I spent time cleaning before Katie's visit. The tomato plants needed transplanting from their little boxes to pots. I set the newly filled pots above the sink in full sunlight, our first frost-free date yet ahead in the middle of May. God stuff and garden stuff. That was my life. On Monday, a packet arrived from Matriarch Meri, addressed to Rev. Janet Sunderland. I held the packet in my lap and stared at my name as if it were a stranger's. How could I possibly be someone revered?

Katy arrived to end my solitude. We wandered and looked and talked and ate. A winter storm dumped snow and rain and in-between, sun. We drove to Bandolier and wandered through ruins, stopped at a flea market, bought peanuts and dried fruit and ate as we wandered, recounted our life stories, like always. Like Mexico. When she left, my little adobe felt hugely empty.

Most days, I rose before dawn and wrapped in a coat to sit on the patio and listen. Stars crackled from the Milky Way. Jupiter hung in the southeast. An owl hooted a sleepy goodnight. We'd had so much snow...and rain...and sometimes snow and rain together, the Jemez would not burn this year. Light grew over a green carpeted desert. Unbidden, the memory of spring thaw, the farm barnyard boot-deep in muck, my zig as a cow zagged plopped me flat out into muck. I'd walked to the house, stiff legged and called out, "Mom!" And like she always did, she called back, "I'm busy. Come to me."

"Not this time," I'd yelled. She came out and washed me down with a hose. Cold, mercy it was cold. We'd laughed and laughed.

A wind chime pinged and birds clicked and twittered.

I went inside. Chama followed: *mom mom mom.*

Every paper I shuffled out multiplied into three more. Sandy, in some letter, had written, "Fly, and if you get scared, don't look down," a line I repeated to myself, often. My wings were tired. I gave finals; I graded papers. Meena, classmate from St. John's and now a colleague at the community college, said, "I have a weekend free. Let's drive up to Chaco Canyon. Take tents." When I shook my head, a half-shrug to one side, she said, "You have to get away; you're getting glassy-eyed!"

At Chaco Canyon, we slept under stars and walked the ruins behind a group guide. We cooked stir fry over an open fire, searing-vegetable smell twining into wood-burning smell, stars crackling, coyotes yipping beyond the circle of firelight. Sunday afternoon, we wandered a petroglyphic wall of symbols—at its top ledge, a line of swallow nests. The ancient petroglyphs ended and dates and names of Spanish explorers began. Between the names, a scratched note: "Sept 26 1910 Joan I cannot get no feed I cannot wait for you." A herd moving on, a woman holding a basket, wondering which way to go. Meena walked on; I stared at the wall. Joan, I cannot get no feed. I cannot wait for you. I watched the swallows. I stared at the sky. A woman climbed from her buggy, walked to this wall, and stood alone. A hawk circled. Purple flowers and yellow flowers and white flowers. A swallow flew into a crevice and fed babies. Sky in Kansas, Mexico, Hawaii, New Mexico: my arms outstretched horizon to horizon; I stood on the earth and I looked at sky.

By mid-May, finals done and grades in, white-bearded thunder gods lifted over the mountains, promised rain, but didn't. I watered the strawberries, bursting with tiny green fruit. I watered peas and lettuce and transplanted the tomatoes outside. I wrote a paper on The Acts and the cosmological significance of wind and tongues of flame. Purple blooming flowers crawled over the fence. I cut the ends of vines and put them in a vase. No matter how much coffee I drank, the kick-starter on my Harley seemed to spin with no catching. Michael would arrive in June and inherit my Chaco tent as a bedroom on the patio. He could sleep later than my early-every-mornings allowed, and his, "Grams, you're making too much noise," would not issue from the bedclothes unless I scraped a patio chair on the stones. "Don't scrape chairs" went on a note taped on the wall in front of the computer screen. I had to-do lists for ordination: motel rooms to reserve; Seaton neighbors to consult who'd offered homes while they were out of town; food stuff to figure out for the reception—nephew Angel said he'd grill; my grocery list included tortillas and fajitas, wine, beer, sodas, a cake. Julia offered to make my invitations in her print shop. Scratch that off. Bless my family. I'd finish seminary reading and papers.

On a Sunday chilly enough for coats, Cliff and I walked to a little café, sunlit windows, small linen-covered tables with cloth napkins, flatware, tiny spring bouquets, and warm air wafting cinnamon rolls and coffee. The café began to empty, but we sat over refills, talked church, talked seminary, talked story. Cliff held my coat for me, as he always did, and we walked down the sidewalk to the church parking lot. We were nearly the same height. Our strides matched. Our arms swung in unison. My hand slipped into his. The inside of me froze while the outside of me kept walking and talking. How did that happen? What had I done? If I snatched my hand back it would be rude. My hand rested in his. They were the same size. Our conversation never faltered. At our cars, we separated, waved, and drove our ways. It didn't seem to change anything. More like we'd become good friends.

He'd call to check in a couple of times a week; we'd go to lunch; he listened the same way Cynthia or Katy listened. Never found fault. And he said one-liners that lifted me out of my worries. "You'll get it done," he said lightly when I complained of the load I'd taken on or worried how I'd take care of Michael's needs amid all these other demands. Inches. I traveled in inches within whirls of necessity.

Katy wrote she was traveling to Africa and wouldn't be at ordination. I'd miss her, but so many were coming—siblings and spouses, assorted children, Cynthia from Austin, Dale from Arkansas to participate in the service, friends from church and school and in general, which meant anywhere between thirty and a hundred people. Susan and Jeff offered their house for the reception.

Sometimes I walked the road and practiced breathing, the roadside ablaze after a wet spring: blue flax and deep burgundy heavy-headed grasses, tiny white flowers and purple and yellow as if it were August after monsoons. I'd wake up cold and wear sweats and wool socks and a few days later, a white-hot descended and crickets clacked. I borrowed Jeff's weed eater and cut grass around the adobe in a four-foot swath to discourage snakes. I had two seminary courses to finish, but they should be done by mid-July. "Should." The operative word in my life. I was close to being crazy but not angry-crazy. Just crazy. Which pointed, in some sort of perverse way, to progress. Cliff checked in every few days. "I'm peddling as fast as I can, and I still have my head above water." He laughed. I laughed too, wondering what kind of a vehicle I'd be peddling if water were up to my shoulders or even waist. I was getting punchy, like a prize fighter after too many rounds in the ring. He talked me through some ideas on a paper. A neighbor said they were definitely leaving in August, and my family could use her four bedroom house. Another neighbor next door to the big house offered her three-bedroom house. Cynthia would sleep with me.

Michael arrived, minus the Going-to-Grandma's suitcase. He'd be ten in a few months and too old for baby things. We wrestled the tent into stability, he blew up the air mattress, spread out the sleeping bag, and lay on his back, looking through the mesh screen at the top. "Bet I can see the stars at night," he said.

I'd passed my usual three-year moving on time. The county came out, renamed all the roads for 911 purposes, and presto, a new address without moving.

And then it was my birthday.

Cards and calls and email arrived. Sandy, wise lady that she was, sent computer games for Michael, a math game, and Mr. Brain. Michael played one or the other every day, my gift of quiet while he played. On Wednesday, my birthday, Alex and Olga and Stacy drove from Albuquerque and took Michael and me for a long lunch, complete with philosophical discussions, after which I dashed home to change, sent Michael to Chris, and drove into town for dinner with Cliff before the healing service. We ate at the Santa Café, a lovely table on the patio, and for dessert, Cliff ordered a little chocolate cake with fudge sauce, ice cream, a candle, and a piece of chocolate bark. We arrived at meditation high on chocolate. Balloons hung over the table at Richard's house and on his table a chocolate-chocolate cake and more cards. We celebrated. In chocolate. Thursday's mail brought more cards and a package from Stephen, a most wondrous clock that not only showed the time, it showed phases of the moon, temperature, barometer, and humidity. Humidity an afterthought in the desert, but it measured how little we had, and it kept me abreast of the moon's travels. My son knew me well.

Michael and I visited Walmart. He wanted to buy me a birthday present, and there hadn't been time. While he shopped, I wandered to other errands, setting my purse in the shopping cart. My purse was not in the cart when I wandered back. I didn't get crazy—no energy for crazy—notified security and the police, and called Richard to ask if he could come pick me up because, of course, along with the little black wallet I'd carried since Mexico and my credit cards and a hundred dollars for groceries, the purse held my car keys and checkbook. I had nothing. Nothing. I didn't even have pockets in my dress. Richard was swamped at the restaurant but said he'd come as soon as he could. After an hour, a clerk came from hardware with my purse. The keys and the checkbook were inside but not the wallet. I called to tell Richard he didn't need to rescue me. We could get into the car and Michael could buy his present since he had money, but I had no identity. I returned home to call the credit card companies.

When I told Alex and Olga what had happened, Alex said, "Janet, you have a whole new identity, and it only cost a hundred dollars. You are like Eve. Now you must find your apple tree." In the desert. Perhaps Adam found a watering hole. My ID from St. John's gone. Only a year left on my driver's license, and it had a photo of me with short hair. My old identity gone. The DMV issued a new license, and over the week, I completed my studies and papers, and for the first time in years, I wasn't a student. I had a new identity and a new address. And so the saga of my birth/rebirth celebration week came to a close.

Things had come close to being over the top and yet I'd remained sane, didn't get depressed, laughed a lot, shook my head in amazement, and became the woman who for a space of time had no identity and reformed herself anew. I remembered my favorite Voltaire quote: "God is a comic playing to an audience who is afraid to laugh." I was still laughing.

After that, I crashed. Michael checked on me from time to time while I slept. He watered the garden, fed Chama, and let me sleep.

I'd asked Jeanne for help finding a suitable thank-you gift for Cliff. I had a leather notebook for Richard, gifts for the servers, but I couldn't find anything appropriate for Cliff. She emailed me: "The universe is generous. I started looking for kikuyu nut leis. You can't buy them. I asked one of my Hawaiian friends where I could find someone to make them, and she said she would be honored. She is a wise woman and a keeper of the knowledge. The kikuyu are used in spiritual celebrations for cleansing and consecrating. The white leis are the most powerful since they are made of the young nuts and the healing sap and energy is in them. They carry the light. The dried kikuyu are dark and carry the earth."

As I crossed another item off the list, I prayed for a sane July.

At the Village Fourth of July, Michael and Chris dashed off to do whatever boys do with sparklers and things that pop. I walked into the Village and played horseshoes, my partner a newly arrived screenwriter researching Armand Hammer and ready for a conversation on Russia and Lenin and the Cold War. An older man joined our rambling talk. In the 1950s, he was a young attorney in Mississippi. How did these people find Seaton Village? I supposed they knew someone who knew someone who owned a house here on the more prosperous west side. I lived on the east side, across the road, in the two room adobe below the castle. And then talk veered off to Kit Carson and movies, so I peeled myself away and walked home. Later, back at the gathering, I sat with others ringing the commons where the boys—little boys to make noise and big boys to organize and supervise—set off fireworks. The little boys the most fun to watch . . . "here, be careful . . . spray water on that one . . . get back!! . . . oops . . . all right!" I laughed a lot. And finally ushered Michael home at 10:30 in a chilly wind. He slept in my bed that night and we bundled close together.

The first big tomato ripened, so I sliced it for dinner, warm and sweet and home-smelling. A promising cloud bank built in the west.

Niece Lia phoned, "Enjoy this whole thing. You're not going to do it again." From the mouths of babes. I lived in a holding pattern where everything swirled around me, and every day I walked to remind my legs it was safe to go forward. By mid-July, things were sorta sane and sorta quiet, but not really. Ordination plans rolled along, a tidal wave.

THIRTY-THREE

ORDINATION

C liff and I sat at the drop leaf table, the casement open to hummingbirds, and worked on the ordination service language. "You can leave that out," he said, or "put it this way," melding mystical concepts with Vatican II simplicity.

I typed it up and designed a cover, but I needed a line to demonstrate my commitment. We practiced the Mass; the next week, we practiced again. On the Saturday before ordination, we would practice the ordination service. Jeanne told me to take ionized minerals when I said it felt like I had electricity running through me and couldn't sleep. I bought and swallowed the minerals. Electricity continued to course through me.

Monsoon season cracked and afternoon rains cooled temperatures, tempers, and stress. Michael entered a week of rock climbing camp. He came home with lengths of rope to practice his knots, quiet and concentrated and proud of himself.

I found my line in Hosea: "I will lead her into the desert and speak to her heart. She shall respond there as in the days of her youth, when she came up from the land of Egypt."

It would fit beside the symbol, a drawing I'd done with a calligraphy pen, a tall, whipping curve, the tail whispering to an end with a crossed line. Here am I.

Michael and I drove to Kinko's and ordered the copies. I'd promised him a Big Mac. Mother bribing child. It should be a bumper sticker.

Richard decided I'd take over as Mass celebrant after my ordination since so many of my family would be here. "Are you ready?" Cliff assured Richard I was ready. Now I practiced as presider rather than co-presider. All my acting and directing linked with Cliff's liturgical skills and we saw what the other saw. We made another appointment to practice. I would be a priest in white.

Only I felt like the White Rabbit, checking my watch and calendar.

A full moon swept stars from the sky as it trundled over my adobe.

I did not see it. I was asleep. Cliff and I met for lunch, our conversation unmemorable, but we told stories and made each other laugh. He especially liked my White Rabbit analogy, although he'd never read the book. Movies. He knew stuff from movies, which, oddly enough since it was one of my professions, I didn't. As we lingered over coffee, Cliff gave me his ordination gift: a set of holy oils in metal screw-top containers.

I could see tears at the rim of my eyes when I looked at him. "Thank you. There's nothing I could have wanted more."

"We are all of us, the thousands ordained over time, chosen for very different reasons and for what we bring to the line of Melchizedek," Cliff said. I stared at him. My head cleared in a connection to this deeper meaning. I would be anointed by the oil of Melchizedek, this child of a Celtic warrior and a Quaker mother. My own personal legend.

Great buckets of water fell in the night, lightening, crackling thunder. Michael and I wrestled the tent inside the kitchen door and he slept beside me, twisting in the sheet as his body was wont to do. I lay awake and watched the jagged flashes through windows. Even with them shut, I could smell ozone. I wouldn't have to water the garden in the morning. I laughed aloud at my oft repeated phrase. Michael twisted and muttered beside me. I curled into sleep.

Five days from ordination. I felt close to tears most of the time. Yet calm. I breathed deep. Hold me in a hand so large the space is infinite, the air still, I prayed.

Stillness lay at the center of me, watching.

Judy and Mom arrived three days before the ceremony. Judy took over the last minute organization after they unpacked in the big house with the deck. My downside of living in the moment meant no short-term memory, so Judy gathered the pieces and lists and made sense of them. Their big house could become the main gathering place.

The family came from west to east and all directions north to south: Judy, Jeanne, Julia, Jack, Jolene, plus assorted spouses and children, as well as cousins Linn and Pat from Nebraska. And Mom and Cynthia. We filled two houses, three counting mine. Cynthia would sleep with me, Michael in the tent on the patio. Cliff stopped by and met the family.

Perhaps it was Jeanne who began the adoption process. From somewhere a piece of parchment was produced, perhaps from Julia as she was the paper sibling. She probably had the good pens to write with, too, since by the time Cliff and I arrived at the big house, having spent the afternoon in rehearsal, they had written up a formal deed, signed it, and tied it with a red ribbon.

Jeanne called the family together, the rolled parchment in her hand. "Cliff, you have been a remarkable mentor to our sister, and we thank you."

Cliff bobbed his head to acknowledge. "But you also feel like family. And as you see, we are a lot of family." She swept an arm toward the expanse of open living room, dining room, and kitchen. Everyone laughed. She gave him the parchment and he unrolled it. "The family adopts you," Jeanne said.

Cliff's laugh was abrupt. "I've never been adopted before!" he said. "Thank you."

The gathering applauded, smiles wide.

Jeanne picked up the white kikuyu nut lei. She told the story of the woman who made it and kikuyu symbolism. "Janet asked for a special gift for Cliff, and this is for her to give him." She put the lei in my hands and I turned to Cliff, put it over his head and onto his shoulders where my hands rested. "You've been a light and taught me what a priest must be. Thank you for being my friend." Cliff took my hand and guided me to turn. Jeanne held another lei in her hands, dark and white nuts, earth and light, balanced. She put the lei over my head and wrapped her arms around me. The family applauded. And then we ate and talked and wandered into and out of conversations and out to the back deck where Michael, who had saved a box of sparklers, handed them around, and everyone played with fire. Cliff and I sat beside each other in wooden deck chairs. I'd taken his hand. It anchored me.

The family came to Sunday's Mass at Loretto, my final Mass as a deacon. Cliff presided. At the homily, he spoke about the priesthood, and the meaning in what I was about to do. At the end, he turned to me and said, "So you see, Janet, no matter where you go now, you are home. Welcome home, my friend. Welcome home." Tears, unbidden, filled my eyes.

At the Eucharist, I raised my hands as he raised the cup, as Richard raised his hands from Cliff's other side.

In the afternoon, I made some sense of my adobe, washed dishes and changed sheets, while Jeanne drove to the airport to pick up Cynthia. I showered, dressed, and drove to Richard's where we met up and drove to Loretto—Richard, Cliff, Gail, and Carol, who were serving. We had an hour, but it was a flurry. Mass booklets and ordination booklets and hymnals to set out. The organist practiced. We set up the altar and the trays and bottles and oils. Bishop Dale and Father Jay arrived, Jay with his deacon. Richard cued the meditation music. We vested. Me in my alb and deacon's stole. I walked into the sanctuary for a last check.

Cliff came to stand beside me. "I'll tell you the same thing the M.C. for my ordination told me: go someplace quiet and sit. You have twenty minutes. I'll find you." I nodded. A big sigh softened my shoulders. The coffee room was empty. I sat by a window. Cliff found me.

We assembled at the rear of the sanctuary: four priests, a deacon, two servers, and me. I saw people from the church community and the community college, from Seaton Village, and from St. John's, Matt Stewart and Meena, Andrea and her daughter, the sanctuary full. I didn't realize I knew so many people. The organ swelled and the congregation sang "The Prayer of St. Francis," a song I had chosen but could not sing, could only absorb "make me a channel of your peace." Gail, swinging the thurible in a cloud of incense, walked first, followed by Carol, me, the deacon, the priests, Bishop Richard with his crozier, Cliff as M.C. beside him. When I reached my mother in the front row, I slid in beside her. She took my hand.

"In the name of God, Father and Mother, Son and Spirit. Amen." Richard said.

I had chosen the music and the readings, but I heard them anew. Dale read from Jeremiah: "Before I formed you in the womb, I knew you, and before you were born, I consecrated you." Richard read the Gospel of John: "In the beginning was the Word and the Word was with God and the Word was God." Richard gave a short homily with an overview of my seminary work and closed with, "She has been a priestess in many lives, and now she has chosen this church to become a priest." Startled, I stared at him. Had he meant to say that? No time to ponder. He instructed Gail and Carol to bring me forward. I squeezed Mom's hand and stood.

Standing before Richard, I listened to his Charge to a New Priest. I knelt for prayers, lay prostrate for the litany, the words swept over me in a wave. Cliff helped me stand while Gail placed a cushion for me to kneel. I felt flushed and unsteady. When Richard lay his hands on my head, a shock traveled down the left side of my jaw, my neck; my body rocked. Dale came next, and then Father Jay. At last, Cliff lay his hands on my head and a flood of peace poured through me.

Richard invited family members to come bless me. Mother came first, placed her hands on my shoulders and murmured a prayer. She kissed my cheek. Joe, my brother's son came next, he, the next generation coming into adulthood and our only male child carrying the Sunderland name. His blessing felt like a promise. My siblings, Judy, Jeanne, Julia, Jack, and Jolene, came in turn. Judy blessed my head and cradled it to her; Jeanne breathed aloha in a long *haaaaaaa* into my crown; Julia kissed me lightly as she held my head; Jack bowed over me, his hand on my head; Jolene lay her hands gently. Richard motioned to my sons. Nathan bent down, his hands on my head. He whispered, "Are you all right, Mom?" I nodded. Stephen, rock solid, blessed me as I touched his hand. I looked at Richard and whispered, "Michael."

Richard's voice boomed, "Michael!" In a moment Michael appeared in front of me. He shrugged his arms wide. "What?" he whispered.

"Just hug me, baby," I said. And he did. "Put your hands on my head and bless me," I whispered in his ear, and as he reached up, he leaned forward and our foreheads touched. A spark flowed between us.

Richard returned to stand before me. With hands on my head, he said, "Receive the Holy Spirit." A ripple, down my head, my shoulders, my back. I breathed to settle myself. He took the thurible and as the cantor sang, "Here I Am, Lord, is it I, Lord," Richard circled me. Incense rose in soft puffs. Spirals of energy rose with the smoke. My body rocked, buffeted. When the song ended, Cliff took my hands to help me rise and steady myself. Richard removed my deacon stole and asked my sons to come forward. Together, they dropped the white chasuble over my head, straightened it, and lay the white stole around my neck. Two chairs appeared in front of the altar. Richard and I sat. He bound my hands with a linen strip and blessed them with holy oil as the scent of frankincense drifted between us, placed my chalice and paten between my fingertips for a moment, removed them, handed them to Cliff, and removed the binding. We cleaned our hands with the bread and lemons, and Richard took my hands in his. "Do you promise to obey me and all my successors?"

"I do so promise," I said, and Richard smiled a quick smile, no doubt remembering all my struggles with authority and with rules. He'd helped me weeks earlier by telling me St. Benedict's definition of obey: to listen without judgment.

We stood. Richard turned me to the congregation. "I present to you Reverend Mother Janet Ellen Sunderland." Applause thundered. Startled, I bowed.

The Mass continued: the Lord's Prayer; the sign of peace with hugs and more hugs; several of the family in a group hug; the presentation of the gifts, which Jolene and Michael brought forward. Mass went smoothly, Cliff on my left, Richard on my right. Gail and Carol flanked me as I offered communion. In my comments after Eucharist, I did a lot of thanking: Richard and Cliff, Dale and Jay and Carol and Gail, the cantor, the organist. I thanked the Seaton Village community, the St. John's community, the church community, and especially, my family. Together, Richard, Cliff, and I raised our hands for the final blessing. We recessed, singing, and I returned alone to the front to offer the first blessing from a new priest. There was a long line.

We left the church in a thundering downpour and drove to Seton Village and Susan's house for the reception. I slid from group to group, smiled and chattered. Carol had made a pair of person-sized blue glittery feather wings, complete with shoulder straps, so I put those on for a bit before transferring them to Michael. I darted from conversation to conversation. I couldn't stop moving. My nephew Angel grilled fajitas and fed people. Trays and bowls of food filled all available countertops and tables. I saw Cynthia and we held each other for a moment. We'd had no time to talk. Finally, I saw Cliff. "The rain stopped. Let's go have that cigar," I said.

Day's before, he said he wanted us to sit and have a cigar and brandy after the ordination. "The last time I had brandy and a cigar was with my dad at Haussner's a few months before he died," he'd said. We slipped out of Susan and Jeff's and walked across the road to my patio table where we half-smoked the cigars, drank brandy, talked.

The party continued without us.

Cynthia walked across the road. She lightly hoisted herself onto the wall beside us, her hands curled into her lap, legs crossed at the ankles. She studied us.

"Do you two know what you're doing?"

We burst out laughing. "We're just friends," we said in unison.

In the morning, family straggled onto the patio and dragged chairs from the house. We made coffee. I stayed in the kitchen. Nathan came in. "Mom, can I talk to you? I understand you had to run away and be quiet before the ordination, but the family's come a long way to be with you." Pay attention, is what he meant, the same phrase I'd used on him over the years. I smiled and walked out to the patio. Cliff stopped by on his way to work. We took group photos. In the afternoon, cars loaded, we drove to Santo Domingo Pueblo for the corn dances. I'd dressed in sweat pants, walked with my head down, feeling shy, almost lightheaded, hoping no one would call out Mother Janet! I'd reached another crossroad, that was clear, and while one side said priest, the destination, as usual, was written in invisible ink. Priest was the journey, but the destination unknowable.

A carnival had set up beyond the dances and Nathan made me ride the Twister with him. The whirling took my spinning away and I laughed. The next day we all drove to Tsankawi and hiked the mesa. On the way home, we stopped for two gallons of milk and a fifth of tequila and ate leftovers. Other than sleeping in the same bed and drifting conversations as we fell asleep, Cynthia and I had little down time for talking. She left with one of several trips to the airport. Most of the time, I felt out of sync with my body as if I were standing half a step to one side.

By the following Sunday, the day of my first complete Mass, Nathan and Michael and Mother were the only ones still with me. I mixed up a couple pieces of liturgy, but Cliff covered. We celebrated one last meal after church, Richard and Cliff and Dale and Nathan, Michael, Mom. And me. Sunday afternoon, Nathan and Michael left, and Mother moved from the big house to mine. I was glad for the company. We cooked simple meals. We talked. We read and rested. Chama, who had mostly lived under the bed during the commotion, curled into my lap and purred. I drove Mom to the airport for her flight back to Judy's; the house empty on my return. Except for Chama. She was there.

THIRTY-FOUR

FROM DESERT TO FOREST

Old Blue carried me to the Pecos Benedictine monastery for three days of retreat. I attended mid-day prayers then walked along the Pecos River, listened to river talk, and smelled the ripe heat of late summer. The walk wound through tall cottonwoods and thick underbrush so unlike my desert abode. Wildflowers crowded the path. Coming to a short waterfall, piled boulders, and swirling eddies, I clambered onto the top of one boulder and sat, breathing to open my heart. All along the walk, my heart had felt heavy; but why? I let it be and watched the water. Was ordination my new foundation, or was there something more? The water rustled. I listened and watched the water, the sky, the hunting hawks floating on air currents. Hawks had circled me on those long walks across farm pastures and at Kalani. My *aumakua*. I longed to see as only a hawk could see. When I returned to my room, I arranged the wildflowers I'd picked and pressed them in a folded sheet of paper.

Later, after vespers, I browsed through the bookstore and found *I Remember Your Name in the Night: Thinking About Death*. I bought it for a friend whose child had died recently and began reading to see if it was any good. It was. I kept reading. Late that night, I wrote, "I have died/or I have re-birthed. The result is the same. I am a slate, waiting for a new message from yesterday's lessons."

Struggle dreams came in the night, shadows restless, taunting.

At 6:45, I rose and dressed for early Eucharist. An older monk, full white beard, bald head, almost fierce looking, celebrated the Mass and used the feminine pronoun from time to time. Not forced or a big deal, he'd say "her." I listened more closely. This was a Mass of Reconciliation, Mother Mary as a medium for reconciliation.

I needed to reconcile me to myself. Not necessarily to God, although that would be part of it, but me to me.

After breakfast, I approached the priest, Father Wilfred by name. "Father, I wonder if you'd have time to talk." He smiled. He said he would.

We waited as a woman spoke about her work with Mother Teresa. He motioned to me and we walked into the hallway.

"I need to tell you something first," I said. We stopped and he turned to look at me. "Two weeks ago, I was ordained a priest, so if you have problems with women being priests, I don't want to force the issue." He laughed and gave me a hug. He pointed to a door and led me inside to a welcoming, low-light room, and shut the door. We sat in easy chairs. Father Wilfred crossed one leg over the other and leaned back. "Tell me about the Church of Antioch," he said. I related lineage and rites and concepts. We inched toward what I'd come to say.

"My ordination was wonderful, but now my heart feels like it's covered in fear."

We wandered around that for some time. Was I afraid of acceptance? No. I didn't want to force the issue of being a woman priest but acceptance wasn't my problem. Was I feeling unworthy? No. We wound through possibilities and answers that weren't answers until a realization coalesced. I couldn't hide anymore. I couldn't hide from who I was.

"The fear comes from stepping into a place of recognizing myself," I said.

Father smiled.

We hadn't talked long, maybe fifteen minutes. I thanked him and left. Walking to my room, I considered the phrase, "fear God," which had bothered me, forever, it seemed, and thought about the conversation with a young woman the night before. She volunteered at the monastery as I had volunteered at Kalani, and we explored what it meant to come closer to that-which-we-call-God, the spiraling in, coming closer to the center core of ourselves. Fear had come up in that conversation too. And as I walked back to my room, I suddenly understood what "fear God" meant, at least for me, in this situation.

What would be required of me?

I stopped on the path and laughed out loud. Same old crossroad.

This new crossroad sign, clearly legible, read, "I am who I am."

I carried all the teachers who taught me: Gloria and Bhante, Kam Nightchase, Marion deNice and Sharon, Saki Lee, Tom Simmons. My job was not to be them, but to be me.

A deep sigh filled my chest and loosened my shoulders. Who I was, was enough, even with the warts and bruises, the fears and insecurities, the mistakes, the unknowing and the struggles—who I was, was enough.

A nap was in order and mid-day prayers and lunch. Stopping in the bookstore, I bought a copy of *I Remember Your Name in the Night* for myself so I could underline passages while reading. One passage asked, "What are your fears?" How could I even list them? Going outside to sit on the railing, I pondered. I'd had a lot of fears: until recently, I was afraid of the dark and realized I wasn't anymore. Somehow that had vanished. I'd feared I would never find something that I could do and do well. And I had. I feared I would always be struggling with money. I'd stopped struggling. I'd feared I'd never have a true partner in my life, and I'd even stopped fearing that. Either I would or wouldn't. Fear of God. I guessed that sort of replaced them all. Perhaps "fear God" meant looking into that place where the real "I" exists. Not I of roles or deeds, but the I AM who is, with no name. Without parameters or boundaries...just energy. Well. That could be frightening...space with no boundaries...and remembered sitting on my patio in the night and seeing the sky so big, no boundaries, and feeling overwhelmed. I was so small, and it, whatever "it" was, so large. My fears paled in the enormity.

I went to vespers and supper and compline, returned to my room and bed, and slept without turning.

Early Sunday morning, out at dawn, a crane flew over my head. I skipped breakfast to walk along the river in an opposite direction from the day before. A circular grove of trees, like the ancient Druids might have built, invited me to sit in the center's open space, listen to wind, and consider my history of Celtic warrior and pacifist Quaker. I held the contradictions within me. Shaking my head, I laughed; the trees rustled, laughing with me. If there's a pared masculine and a feminine energy in all of nature, including humans, including me, no doubt that's also true for the Divine.

Before lunch, I packed and loaded the car. After lunch, I thanked several people, Father Wilfred last.

I held his offered hand in my two. "Thank you," I said. He looked at me a long moment, smiled, and nodded.

Driving home, the sky beautiful, the red rock cliffs shining in late afternoon sun, my heart felt light and clear. As I carried my overnight bag into the adobe, Chama, alone for two nights, wound around my feet, *mom mom mom.*

Monday morning, I called Cliff to tell him what I'd learned.

"Maybe it takes time to recognize who we are," he said.

Suddenly, fall semester was upon me. Without my own courses of study, time stretched. The routine was the same, school and church and home, but the tension of so much on my plate at one time had dissolved. Richard, Cliff, and I rotated leading at Mass; we continued our Sunday lunches. Often in late afternoon, the desert called, and I walked among the painted hills.

One night, a dream of buying the Barnes, Kansas, house—the house of childhood when my father was alive—woke me from a sound sleep. The dream house had a lot of property, but needed cleaning and fixing up. The dream vivid, compelling, and the next morning, I sat at my casement window, writing it into my journal, and wondering what it could possibly mean. A hummingbird flew to the window and hovered.

A neighbor in Seaton Village called and asked me to come do last rites for her mother. Several people came to me for energy healing. At first, since most were neighbors or close friends, using my made-up bed for treatments worked, but as more and more called, I rented a treatment room in a downtown building and set up appointments.

Matriarch Meri notified Richard she was retiring and moving closer to her daughter. The school and church leadership would fall to Richard, although she would remain Matriarch. Boxes of church records and books began arriving at Richard's house. He stacked them in the basement, set up a desk area, and appointed me Dean of Sophia Divinity School.

And just that quickly, life sped up again. After teaching, and on days when I had no healing appointments, I went to Richard's office in the basement and began organizing the seminary.

At convocation that fall, Richard appointed Cliff to Director of Liturgy and requested he be elevated to bishop. The other bishops agreed. Our Sunday lunches after church now turned to organizing our Christmas service, Lent and Easter services, and Cliff's consecration to Bishop in March. I would be Richard's M.C. It was as if all my theatrical directing would be put to use.

Once more, or perhaps as always, my life revolved around healing practice, church, school, and home to feed Chama. Sometimes, I sat still in the evenings and stared at the television.

Cliff and I met for lunch when we could. He'd come by the house and we'd work on his consecration service as he and I had worked on my ordination service, changing words, melding mystical practices with Vatican II simplicity.

His consecration became another powerful experience. Matriarch Meri presided with Richard and Bishop Dexter. I circled among the three bishops, assisting each, inside their energy field around Cliff as if we were alone at the altar, a combined unit, although the church as overflowing with friends and church community as at my ordination. In the space of two hours, Cliff seemed to change, an anchored quality about him. His wife attended and his brother Ken. After, I went to the party at Richard's house, sat briefly by the door, and slipped out unnoticed. That night, I dreamed of driving in a car to the end of a road and realizing I'm almost out of gas.

THIRTY-FIVE

A New History

Months later, when Cliff dropped me off after a Wednesday night service, our cheeks brushed as we hugged goodnight. My body reacted in a rush of fire.

I heard Kelsey's words, "I wish you a love that burns the flesh," and Cynthia's "Do you two know what you're doing?" tumbling through my head one after the other.

Pushing him toward the car, I said, "You have to go. Now."

He looked confused.

Cynthia was right. We didn't know what we were doing. At least in our conscious knowing. Hindsight is so much wiser, most often wiser, than in-the-moment sight. We were good friends, but we couldn't see how we looked when we were together. And although we may have been a "match made in heaven," so to speak, or, more precisely, dreams, the logistics of working it out at ground level proved troublesome. Cliff and his wife had grown apart as some marriages do, but he didn't want to hurt her. I wouldn't break up a marriage. We remained good friends, presiding together, working together, laughing together.

Cliff and I drove to the mountains sometimes and sat, talked, wondered. I told him many of my old dreams. The first one, nodding at me in the mirror, the room all white, remained my favorite. I had no inkling from that dream I'd become a priest, but the dream opened a door. I told him the dream man once said he came from Union Country. Cliff laughed. "Baltimore is Union Country," he said. He'd moved to Santa Fe because his wife had found a life that called her. Along the way he'd learned homeopathic healing and participated in shamanic workshops. I related the dreams that told me he practiced shamanic techniques. Neither of us knew what to think of the string of dream-stories. They'd even shown he had allergies! He did, especially when chamisa bloomed. When I told him the dream story of being given his "true name," Krasinski, he looked at me, his eyes startled wide.

"That is my true name," he said. "My grandfather changed it to Kroski when my dad was in high school."

He told me stories of growing up in Baltimore and how, at eight years old, he began serving as an altar boy and at twenty-five was ordained. I told him about the farm. We told our stories; we struggled with our present.

Opening old journals, I searched through the dreams. In that first dream, the one in the cathedral all white—his hair, vestments, the frame around the mirror, the light. But in the other dreams, unless he was being a spaceman, he had dark hair. Cliff said he wasn't a spaceman, he was Batman. He could see in the dark. I'd never dreamed of Batman. Not once.

"And I had dark hair. It started getting white in my 30s," he said.

We fell into each other's life and we could not let go. When he stopped by to say hello, he'd call, "Honey, I'm home," as he crossed the patio. No matter how absorbed I might be in something, my head lifted and I'd laugh.

We moved alike, Cliff an inch or so taller.

We could not not be together.

Cliff also searched. He didn't know anymore how or why than I did. He said the first time he saw me in church, that first day I attended, his head whipped to see me; unsettled, he'd turned away, but he'd seen me.

Stories of love often fill with chaos. Love is dangerous. And it isn't easy. Whatever else it is or isn't, love is rarely easy. That's why the stories of ladies in towers and princes fighting thorns, brambles, and dragons have merit. Love isn't easy. Forgiveness isn't easy, either. But love without forgiveness is empty.

I knew I had to leave, but I didn't know where to go.

On a January morning, frost at the bottom of the windows, I woke from a dream that said a job waited for me in Kansas. I got up, fed Chama, fixed tea, and built a fire, all the while wondering at the strange message. We were, once again, blanketed in snow, classes canceled, so I booted up the computer. For a couple of hours, I searched the Internet for "jobs Kansas," focusing on familiar places: Manhattan; Topeka, where my brother lived; Marshall County, where the farm lived. The Graduate Theatre Department at K-State in Manhattan, where I'd done graduate work after my B.F.A.—before moving to Austin and meeting Bill Joyce and making movies, etc. etc.—and where I knew people, advertised for a Drama Therapy teacher. Many clients had come my way after ordination for counseling and for healing. I was a professional actor and a college teacher. I applied.

My dreams did not give me the insight to say the "job" was to bring my mother home so she could die. Some crossroads you'd rather not see.

But like Odysseus or Dorothy or Alice, I kept yearning for home.

And while I didn't find a job, or even an interview, I looked east to Kansas and caught the train to visit my brother in Topeka over spring break. Jack and I drove to Kansas City and passed by the newly renovated train station, the same station where my mother hid under benches during the FBI/Mob shootout, and where, years after her adventure, my sister and I changed trains every summer on our way from Barnes to visit Aunt Olive and Uncle Glen in St. Louis. The Kansas City station held family stories.

Jack circled the drive and turned up Main Street. As we drove up the hill, I recognized the trees Judy and I used to sit under when Aunt Esther and Uncle Howard, who lived in Kansas City, met us with a picnic lunch and made sure we got on the right train to St. Louis.

My heart did that bloop-open thing.

I glanced at my chest and looked at my brother. "I guess I'm moving to Kansas City."

In June, three months after driving through Kansas City, my children arrived in Santa Fe to help me move: Nathan and Kyong and Michael returned from Hawaii where they'd moved, briefly, and Stephen drove down from Denver. A family in the Village welcomed Chama and her dish and cat box. Cliff came by to say goodbye. We both looked ragged and our conversation constrained. He left, both of us edging at tears. I'd cried my way though weeks of deciding and all through Mass the previous morning. Now I packed, my sons filling the nooks and corners of the U-Haul trailer—since it was Stephen, well-balanced—and attached it to Stephen's Cherokee. I stood one last time at the kitchen window where early tomato plants once gloried in sun and looked over the desert to the western mountains. In my heart, this adobe would ever be mine—a small, quiet place where I read and wrote, and where Cliff and I sat at the casement window and watched hummingbirds visit. I heard car doors slam and Nathan call, "Mom?" It was time to go.

We drove to Kansas wagon-train style, Stephen towing the U-Haul in the lead; me in Old Blue; Kyong and Michael in her car, which they'd shipped to and back from Hawaii; Nathan brought up the rear in the Mustang he'd bought when they landed in California. We traveled the plains in a nighttime rattling thunderstorm, dancing woo-li-masters-lightning-flashes horizontal across the sky like a psilocybin-infused dream. I cried all the way.

I found an apartment; the kids found one just down the street. Stephen drove back to Denver. Nathan and Kyong found restaurant jobs. I became full-time grandma, enrolled Michael in school, took him to music lessons. I'd moved the psychic line with me.

Cliff and I talked on the phone when we could.

In late July, near the time of my father's death, I decided to visit his grave in Barnes, Kansas. I took my white stole and holy oil for anointing the dead. I had forgotten how hot the high plains become on a late July day. I had not brought a hat, so stopped at a roadside machine shop for a farmer hat, the kind with a bill and a business logo printed in front. I didn't notice what it said. I was driving to a cemetery to visit my father.

At the second gravel drive, I pulled in and parked. His headstone lay in the row closest to the road, Little Joe's next to it. Wearing my stole and carrying the vial of holy oil, I walked over, took off my shoes and sat on the ground, legs stretched lengthwise down his grave. I anointed my body in lieu of my father's, first my feet, pulled open my shirt to reach my solar plexus, my heart, my throat, and lastly taking off the cap to anoint my head. Grief poured out of me, tears to water the earth in this holy place. After anointing my forehead and crown, I sat with open palms, listening. The wind, the prairie wind, slow and sleepy, the sun warm on my skin. I sighed deeply, opened my eyes, and wondered what someone might think, had they seen me there, skirt askew, shirt open, sitting on a grave. But I was in a little country cemetery two miles from town on a gravel road few drove. A butterfly, bright monarch wings, landed on my big toe, lifted, fluttered around my feet. In Mexico, they say when a warrior dies, his soul becomes a butterfly.

It takes such a long time and such a lot of work to become an adult who forgives.

In the fall, that being an over-full year of transitions, Mom came to visit. We drove up to her home church in Wymore where everyone was happy to see her, and the young people who'd once measured themselves against her height now towered above her in their hugs. We sat in her usual pew, not too close in and not far back. Her fingers combed bangs back over her forehead. When the opening song began, her clear alto rose once more in the familiar melody.

After church, we went to the truck stop for lunch, just as she and Dad used to do. The mashed potatoes and gravy, the thinly sliced roast beef reminded me of my childhood. As Mom counted out bills to pay, she said, "I want to go down and visit Lavern at the Good Sam." Remembering the Good Samaritan nursing home where Grandma Sunderland died, I hated the thought, but we drove down. I started to park in front of the old red brick building, but Mom motioned me to a parking lot across the street in front of a long, new white building.

"This is the Good Sam?" I said. It was.

I waited in the lounge while Mom visited with Lavern. No one came in. I sat alone, remembering family elders who had died in the old brick building: Grandpa Joe who had come here when he couldn't live in Barnes anymore, Grandma Sunderland who baked the best sugar cookies in the entire world, Grandpa Albert who used to tell us ghost stories on summer farm evenings as we sat outside.

Driving back to Kansas City, the late afternoon sun burnished ripe milo heads into ruby red. Mom sat quietly, staring out her side window. She sighed.

"It's time for me to move to the Good Sam," she said. "I'll know people there."

And just that quickly, a two-week visit turned into forever.

Along with grandmothering, I daughtered, driving the three hours up and three hours back to move her in and to visit. I reacquainted myself with Highway 36 across the top of Kansas, the first highway I remembered from childhood's drives between Barnes and Grandma Sunderland's house, and where a red neon sign, shaped like a cross, said EAT GAS, the A holding the center for both words. It made me laugh as a kid. Now it, too, was gone.

A year and a half later, Mom had a seizure that sent her to the hospital; the doctors didn't think she'd survive. I called the family home and we circled her hospital bed. Jeanne brought sacred ti leaves. We spread them around her, held hands, and sang. Mother opened her eyes, looked around, and said, "Am I having another baby?" A plaintive cry. We laughed, hugged her, said no she wasn't. She moved out of intensive care, and after another week, the family began to leave. Mom went back to the Good Samaritan, and I stayed a few more days, sleeping at a small, roadside motel.

One afternoon as she was curled into her blankets, I curled behind her. "Mom, are you ready to go?" I said. She turned her head to look up at me. "Oh, my yes. There'll be folks to laugh at my jokes on the other side." Tears streamed down my face; my nose was running; I swiped a sweatshirt sleeve across my upper lip. Mom watched. "Didn't I ever teach you not to wipe your nose on your sleeve?" she said. "Yeah, Mom. You did," I said. And laughed.

That evening, driving back to Kansas City, an old rusty-colored truck pulled out in front of me from a side road. I glimpsed an old man in the truck cab, swerved hard to the left, shuddered off the truck's front steel bumper, and landed in a ditch with a bone-shaking crash. I crawled out of the car and stood in the ditch, wind whipping my hair. Old Blue was dead, but I wasn't. Nor was the old man, but our two vintage steel-framed vehicles, while keeping us both alive, had done each other in. A highway patrolman drove me into Marysville to my aunt and uncle's house. My uncle helped me buy a used car, a blue car which I immediately named New Blue. After resting a bit, I drove down to the tow truck lot and cleaned out Old Blue.

A deep sadness weighted me. Dad had taken his car back. I figured he'd take Mom soon.

A week later, I drove up to see Mom and found her in a wheel chair near the dining room doors. She pointed to the door and said, "Let's get out of here," and immediately went into a seizure. I would not send her back to the hospital. She'd told me what she wanted. I took her back to her room and put her into bed. I sat for the longest time, holding her hand, soothing her with words, telling her it was okay, tears running down my face. I didn't know what to do, but I knew she was dying. I called Cliff, close to hysterics.

"I don't know what to do!"

He calmed me. "You've already done everything. Now you have to back up and let her go. She won't leave as long as you're there. Sometimes the dying need privacy."

When we hung up, I noticed Mom's friend Lavern in a wheelchair at the open door and walked over. "Lavern, Mom's dying," I said. Lavern nodded, turned her wheelchair, and Mom's clock, a clock with birds all around the perimeter that chimed a different bird call each hour on the hour, sang like a nightingale. I glanced at the clock and at Mom. She had stopped breathing.

Before notifying the nurses, I ran a basin of warm water and washed her face, hands, body. It was an old ritual to ready both of us for our future.

The nurses called the mortuary. They arrived with a stretcher and a black body bag. I could not watch her be put into a bag, so went outside and sat in New Blue in a blinding snowstorm, the heater on, the windshield wipers wiping until they rolled out the stretcher and lifted it into the hearse. I slowly drove to my cousin's to call the family. They all flew back, and we buried her next to Dad. That's what she wanted.

AS THIS MAN IN THE EARLY COFFEE SHOP DREAM FROM YEARS BEFORE said, sometimes it's hard to move forward. My grief trapped me as Cliff's grief over his marriage trapped him. Seven months after my mother died, Cliff moved to Kansas.

In November, Cynthia died, and I went to Austin to preside at her funeral.

It was not an easy year of letting go to begin again.

We started at the bottom. I'd returned to my old standby, bartending. Plus the psychic line. I'd kept my SAG card active so a talent agency took me on, and during a small film job, a co-actor said he was a speech teacher; I said I was too, and he suggested me to his department as adjunct faculty. I went back to teaching public speaking. Cliff started as a substitute teacher in the public schools, but a chance meeting at a local college with the department head of philosophy gave him a college teaching job.

We bought a house in Kansas City and moved across the state line into Missouri. As the "Barnes house" dream told me, our 1924-built house resembles Grandpa Joe's big house where we'd lived when my father died. If cut in two and made into a row home, it would look like the Baltimore house Cliff grew up in. We have a lot of gardens. José would be proud, although hardly pleased with the sometimes messy upkeep. Grape-pop smelling iris and roses fill separate garden plots. One cousin gave me peony roots that had come from Grandma Sunderland's.

A year after buying the house, Cliff arranged a birthday dinner at the Peppercorn Duck Club, a posh restaurant in the Hyatt Hotel. For an after-dinner drink, we went to the rooftop revolving bar and sat, holding hands, gazing at the expanse of city lights below us.

When we left, he led me across the street to Union Station and up the hill to the same trees that had called me to Kansas City, the trees I sat under as a little girl.

Carefully removing a ring from the case in his pocket, he asked me to marry him and slipped the ring on my finger. He'd brought a tiny flashlight so I could see the sparkles in the antique blue diamond.

We married in November. In the same way the flock of family descended for my ordination and Mom's funeral, they flew in for the wedding. The house was full of people—sitting on the stairway, around the table, weaving orchids into leis for us to wear as we said our vows, or making whatever they were making. Ken and Jodi, Cliff's only brother and sister-in-law, tentatively entered the fray. The orchids came from Robert's Hawaii gardens. Orchids decorated the cake, and armfuls filled vases for the altar. And food. We had food. I won't detail the Costco shopping trip my sister engineered, Jeanne with one cart, Cliff with another, trotting behind his whizzing soon-to-be-sister as the carts piled high and the rest of us trailed. He likes that story. He tells it well. I like the story of Cliff and Ken dancing with each other at the reception and then neck wrestling.

Needless to say, the days before our wedding precluded much deep thinking, so when we came to our vows, we winged it. Richard presided. Cliff vowed to keep me safe and always protect me, to laugh with me, and listen to me; I vowed to listen to him, to always be at his back, to love him every day. "And when you tell me to stop, I'll stop," I said. Well. The church erupted and laughter bounced off the walls. "No!" I said, holding Cliff's hands and turning to the congregated frivolity. "I mean it!"

Richard pronounced us. We stepped from the altar, and to the sound of K. D. Lang and Tony Bennett singing "Exactly Like You," Cliff twirled me once, and we danced up the aisle.

EPILOGUE

As we learned the things of living together, we counted the odd things between us. When Cliff was confirmed, he'd taken the name John. His mother's name was Rosalie, although most called her Rosy, and my mother's name was Rosy Jeanette, although she preferred Jeanette. Cliff's mom filled the Mom-gap my mother's death had left. When she phoned, we'd laugh our way through stories about Cliff and Ken, stories about her family. She came to Kansas City after a stroke left her incapable of living alone, but she was tired of living. Cliff let her go as I had let my mother go. We flew back to Baltimore and buried her beside Cliff's dad.

Rereading the old dreams, I shake my head, seeing the many times a cliff entered into them, and while I've read book after book on mystics, dreamers, intuitives, and muses, I still can't nail down why my brain works the way it does.

What I do know, and respect, is the way our partnered energies celebrate the divine masculine and divine feminine at home and in church. Cliff primarily does the cooking and laundry; I hammer and fix things and do outside yard work.

When Barnabas, so many years ago, said, "forgive yourself," I had no idea what that meant. Now I understand. It doesn't mean what happened was okay. It means forgiveness lifts the pain and grants freedom to change. Forgiving allows hope.

Faith, I finally learned, comes from trusting the journey.

Cliff, in his philosophy classes, lectures on fate and free will and tells the story of how he was born six weeks premature, seventeen minutes before my father died; how our mothers' names, family names have similarities, of my dreams. And as they sit, mouths agape, Cliff imitates the soundtrack music to Rod Serling's *Twilight Zone*: do do do do—do do do do.

We have a legendary love, you could say. Like Ohi'a and Lehua, we are each other's strong trunk where we bloom.

Our 1924-built house looks much like a child's drawing: peaked roof, windows flanking the door, a tree out front. If I were to draw it, I'd write "Honey I'm Home" across the bottom of the page. In early mornings, I sit at an upstairs window looking over the backyard gardens, fix tea, and write in my journal. That's the small office where the same file cabinets hold the same plywood sheet-top desk, refinished, with the same under-carriage I installed in Santa Fe for the keyboard. It does not wobble. *The Magic Garden*, the lady, the king, the dragon, and the widespread tree sit on a bookshelf. Across the hall, my writing room has a big window with a Romare Bearden quote taped to the window ledge: "Artists are like mice. They need old houses where no one can bother them and they can just go about their business and do what they have to do." I'd really like to keep this. Bearden died in 1988. His wife and both his children have also died. A corner shelf holds the collection of stones that bind me to Moloka'i, to St. Lucia, to Mexico, to Santa Fe. My memory forgets many things, but not where I gathered those stones, talismans of love from places I could not stay. Now Cliff and I gather stones from places we visit and cannot stay. Together, they hold our history.

Once more, I was called to Hawaii to preside at nephew Damion and Aimée's wedding. Cliff encouraged me to go. He was teaching and couldn't leave.

We Aunties tied bows around the small jars of homemade lilikoi butter and attached place names to the tops, arranged flowers, laughed and told stories. The wedding began with Aimée's Hawaiian brother-in-law blowing a conch shell greeting as clouds gamboled toward us. Rain blew in from the sea, and we rushed through the ceremony, standing as we were on the edge of a bluff, overlooking the sea. Daemion and Aimée spoke the vows each had prepared; I anointed them with holy oil on forehead, heart, and hands, did a final blessing, and we dashed for cover. Jeanne danced a wedding hula for the newlyweds, we ate and feasted, and two days later, Lia, my sister Julia, and I drove south into Puna to visit Kalani Honua and spend the night at my long-ago home in the jungle.

Slipping off sandals, I walked to the room barefoot, toe-tips elevated against a stub from tree roots growing through grass, same tree roots, same grass. We unpacked in a guest hale whose wide-screened windows breathed the evening story of musk, fungus, heat, and wide-mouthed flowers closing for the night. Walking into the powdery dusk, thick like you could hold it in your hands, I circled the familiar gravel road around the compound. Overgrown weeds and grass covered the garden José and I planted and tended. The mound where Ben build a sweat lodge now held a sculpture, the office wore clean paint, but the sweet scent of plumeria and the ever-circling jungle wrapped me in end-of-day familiarity. A sleepy twitter welcomed from a bush. That night, I slept in the sound of rustle and breeze and woke as twitters morphed into song.

Lia, in her official capacity as marketing director for her parent's lodge, toured the grounds with the Kalani director. Julia and I tagged along, riding a golf cart through the extended grounds and walking into the jungle to visit upscale individual guest hales where I'd once dumped lava chunks. At the end of the tour, the director offered watsu water massages.

The masseuse, Sylvie, a woman immersed in water and in healing, swirled me as a willing mermaid, captive in a warm circular pool arched with black tarp. A womb, you could say. We were alone. My eyes closed. I lost all consciousness of space or time. I was water. Sylvie moved me.

She said, "Your heart," as she pressed a sore spot where my ribs joined.

"My father died when I was eight," I whispered. "That's a forever-sore spot."

Sylvie lifted and manipulated me in boneless emotion, lifted and swirled. As my chest released, I heard, *I couldn't stay but I sent you Cliff.* My eyes blinked wide and my arms flailed, sloshing water in my face, in Sylvie's face, as I struggled to stand. And then I laughed. Sylvie helped me balance as water sloshed over the pool rim.

I've not heard his voice again.

From a page in my Santa Fe journal, I offer a quote from the book I bought at the Dominican Retreat Center, *I Remember Your Name in the Night*, by Father Donagh O'Shea.

"I need to give myself profoundly to the future; that is part of what it is to love time, to love life itself. Love casts out fear. If I can be courageous in the face of the future, then when my future comes it will be mine. And only when it is mine can I give it away. To God and to others. For you I will be who I will be."

The End

ABOUT THE AUTHOR

 **Janet Sunderland** is an actor, writer, teacher, editor, and spiritual counselor/healer, practicing the hands-on technique, Huna Lomi. She earned a B.F.A. at Kansas State University in Manhattan, Kansas, majoring in fine arts and theatre, an M.F.A. in the Great Books Program of St. John's College, and an M.Div. from Sophia Divinity School. She is a published writer, both in poetry and memoir, and holds a Screen Actors Guild membership. She has been interested in and has read the work of Carl Jung for many years.

SHANTI ARTS

NATURE ▪ ART ▪ SPIRIT

Please visit us online
to browse our entire book catalog,
including poetry collections and fiction,
books on travel, nature, healing, art,
photography, and more.

Also take a look at our highly regarded art
and literary journal, *Still Point Arts Quarterly*,
which may be downloaded for free.

www.shantiarts.com

CPSIA information can be obtained
at www.ICGtesting.com
Printed in the USA
BVHW041302290721
613184BV00011B/237